Brilliant Manoeuvres

Brilliant Manoeuvres

How to Use Military Wisdom to Win Business Battles

RICHARD MARTIN

GLOBAL
professional
publishing

Global Professional Publishing Ltd
Random Acres
Slip Mill Lane
Hawkhurst
Cranbrook
Kent TN18 5AD
Email: publishing@gppbooks.com

Global Professional Publishing Ltd believes that the sources of information upon which the book is based are reliable, and has made every effort to ensure the complete accuracy of the text. However, neither Global Professional Publishing Ltd, the authors nor any contributors can accept any legal responsibility whatsoever for consequences that may arise from errors or omissions or any opinion or advice given.

ISBN 978-1-906403-85-0

Printed by IBT

For full details of Global Professional Publishing titles in Finance, Banking and Management see our website at: www.gppbooks.com

Contents

Acknowledgements

As this is my first book, I feel compelled to thank so many people, but I will limit my outright acknowledgments to those who have accompanied and encouraged me from the start in this endeavour. I thank my business mentor, Dr. Alan Weiss, who encouraged me to leverage my military knowledge and experience and to combine it with my business experience to create this book. Thank you also to Chad Barr, of the Chad Barr Group, for suggesting the 'brilliant' title *Brilliant Manoeuvres*. My agent Arnold Gosewich believed in my book idea and me enough to take a chance on a first-time author. Arnold gave me the benefit of his tremendous experience in the publishing industry and was always willing to take the time and show the patience to educate me about its intricacies. I'm extremely thankful. A special thanks goes to Libby Wagner of Libby Wagner and Associates, who put me in touch with Eric Dobby at Global Professional Publishing. Libby's assistance greatly accelerated the process of finding a commercial publisher, and I have appreciated Eric's flexibility, professionalism, and willingness to consider my opinion. Thanks also to my editor, Kevin O'Connor, who transformed my manuscript into the professionally presented book you are now holding. I also extend my heartfelt appreciate to all the members of Alan Weiss's global community of consultants, singling out Roberta Matuson, Andrew Miller, and Dave Gardner for their constant support and advice, as well as Alex Goldfayn, Seth Kahan, and Guido Quelle. They provided the power of personal example, as well as prodding, encouragement, and direct assistance at various times and places. Thanks to all of you.

On a more personal note, my big brother Mike has been an inspiration since my childhood and has constantly encouraged me to deepen my knowledge of many areas and to write. He gave me massive amounts of encouragement and helped me immensely with my writing. For this I'm eternally grateful. Finally, I wish to thank my wonderful wife Brigitte from the bottom of my heart for her ceaseless encouragement, love, and devotion. She is my biggest fan and cheerleader, and without her backing (and occasional kick in the derriere), I never would have persisted in my business dreams, much less the writing of this book. This book is dedicated to my three lovely daughters, Elizabeth, Victoire, and Leila.

Foreword

As a student of military history (my father was in the first volunteer parachute regiment ever formed in the US in 1940) and as a successful global consultant, I've often been struck by the application of military principles to competitive business.

While business defeats are seldom fatal, and successes often ephemeral, they do lend themselves to analysis and deconstruction for learning purposes and in the pursuit of excellence. Unfortunately, there is no West Point or Sandhurst discipline for business executives.

To be able to lead people in ethical, aggressive, and compelling campaigns is a vital role for contemporary leadership. It's important to lead from the front. The highest casualty rate among any officers in the US Civil War was among brigadier generals, since they mounted the lone horse in front of a brigade and shouted, "Follow me!" Too many current military leaders are safe behind the lines in bunkers and compounds (or thousands of miles away in remote bases). Business leaders have no such luxury.

We also are witness to ethical lapses of immense proportion in business today, with sad examples at Enron, Anderson, Tyco, Murdoch's publishing empire and others sullying once revered names. We can learn from the military here, as well:

> *"Men who take up arms against one another in public war do*
> *not cease on this account to be moral beings, responsible to one*
> *another and to God."*

This admonition was from the US army military regulation of 1863, during the height of the Civil War.

During that war, the highly successful Confederate raider, General Nathan Bedford Forrest, was quoted as explaining his success by "I get there firstest with the mostest." (Many scholars consider this apocryphal since Forrest was an educated man.) Yet isn't that what Steve Jobs did at Apple, breaking new ground with successful, albeit not perfect, innovations? The iPhone is one of the most dramatic new products since the Civil War.

Rich Martin, an acclaimed military officer and brilliant consultant, has distilled the best of military maneuvers into business brilliance. Very few people have the experiential base to do that. But Rich has mounted his horse and said, "Follow me!"

Congratulations on getting this far. Now start running after him.

Alan Weiss, PhD
Author, *Million Dollar Consulting* and *The Consulting Bible*
Former consultant to the US Air Force

Preface

There have been many books over the years on how to apply elements of military strategy and leadership to business. In fact, we can say that it forms a kind of sub-genre within management and business literature. Probably the most famous work of military strategy is *The Art of War* by Sun Tzu, an ancient collection of aphorisms to guide military and political leaders in preparing for and prosecuting wars. It has been a mainstay of business executives and entrepreneurs who have sought inspiration in military wisdom in order to achieve business success. Clausewitz's masterwork *On War* has also been a source of inspiration for some. There have also been many books highlighting aspects of military leadership and strategy as relevant for a business audience.

However, I think this book is quite different from all of those other books. I say this for three reasons. First, it is based on my combined knowledge and experience of military command and business. I served for over 25 years as an infantry officer in the Canadian Army. After that, I started and have built a successful management consulting practice. I have been able to see the commonalities and the linkages between military and business strategy in action. The second reason this book is different is because it explains the relevance of various aspects of military wisdom and shows what is applicable and how, and what isn't applicable.

The third reason *Brilliant Manoeuvres* is different is that it is much more comprehensive and complete than any other book I know of that discusses the parallels between military wisdom and business. I haven't limited my survey to strategy or leadership, as important as these are. In this book you will find chapters on offensive and defensive strategies and tactics. There are details on military planning, decision-making, intelligence, and logistics that are simply not found anywhere outside highly specialized military doctrine manuals. I've presented the military concepts in such a way that the business leader will be able to apply them to strategic, operational, tactical, and leadership challenges. I've included a chapter on how military planners and leaders deal with the uncertainty, friction, and risks of conflict. I also explain how the military techniques for dealing with these realities can be applied to business. Finally, the reader will find extensive discussions of organizational dynamics, including morale, mood, cohesion, and motivations, as well as an in-depth look at the military philosophy of leadership.

Whether you're a business executive or manager, an operational supervisor, someone involved in sales, a small or medium-business owner, or even just self-employed, I am sure that you can find something of value in the military wisdom I've revealed in this book. I also think that managers and leaders in all types of organizations, not just in business, can get a lot out of this book. Throughout, my intent has been to provide the best possible understanding of military wisdom for application in business and other non-military endeavours. I have chosen the word 'wisdom' carefully, because I think that it is the only word that fully conveys the richness of pragmatic thought that is applicable in the business sphere.

Chapter 1

How Can Military Wisdom Apply to Business?

Rather than comparing war to art, we could more accurately compare it to commerce, which is also a conflict of human interests and activities; and it is still closer to politics, which in turn may be considered as a kind of commerce on a larger scale.

Carl von Clausewitz

How Business Concepts Helped Me Achieve A Military Mission

I commanded an infantry company on peacekeeping duty in Bosnia from August 1999 to late February 2000. The mission of my unit, a company comprised of around 150 soldiers, was to patrol a sector of about 4,000 square kilometres in northwest Bosnia, which included the small towns of Drvar and Bosansko Grahovo as well as several dozen villages and hamlets, hundreds of farms, and a forested mountain area. The area had been predominantly Serb until August 1995, when a Croat offensive led to the forcible expulsion of the 17,000 Serbs who had lived there. Within weeks, the Croat forces had resettled Croats in the newly acquired territory. These Croats were originally from central Bosnia, and had themselves been expelled from their homes earlier in the war.

Our force had to conduct patrols and actions in support of the Dayton Peace Accords that had been negotiated and agreed by the belligerent parties in December 1995. This was a mission led and conducted by multinational forces of the North Atlantic Treaty Organization (NATO). We also had to keep the peace, which involved supervising the activities of the Croat militia, Croat-dominated police, Croat-dominated intelligence operatives, or any other opponents of the peace accords, such as Croat politicians and criminal elements. The summer of 1998 had been particularly agitated. The Croat militia had staged a major riot in the main town in my sector, Drvar, in order to prevent the return of Serbs to their homes. When we took over from the previous Canadian unit in early August of 1999, tensions were high once again in the sector. Ordinary Croats who had been resettled to the area held considerable animosity toward the NATO forces, and specifically us. However, it quickly became apparent that we were dealing with a situation where the Croat elites, by and large the same people who openly opposed the Dayton Accord, and militia had a stranglehold on the towns of Drvar and Bosansko Grahovo, and that they were aided in this by the local police and judicial system. In fact, many of the Croats, although hostile to Serbs, were more afraid of the Croat forces and criminal elements that had infiltrated businesses and corrupted local politicians than of the returning Serbs.

The conflict had basically gone underground by the time we had arrived in August 1999 but it still showed the pattern of a low-level insurgency. NATO, including the Canadian military forces, represented the government side, the side of law and order and of legitimate political authority. There were some politicians and elites at the local and Bosnian levels, people such as the Serb mayor of Dvrar Momcilo Bajic as well as the Croat member of the Bosnian Presidency, Ante Jelavic, who supported the Dayton Peace Accords and the attempts to restore the rule of law. The majority of those with any kind of power in the sector, however, did not support the Dayton Peace Accords. The forces of peace and order and the forces of the opposition did not confront each other in open battle but rather were fighting for the "hearts and minds" of the population. If this term sounds familiar, it should not be surprising. It's a pattern that has appeared in military counter-insurgency operations for decades. The British in Malaya (now Malaysia) in the 1950s claimed to be fighting for the 'hearts and minds' of the local population. The same was claimed in Vietnam, and then once again more recently in Iraq and Afghanistan.

As we settled into our sector in that hot summer of 1999, I conducted my estimate of the situation and realized that operational success would depend on us gaining the confidence of the local populace while simultaneously discrediting the opponents of the Dayton Accords. We had to ally ourselves with the various agencies of the international community and non-governmental organizations (NGOs). The former included the UN High Commission for Refugees, the Office of the NATO High Representative, the International Police Task Force, and the Organization for Security and Cooperation in Europe. The NGOs included the Red Cross, CARE, Oxfam, and several other European based humanitarian relief and development organizations. In fact, we had to support anyone in the populace and the International Community who was trying to rebuild the country along the lines of the peace accords.

Our tactics were to be strict in enforcing the peace accords in our dealings with the Croat militia and politicians as well as Croat strongmen, politicians, businessmen, media, local organizations, and the Catholic Croat and Orthodox Serb clergies. We ourselves would oppose those who opposed the peaceful return and resettlement of Serbs using the most effective military weapons we had at our disposal. This involved constant patrolling, the actual physical presence of forces, inspection of military and police units, use of vehicle checkpoints, dialogue with the local population and officials, media activities, distribution of leaflets, and assistance to those in need either directly through our own humanitarian relief efforts, or more commonly by supporting and ensuring the security of the various international relief and security agencies and NGOs.

When I explained to my troops our role and my plan to achieve our mission, I deliberately compared what we were doing to a business situation. I told my troops that we selling a product to the population, and that product was peace and security. To do that, we had to win them over to our position and prove to them that we were worthy of their trust. In other words, we had to show consistently and unwaveringly that they were better off supporting the Dayton Peace Accords and the central Bosnian government than the Croat criminal elements, corrupt politicians and policemen, and the Croat militia. I deliberately compared this to marketing, advertising and promotion. We would repeatedly tell the local people the same thing, and then act in accordance with our 'brand,' as it were. I told our soldiers we would be consistent, and that these methods would be effective over time.

My collaborators and I saw the obvious parallels on the ground between our combined peacekeeping and counter-insurgency role and a business that is working to distinguish itself from competitors to win customers to its products and services. Early in my military career, I had acquired a Bachelor's degree in business administration at the *Collège militaire royal de Saint-Jean* in St-Jean-sur-Richelieu, Quebec in Canada. This basic, theoretical knowledge, plus my experience in working with industry as a project manager on weapons systems development and acquisition projects in the mid-1990s proved to be essential in helping me understand the military and security situation in Bosnia, and to develop a strategy and operational plan to achieve our mission.

I have recounted this personal story to illustrate how business knowledge can be of use in the realm of military strategy. The aim of this book is, however, to do the converse, that is, to show the applicability of timeless military wisdom to achieving success in business. I will demonstrate the metaphorical, conceptual and practical similarities and linkages between war and business, and between military thinking and business thinking. I will provide practical tools to apply the military principles and techniques of strategy, operational art, tactics, logistics, decision-making, and planning. I will also explore the principles of military leadership, cohesion and morale and their application to organizational dynamics and leadership in a business context.

In the remainder of this chapter, we consider the influence of military theory and practice on business and organizational management as it has evolved since the late 19th century. I will then provide a bit of my background so the reader can appreciate how I came to understand and elaborate the usefulness of military thought for business and management. Next, this chapter will serve as a primer on the structure of military thought, especially as it concerns the levels of war: strategy, operational art, tactics, as well as the relationship of the levels of war to the disciplines of logistics and planning and to the physical and moral planes of war. This will provide the framework for understanding the linkages in each of the subsequent chapters.

How Military Thought Influences Business Practice

There are three ways in which military thinking and experience influence business. The first is metaphorical. As an example of such metaphorical language, Warren Buffett has often stated that he looks for "economic castles protected by unbreachable moats". By this, he means that he seeks to invest in businesses that have a virtually unassailable competitive advantage. By the way, Buffet has also called investment derivatives "financial weapons of mass destruction," a pointed comment about the financial meltdown that shook the world in 2008 and 2009.

In my work as a consultant, I have often noted how entrepreneurs and executives use colourful military language as well as examples from military history to illustrate points they are trying to make when motivating employees. In fact, this metaphorical use of military language is so common that we can deduce that many business executives, especially CEOs, like to see themselves as warriors and generals, fighting off competitors and conquering new markets. They talk about attacking competitors, defending turf, firing warning shots, establishing beachheads, bypassing the competition, rallying the troops, and so on. This metaphorical language indicates that there does exist a profound linkage between business and military strategy, at least in the minds of many business people.

The second type of linkage is conceptual. This implies that there are underlying similarities between business and military theory and practice, which can be of practical import. The opening story of this chapter is a perfect illustration of this conceptual linkage. The conceptual similarities between the situation in Bosnia and that of a business working to differentiate itself relative to competitors was readily apparent to any thoughtful observer. I believe that it is these conceptual similarities that people intuit when they use military examples in a metaphorical sense.

One of the most prevalent similarities can be found in the area of strategy. Strategy in and of itself was originally a purely military concept. The term comes from the Greek word for generalship, *strategeia* from *strategos*, which means general or field commander. The term became increasingly associated with the highest levels of decision-making and the general policy framework of business organizations. Peter Drucker claimed that his book *Managing for Results*, published in 1964, was the first book to talk about business strategy even though it didn't explicitly use the term. Another early major use of the term in a business context is actually attributable to Alfred Chandler in his book, *Strategy and Structure*, which appeared in 1962, though it had probably already entered common colloquial usage by then. By the same token, salespeople will frequently talk about tactics when they describe selling and closing techniques. They've obviously intuited the fact that tactics are much more situational than strategic, and that they are applied in the heat of battle to achieve immediate results.

Much of the discussion in this book builds on the metaphorical and conceptual linkages between war and military thinking with a view to isolating techniques and practices that can be adopted for resolving business problems such as strategy, positioning, competitiveness, leadership, planning, and decision-making. Since the end of the 19th century, business theorists and captains of industry have consistently used methods and practices developed in the military for application in business. For instance, in the late 19th century, the French management theorist Henri Fayol explicitly adopted the concept of unity of command, which is a vital principle of military command theory, and applied it to the nascent discipline of business organization. Fayol looked at how military units were commanded and organized, and determined that a key factor in ensuring effective and efficient command of forces was that soldiers only took orders from one person, their immediate commander. Thus, military forces were organized into a nested hierarchy of progressively smaller and more specialized units, each one commanded by only one individual. He advocated the same type of structure for businesses. Peter Drucker claimed that business structure, particularly the hierarchical framework and the multi-divisional structure, was inspired by the composition of armies and the Catholic Church. Indeed, there are only so many ways to structure a major enterprise involving large numbers of people and significant resources. In his history of American business strategy and structure, Alfred Chandler traced the line of influence from the railroads in the 1850s to the multi-divisional corporations of the 1920s. He showed how the railroads created multi-functional units under the authority of a single individual with a central headquarters to coordinate planning and allocation of resources. This led to the distinction in business of line and staff managers. Although Chandler didn't explicitly note the similarities to military structures, the fact that line and staff are military terms clearly indicates the influence of military conceptions of planning, decision-making, command relationships, and communications. He also noted that the executives and staff officers in headquarters were expected to make strategic decisions, whereas the line managers in field units were expected to make tactical decisions.

The final linkage is technical. There are many technical areas of expertise that were either developed for military use, or that developed as a result of wartime efforts. For example, as described in the *Wiley-Blackwell Handbook of Individual Differences*, psychometric testing for ability and temperament was in its infancy in 1917 when the United States entered the First World War. However, the need to raise a huge army in a short period of time, and to select for various military jobs such as officers, pilots, and technicians, led the U.S. Army to use the various extant measures of IQ and to also develop its own selection tests, the Army Alpha and the Army Beta tests. This relationship continued during the Second World War. A workforce of 1,500 psychologists was employed by the U.S. Army Air Force to develop selection and training programs. For instance, Air Force psychologists were able to predict future success on pilot training using various psychometric measures of ability. Another technical field that originated through military necessity is operations research. The Allies in World War II faced a number of problems that called for mathematical modelling to optimize allocation of resources and decision-making. The first major application was for the Battle of Britain during which the Royal Air Force had to determine where to position its radar sites to maximize coverage of the air approaches to Britain. They then had to optimize the deployment of their limited fleet of fighter planes so they could most effectively intercept and destroy the German bombers attacking the country. Later on in the war, British, American and Canadian naval forces and convoys had to be optimally assembled, routed and protected in order to maximize the chances of survival against German submarine attacks during the Atlantic crossing. This technique was combined with the decrypts of German radio signals to limit the impact of German U-Boat warfare on the course of the war. During the 1950s, operations research was applied to the management of the massive U.S. Navy Polaris missile and nuclear submarine programme, initially in the form of the PERT-CPM scheduling approach. This, along with the need to more adequately manage the massive spending on weapons system development during the Cold War, led to the full development of project management as a discipline.

These are just some of the technical disciplines that either originated as a result of military necessity or were greatly accelerated owing to wartime exigencies. The main point is that there has been a flow of theory and practice from warfare and military forces to civilian applications, mainly in business and organizational management. In her excellent work, *The Capitalist Philosophers*, Andrea Gabor wrote that the expansion of the Army Air Forces during WWII "needed new management systems and a new breed of manager. Modern logistics, cost accounting, and systems analysis owe much to the systems developed by the Army Air Forces during World War II. As managers and experts attached to the Army Air Forces moved back into civilian life after the war… these men left their mark on everything from the revival of consumer production after the war to military and government policy during the Vietnam War era."

How I Came to Realize the Usefulness of Military Parallels for Business

It should be fairly obvious by now that I am not the first person to see the parallels and usefulness of military wisdom for business theory and practice. However, I didn't come to that realization easily. In fact, it had to be coaxed out of me to a certain extent. The story of how I gradually changed my thinking is germane since I believe someone without my combined military and business experience and expertise might not see the usefulness, thereby missing the lessons of this book.

I joined the Canadian Armed Forces right out of high school, when I was 18. I had wanted to be a soldier since at least grade 8, and my parents often remarked that, in fact, I had wanted to be a soldier when I was quite young even before I actually can remember. When I was a teenager, military history, aircraft, and weaponry fascinated me. I could name the different types of tanks and fighter planes as well as many of the Canadian, American, British, and Soviet classes of naval warships. In other words, I was a military nerd, a military geek in high school. Thus, I applied for military college in my final year of high school. I was reasonably good in mathematics and the physical sciences, so I imagined I wanted to study engineering even if another part of me never doubted that I actually wanted to be an infantry officer. Military college was a fabulous experience for me. I made many lifelong friends and met the challenges of being an officer cadet, learning the basic principles of management and leadership, this at an age when most young men were struggling to pay their way through school by bartending or doing similar non-supervisory jobs. I was trained formally in leadership when I attended Basic

Officer Training Course in Chilliwack, BC, during the summer of 1981, and then subsequently in leadership and tactics so that I might become a platoon commander after my Infantry Officer Basic Course. I followed the usual military college pattern and did this in phases during successive summers from 1982 to 1984.

Meanwhile, I realized during my first academic year at *Collège militaire royal de Saint-Jean* that I wasn't really cut out for studying science and engineering. Instead, I found myself attracted to the study of business administration. That's the program I chose to pursue, and so I completed a Bachelor of Administration degree in 1985. I was then commissioned as a second lieutenant in the 3rd Battalion of the *Royal 22ième Régiment*, stationed in Valcartier, located just north of Quebec City. I served initially in Valcartier from 1985 to 1988, fulfilling my role as a platoon commander and then assistant operations officer in the battalion headquarters. In the summer of 1988, I was posted to the 1st Battalion of my regiment in Lahr, Germany, where I commanded a rifle platoon for another year. Following that, I was promoted to Captain and served as a junior staff officer in the headquarters of 4th Canadian Mechanized Brigade Group and then 1st Canadian Division, both in Germany. During that initial five-year period, I participated in numerous exercises and training opportunities in Canada, Germany, Norway and France. I got to hone my skills as a junior officer in charge of senior NCOs and junior-ranking soldiers, both in garrison and on exercise. I also learned the rudiments of basic staff work and administrative writing, and attended a number of courses on advanced tactics.

Up until then, my path had been quite conventional for a young infantry officer. I can't say that I got to apply my business degree very much. My knowledge and expertise in all-arms tactics, as well as command and leadership evolved considerably during this period, but my knowledge of business remained as theoretical as the day I had graduated from military college. I was developing in terms of military theory and practice but not on the business and management side of things. This began to change in 1992, when I was selected to attend a yearlong British Army technical staff course at the Royal Military College of Science in Shrivenham, England. I had always been very interested in military technology and history, as well as the detailed characteristics of weapons systems. This course allowed me to indulge my passion in this area by discovering the intricacies of system development and design. It was also a wonderful experience to live in the UK for a year. This was also my first real contact with industry, as the curriculum included industrial visits to factories and facilities of companies and agencies involved in research and development and weapons systems manufacture. I visited factories such as those at Alvis, the Royal Ordnance Factories, and GKN Sankey in the UK, and GIAT and Michelin in France. For the first time, I saw the practical application of many of the business management principles I had learned in theoretical terms during my academic studies.

I was posted back to Canada in early 1993 to serve in National Defence Headquarters (NDHQ) in Ottawa. I was employed as a technical staff officer in a project management office for acquisition of an anti-tank missile system. This brought me into close working relationships with project engineers, technicians, research scientists, marketing and sales representatives, and employees of other federal government departments. It was a real eye opener since I noticed the utility of tactical planning and decision-making tools for general problem solving and managerial tasks. It was also the first time in my career that I could apply some of the basic business management skills such as bookkeeping, marketing, operations management, production management, etc. I ultimately served five years until 1998 in the anti-armour project management office and the Directorate of Land Requirements in NDHQ. Early in that period, I was assigned to develop a project schedule and work breakdown structure for a project using a project management software package. This got me interested in the field of project management, so I applied for part-time study in the Masters of Project Management at the *Université du Québec en Outaouais* in Gatineau, Quebec, just across the Ottawa River from Ottawa. I completed the degree in 1997 and learned along the way that the discipline of project management was almost completely a creation of the defence and weapons system sector.

In the second half of 1997, I attended the Canadian Land Force Command and Staff College in Kingston, Ontario to complete my Army Command and Staff Course. This is the course an officer needs to be considered a qualified senior line or staff officer, at least in the Canadian Army. In early 1998, I was promoted to the rank of major, and took command of an infantry rifle company in the 1st Battalion of the *Royal 22ième Régiment*. It is in that role that I commanded a company group on peacekeeping duty in Bosnia from August 1999 to February 2000, as described in the opening section of this chapter.

In this role, I honed my command and leadership skills, and I finally got to apply the training and development I had undergone over the years. The environment in Bosnia was not one of high intensity warfare but there was definitely a tension, as described above. This was the high point of my military career since I had to apply all of my resolve and diplomatic skills in dealing with local authorities, citizens, and representatives of the international community. In fact, under my leadership, my company was instrumental in securing the safe return of over 2,000 displaced persons during our six-month rotation in theatre. University of Calgary military historian David Bercuson, who had visited our camp in early September 1999 with a senior delegation representing the Canadian Defence Minister, described our work and wrote about it in the *National Post* after returning to Canada, writing that my company and I "could do no wrong."

As the tour in Bosnia came to an end, I was faced with the question of what I wanted to do next. I had been on a high, living on adrenaline for almost a year by then. I was 38 years old and fast approaching 20 years of service. I would have been allowed to retire after 20 years with a modest pension. I seriously considered doing so, thinking that I could work in the defence industry. However, I also developed a passion for study and research when I had done my masters in project management. With my knowledge of military technology and passion for military history, I decided that I would like to try a shot at university teaching. The only available positions were at the Royal Military College of Canada in Kingston. As there were no teaching positions open for officers that year and I didn't have a PhD, I accepted a job on the military staff at the College, with the hope of applying for the War Studies doctoral program at RMC. I was posted with my family from Valcartier to Kingston in the summer of 2000, and applied to the War Studies program during the following months.

I was accepted and started full-time doctoral course work in the fall of 2001. Although I initially enjoyed my studies, I came to realize that I wasn't really cut out for the War Studies program, as I found it too focused on military history. I simply couldn't see myself doing a dissertation and then teaching military history as a second career. I wanted to be in business for myself, possibly building a training company. With that being said, however, I studied with one of the most prolific Cold War historians in Canada, Dr. Sean Maloney, an expert in the history of UN peacekeeping and in Canada's military operations and deployments since the end of the Second World War. Amongst other things, Sean led me to the study of all the major theorists of war, from Sun Tzu and Thucydides to Mao Tse Tung, Clausewitz, and Sir Robert Thompson. I also developed a deep understanding of the dynamics of the Cold War and the role of UN peacekeeping, especially smaller countries' contribution thereto and to maintaining the balance of power throughout the Cold War. In his course about contemporary warfare, Maloney also delved deeply into the Balkans and other post-Cold War conflicts. Thus, I was able to relate what I had experienced in Bosnia to the theoretical constructs he presented, which was indeed fascinating.

After setting aside my PhD ambitions for the time being, at least in War Studies, I was posted to the Directorate of Army Training in the Land Force Doctrine and Training System, also located in Kingston, where I served until my retirement from the Army in May 2006. This assignment influenced my current thinking, including my realization of the general utility of military decision-making and problem-solving approaches. I worked closely with a number of training development and personnel selection officers on the modernization of the Army's junior officer and NCO leadership development programs. I was also able to use all my knowledge and expertise in various fields such as project management, training management, tactical command and leadership, research and development, scholarly research, personnel management, staff planning and decision-making processes, as well as using my general analytical and synthetic skills.

I retired in early May 2006 after 26 years of service in the Canadian Forces. I was proud of my service, but I would be lying if I said that I wasn't relieved. Military retirement can be a difficult and emotional process for career soldiers, and I certainly experienced my share of angst. To ease the transition, I had accepted a one-year contract position with a defence contractor with offices in Kingston. My plan was to work for that company for a year, and then to move to the Montreal area to start a training business, as I had promised my wife six years before when I had been posted to Kingston. However, no sooner had I left the military and started in my defence contractor job that I wanted to start my own business. One day, I was browsing the business section of a local bookstore and saw a book by Alan Weiss, called *Million Dollar Consulting*. I bought the book, read it over the course of a few days, and decided right then and there that I was going to be an independent management consultant. By early June, I had enrolled in Weiss's "Million Dollar Consulting College" held in Boston in October 2006. By the end of June, I had registered my business as Alcera Consulting, obtained my tax numbers, and started developing a website and collateral materials. I had never been in business, even though I had basically two business management degrees. With the help of Weiss's books, training, and mentoring, I now had a business model. I left the defence contractor in August of that same summer, and started marketing my services. My first client was the military unit where I had been hired to work for the defence contractor. It was pretty iffy at the beginning and completely based on my previous military work, but at least I was in business and I began earning revenue.

When I first started marketing my services to civilian organizations and business clients, my impulse was to play down my military background, and to under-emphasize the relevance of military processes and practices for business. Even though I knew the knowledge and skills I had acquired in the military were all highly relevant to business—I used many of them everyday myself—I hesitated to point out what I felt were obvious similarities and applications of military thinking to business. In fact, I was so reticent to make these linkages, that I would deliberately avoid making them. For instance, I had gotten a mandate to develop and deliver a training package on adaptation and change management for a major corporation in the financial sector. My buyer was a VP, and he had specifically hired me because of my military background. I was delivering one of the workshops when one of the participants asked me to tell some military anecdotes. In fact, he was asking me to show how military knowledge could be useful to the topic at hand. I hesitated, and then told a quick anecdote. I refused to continue in this vein even though several course participants wanted me to elaborate, finding the military example fascinating and relevant. It was only a few years later that I finally realized that I had unique insights to offer to business managers, executives, entrepreneurs, and managers in other sectors. With encouragement from my business mentor, Alan Weiss, numerous consulting colleagues, family and friends, I started to write more and more about the applications of military concepts and practices for successful business outcomes. I also started to pepper my conversations with clients and prospects with personal military anecdotes, illustrations and comparisons of business and military principles and concepts, historical examples, and metaphors. I immediately noticed the interest this change produced, as well as the power of the metaphors and examples I used to convey the military principles and teachings I increasingly found were relevant to business.

I finally realized just how deep the interest and need is for a detailed and practical exposition of the most relevant principles, teachings, techniques, and concepts from military theory and practice for business. Thus, the book you are reading. As you can see from my overview of the history of the use of military applications in business and organizational settings, this is not a novel idea. There have also been other books in the genre, and the popularity of such works as Sun Tzu's *The Art of War* and Robert Greene's *The 48 Laws of Power,* and their presence on the shelves of the business section in bookstores prove there is a continuing fascination with and applicability of military theory and practices for business and management. Furthermore, as I showed from my personal story and experience in Bosnia, I feel that I am uniquely qualified as a former career soldier and now a management consultant to interpret military insights for a business audience.

Of Levels and Planes

The title of this section may have implied that I would be talking about carpentry, but in actuality I want to explain two important concepts from military thought that have theoretical and practical importance for business, and will be critical as this book progresses. The first concept concerns what are known as the 'levels of war'; the second concerns 'planes of war.' It is important to understand these concepts in their military usage in order to better apply them to the sphere of business. The ideas of levels and planes of war provide a conceptual framework for warfare and military thought, and they also provide a conceptual framework applicable to business.

There are three levels of war: strategy, operational art, and tactics. In its purest form, strategy is the theory and practice of raising and employing armies to achieve political ends. I use the term 'army' in a generic sense for all military forces, including navies and air forces. Historically, it is only in the modern period that states have consistently raised and maintained large standing armies. There were exceptions in the past such as in ancient Rome but they were few. To raise and maintain an army for any length of time, one has to be able to both justify its existence and to finance it. The first need is largely political in nature; this means you have to have a good reason to create and maintain the army. The second need follows logically from the first, as soldiers, weapons and their upkeep require huge amounts of capital, labour, time, and other resources. They are a huge drain on a country's treasury and resources. As Sun Tzu said in *The Art of War*, "Warfare is the greatest affair of state; it must be thoroughly pondered and studied." The raison d'être of the army and its payment, equipping and financing require considered attention from politicians and the highest military commanders. However, it isn't enough to have an army or any other type of armed force. One also must know how to employ it judiciously. Theorists usually distinguish between 'grand strategy', which involves the political leadership of the country in making fundamental existential decisions and setting goals, and 'military strategy', the realm of military leadership, which involves the actual employment of military forces to achieve political ends. In other words, grand strategy is about setting war aims and broad parameters for action including the political, social, and financial mobilisation of the country, and military strategy is about actually fighting the war, whether it is all-out war or a more limited form of conflict or deployment of forces.

There are obvious parallels between the pure military conception of strategy and its application to business. Previously, we described how business theorists and practitioners have come to the realization that the most fundamental decisions about a business, that is, its goals, purpose, character, and resourcing, were conceptually similar to the domain of strategy. Thus, strategy in the business and organizational realm seeks to ask and answer the same type of questions as strategy in realm of warfare and conflict. What is our purpose? What are our fundamental values? What is our market? What are our goals? What are our key advantages and how should we exploit these to outwit the competition and secure our future? How should we be structured and organized? Where and when should we operate? In exactly what business are we? What resources are required? How should we pay for it? How will we know we've achieved our aims? In business, this corresponds to corporate strategy, and it is equivalent to grand strategy in the military realm. On the other hand, competitive—or business—strategy is concerned with achieving transient or sustained competitive advantages through superior positioning and execution. This is equivalent to the notion of military strategy in the military domain.

Another level of war that most people readily apply to business is that of tactics. Simply put, tactics are the theory and practice of achieving your aims in the heat of battle. One way to remember the distinction between strategy and tactics is to look at their etymologies. As noted previously, strategy comes from the Greek word for general. Generals usually aren't involved in hand-to-hand combat with the enemy, unless something has gone terribly wrong. Tactics comes from the Greek term *taktike*, which means to arrange or order things. In other words, tactics refer to how to arrange troops on the field of battle and manoeuvre them to achieve success. I sometimes use a mnemonic device that helps to distinguish between the two and explains their inherent meaning. When thinking of strategy, think of 'stratosphere'; in other words, strategy implies one is at an altitude, overlooking the battlefield but not getting bloodied or muddied. When thinking of tactics, think of the word 'tactile'; in other words, actual contact and combat with the enemy.

Most day-to-day situations in business are tactical in nature. For instance, company strategy aims to offer certain products or services in particular markets to meet specific needs relative to competitors. However, the actual business of finding customers and closing business, making the sale, is tactical in nature. Another example: A company president decides to change the company's culture. Working with her team of senior executives, she identifies key objectives, values, and processes to support this goal. Managers and employees at the different levels of the organization then have to implement the strategic change on a day-to-day basis, in myriad situations, with many different people, both internally and externally. These micro-decisions and actions are clearly tactical in nature, as they are if taken in the heat of battle.

Strategy and tactics also differ in terms of how they are conceived, developed and communicated. Strategy is somewhat amenable to systematization, but it is ultimately very artful. No two situations or organizations will ever call for the same strategy. It also requires great intelligence and opportunism. Tactics, on the other hand, are inherently repetitive, mechanical, and process-oriented. Should such-and-such occur, or the enemy or competition or customer do this, then take such-and-such action. If that doesn't work, then try this other action. Tactics are therefore fairly easy to systematize and indeed must be systematized and as a result, tactics can be taught and evaluated. In summary, we can say that each strategy is ultimately unique, whereas tactics are repeated.

In centuries past, the levels of strategy and tactics covered the whole of warfare. This was because military forces were smaller, more ephemeral and less capable with shorter range of action and less staying power. Armies were raised for purposes of war when there was a clear threat or when a ruler wanted to conquer another state. Soldiers were often paid from the proceeds of campaigning, even by rape and pillage, and were expected to live off the land, at the expense of its inhabitants. There was no personnel management, discipline was harsh and inhumane by modern standards, and logistics basically involved raising taxes or stealing money to pay for the war. In addition, armies were poorly articulated. This means that units had few sub-divisions, were mostly uniform in form and function, and tended to be deployed in simple close-order formations using only mechanical manoeuvres learned by rote.

The wars of the French Revolution and Napoleon changed all of that. Probably for the first time in history, a country raised huge armies consisting of untrained conscripts armed with standard weapons, and formed into large articulated units with fairly consistent leadership. Napoleon's *Grande Armée* also included large artillery forces, heavy and light cavalry, engineers, and a *corps d'intendance*, an administrative element that accompanied armies to ensure their supply and maintenance in the field. The French army was huge by existing standards. It therefore required a whole different level of organization and structure. Consequently, balanced divisions consisting of all arms were created, and these were then grouped into army corps and field armies, under generals of progressively higher rank. Senior command was attributed almost solely on the basis of competence in battle. Furthermore, political ideology and propaganda became part of the armoury of the French nation at arms. This was truly a formidable and frightful force.

The French had multiple enemies on numerous fronts, and had to fight enemies on many fronts simultaneously for years on end. Whereas wars had until then tended to be rather short, they were now protracted, intense, and costly. The old strategy and tactics were clearly insufficient. The French, therefore, developed the first notions of 'operational art,' and this level became increasingly elaborated throughout the 19th century, reaching its full development in the world wars and modern theories of war. In a nutshell, operational art is the theory and practice of combining campaigns and battles to achieve war aims and to create the conditions for battlefield success, whether these are material, human or technical. To do so, you need to develop clear war aims, campaign plans, permanent staffs of specialized planners, communication methods, intelligence analysts, and logisticians to create detailed operational plans and orders. While most military theorists treat logistics as a separate domain, for the purposes of comparison and application to business situations, we might consider it part of operational art even though it's more of a science. The same can be said of the many technical approaches that are used in modern military forces, such as in operations research, personnel selection, and training and development. Operational art in its widest sense is probably the level of warfare with the greatest number of extant applications of military theories and practices in business. Moreover, all of the specialized areas of business management, such as finance, human resources, business intelligence, marketing and promotion, operations and production management, and provisioning have clear parallels in the military realm. The key commonality is that these domains all support the aim of achieving strategic success by enabling and supporting successful tactical execution. Operational art and its various technical and managerial manifestations is the conceptual glue that links strategy and tactics, both in the military and business realms.

There is another way in which war and conflict can be relevant to the realm of business, and this is the notion of planes of warfare. Wars and other military conflicts play out on a physical plane and a moral plane. The physical plane is the whole material underpinning of war and combat: force ratios, weapons characteristics, material resources, money, people, etc. However, every historian, theoretician and practitioner of war and conflict knows that war and conflict occur just as much in the head and heart as on the field of battle. History is full of examples of large armies being defeated by much smaller forces. This is because psychological forces can sometimes be just as effective and efficient as physical forces. This is why leadership, morale, cohesion, subterfuge, surprise, and cunning are so fundamental to success in battle and in conflict in general.

The same applies to business. There is clearly a physical plane, involving calculations of resources, finances, technical characteristics of products and services, markets, costs, prices, etc. But there is also definitely a moral plane, where psychological and ethical factors play out and determine the relative success of strategies, business models, and business tactics. The moral planes of war and business are also similar in that both reflect the fundamental uncertainty and emotions involved in competing interests and random causal factors. This is why Clausewitz compared war to commerce: They are both "conflicts of human interests and activities."

The aim of this chapter has been to establish the fundamental utility of military thought and practice to business. Through my personal experiences in Bosnia and throughout my military career, I showed how I came to see the profound metaphorical, conceptual and technical linkages between the two domains. I also showed how the basic logical framework for thinking about war and conflict—the levels of strategy, operational art, and tactics as they play out on the physical and moral, psychological planes—provide a ready-made and accepted framework for thinking about business.

How This Book Is Organized

The remainder of this book provides detailed applications of military theory and practice for business. Chapter two shows how to apply offensive principles of war to business strategy, operations, tactics, and organizational dynamics in general. In Chapter three, I do the same thing, but for defensive situations. We will see how the key difference between offence and defence is in who has the initiative, you or the enemy. Chapters four and five provide a deeper look at three key principles of war, respectively the principle of the objective and the linked principles of mass and economy. I consider these to be particularly applicable in business, because everyone needs to know where they are going (objective), and there are never enough resources to do everything you want to do (mass and economy). Chapter six is a primer on military decision-making and planning, and how they can be applied to business situations. This chapter will also include a discussion of military notions of uncertainty, friction, and risk, because I have found in my consulting practice that this is an area that needs to be considered much more than it usually is. Chapter seven describes the most relevant concepts of military intelligence and how they can be applied in competitive business situations. Chapter eight examines the key concepts of military logistics and other technical aspects of warfare and how they can be applied in business. Chapters nine and ten close out the book, and examine morale, cohesion, motivation, and leadership from a military standpoint and their application to business and organizations in general. The final section in chapter 10 provides a list of ten principles of military leadership, along with diagnostic questions for each one and some techniques for building skills in those areas.

Throughout the book, each chapter will include examples from military history, personal anecdotes, business examples, and explanation of the key military concepts and how they should be applied to business problems and situations. I will also include exercises and diagrams that help business executives, managers, and entrepreneurs apply these concepts and tools to their own reality. Finally, each chapter includes a number of highlighted 'Brilliant Manoeuvres' that encapsulate the lessons of military wisdom to win business battles.

Chapter 2

Offence: Seizing and Maintaining the Initiative

The best form of defence is attack.

Carl von Clausewitz

Military tactics are like unto water; for water in its natural course runs away from high places and hastens downwards. So in war, the way is to avoid what is strong and to strike at what is weak. Water shapes its course according to the nature of the ground over which it flows; the soldier works out his victory in relation to the foe he is facing. Therefore, just as water retains no constant shape, so in warfare there are no constant conditions.

Sun Tzu

The first and most important principle of war and the only sure road to victory is offence. Defence is only a temporary measure. Offence, however, isn't just about attacking. It is also a mindset of seizing and maintaining the initiative by keeping the enemy off balance. No battle or war was ever won by purely defensive action. Offence is about taking the initiative and attacking the enemy at a time and a place of one's choosing. Speed, shock and surprise are essential to generating momentum, but they all depend on the willingness to take calculated risks, and to put the enemy in a defensive posture. To win requires seizing and maintaining the initiative; going on the defensive only buys time to withdraw, reorient or reconstitute one's forces. The same fundamental logic applies in business.

Brilliant Manoeuvre

To win in war and business requires seizing and maintaining the initiative; going on the defensive only buys time to withdraw, reorient or reconstitute one's forces.

We will discuss the principles of defensive strategy in detail in Chapter 3; this chapter is devoted to the key principles of offence. Each section in this chapter examines one of the four most relevant principles of offence (see the text box) for business strategy and tactics and how they are best applied to business situations.

Principles of Offence

- **Seize and Maintain the Initiative.** Offence is about taking the initiative and attacking the enemy or competition at a time and a place of one's choosing. To do this requires freedom of action, which is the ability to choose the time and place to act.

- **Manoeuvre for Advantage.** Create dilemmas for the enemy or exploit his dilemmas so that he commits to one course of action, which then creates vulnerabilities that can be exploited through superior intelligence and speed. Attack when and where the enemy least expects it.

- **Use the Indirect Approach.** The best way to defeat an entrenched enemy is to go around him, exposing weaknesses and gaps in the defence, and exploiting them to go beyond his defences in order to threaten his whole position.

- **Probe and Follow the Path of Least Resistance.** You can't know definitively at any time whether your moves are certain to work owing to incomplete information. It is therefore best to advance by probing, finding weaknesses and reinforcing successful incursions by following the path of least resistance.

Seize and Maintain the Initiative

One of the best examples of the need to seize and maintain the initiative occurred during the Falklands War between Britain and Argentina in 1982. A Victoria Cross was awarded posthumously to Lieutenant Colonel Herbert 'H' Jones of the British Army for his gallantry and initiative in the capture of Goose Green and the liberation of Darwin. Here are excerpts from the official citation as published in *The London Gazette* of October 8th 1982 (ellipses omitted):

> *"On 28th May 1982 Lieutenant Colonel Jones was commanding 2nd Battalion The Parachute Regiment on operations on the Falkland Islands. The Battalion was ordered to attack enemy positions in and around the settlements of Darwin and Goose Green. During the attack, the Battalion was held up just South of Darwin by a particularly well-prepared and resilient enemy position of at least eleven trenches on an important ridge. However, these had been well prepared and continued to pour effective fire onto the Battalion advance, which, by now held up for over an hour and under increasingly heavy artillery fire, was in danger of faltering. In his effort to gain a good viewpoint, Colonel Jones was now at the very front of his Battalion. It was clear to him that desperate measures were needed in order to overcome the enemy position and rekindle the attack, and that unless these measures were taken promptly the Battalion would sustain increasing casualties and the attack perhaps even fail. It was time for personal leadership and action. Colonel Jones immediately seized a sub-machine gun, and, calling on those around him and with total disregard for his own safety, charged the nearest enemy position. This action exposed him to fire from*

a number of trenches. As he charged up a short slope at the enemy position he was seen to fall and roll backward downhill. He immediately picked himself up, and again charged the enemy trench, firing his sub-machine gun and seemingly oblivious to the intense fire directed at him. He was hit by fire from another trench, which he outflanked, and fell dying only a few feet from the enemy he had assaulted. A short time later a company of the Battalion attacked the enemy, who quickly surrendered. The display of courage by Colonel Jones had completely undermined their will to fight further. Thereafter the momentum of the attack was rapidly regained, Darwin and Goose Green were liberated, and the Battalion released the local inhabitants unharmed and forced the surrender of some 1,200 of the enemy."

And now a business example: Lee Iacocca took the helm of Chrysler Corporation in the late 1970s after the US government temporarily saved the company. He had to do something significant to go on the offensive. Despite market research that showed little interest in a convertible, he ordered his engineers to cut the roof off a Chrysler New Yorker sedan to make a prototype convertible he could drive. Reactions were immediate and very positive so he decided to go ahead with a new line of convertibles, thereby re-invigorating the brands and the reputation of the company. The highly successful introduction of the minivan, a category-buster that combined the size of the station wagon with the comfort and space of a van on a car chassis, followed. It was so successful that imitations started pouring out from the competition. Unfortunately, Chrysler was not able to sustain this level of innovation over time, and has declined almost to oblivion since then.

As illustrated by Jones's charge at Goose Green, the purpose of offensive action is to seize and maintain the initiative; the means to this is to attack the enemy at a time and place of your choosing. If the timing is right, an attack can have a devastating effect on the enemy. The example of Lee Iacocca when he was at the helm of Chrysler Corporation is also an excellent illustration of seizing the initiative through offensive action. He knew he had to do something, if not drastic, then at least significant enough to stir his troops, and make an impact in the market. The reintroduction of the convertible sent a clear message that Chrysler was back, and that the company intended to compete vigorously.

The key to Jones's and Iacocca's successes in the examples above was the creation and exercise of freedom of action, a concept that will be elaborated further in this section. Moreover, they didn't wait for the situation to evolve but rather took matters into their own hands. They moved with great speed, surprising the enemy and competition, and showed resolve in pursuing their chosen course of action. In business terms, this is the difference between seeking out opportunities to expand and better meet the needs of markets and customers, or to hunker down and wait for the competition to move so you can imitate them. The latter can be a viable option, as we have seen over the years with the car rental company Avis, whose motto was "We try harder," a clear example of follow-the-leader. However, the danger in this approach is leaving the initiative in the hands of the market leader, which was Hertz. As shown by Jerry Porras and Jim Collins in their bestseller *Built to Last*, it pays to be the market leader in terms of growth and value created for shareholders. Ultimately, giving up initiative can lead to a full defensive posture. This should only be a temporary measure to buy time to reconstitute and to plan for retaking the initiative and going back on the offensive. Ultimately, in both war and business, lack of initiative equals stasis, and stasis leads eventually to death.

Freedom of action is essential to initiative, as it underlies the ability to act according to one's will and timetable. It allows the attacker to act with minimal constraints from the enemy or competitors at a time and place of one's own choosing. Freedom of action can result from the absence of a threat but, more often than not, it is a state of mind. Lieutenant Colonel Herbert Jones could see that his entire battalion's advance was being held up by a strong enemy defensive position. However, the enemy was really only strong in this location. It is the latter fact that gave him freedom of action because he knew that if he acted with vigour, his attack would surprise the enemy and rally his forces to continue the attack. He chose to act with temerity and resolve, and this led to the resumption and ultimate success of his battalion's offensive mission, though he paid with his life. In other words, he manufactured his freedom of action.

Brilliant Manoeuvre

Freedom of action is essential to initiative, as it underlies the ability to act according to one's will and timetable. It allows the attacker to act with minimal constraints from the enemy or competitors at a time and place of his choosing.

It can take a lot of nerve to create or leverage freedom of action, either in the military or business spheres. This is because the current situation seems so familiar. There appears to be no reason to change one's habits or to make a bold move. Conversely, it can be enticing to give up, which is why morale and cohesion are also required to seize and maintain the initiative. Morale and cohesion are so critical in all undertakings whether in business, politics, war, or any other social endeavour that they merit a full discussion in Chapter 9.

In business, freedom of action and the initiative it enables are often the result of a strategic re-definition. Companies often have to undermine their main business lines by investing in new ones, thus transforming themselves in the process. Consider the example of IBM, a major company that has successfully negotiated several major technological transitions throughout its existence. The first transition was from mechanical office machines such as punch card readers to analog electronic computers and electric typewriters. Then, it made the transition to digital computers and the requisite software. When the microcomputer came out in the late 1970s, IBM was at the forefront of this shift through the introduction of its Personal Computer, the PC. It stuck with its PC division until the mid 2000s when it sold it to Lenovo in China. In the meantime, IBM transformed itself into the largest software and digital services developer and provider in the world.

Throughout this process of change, had IBM seen itself as simply a manufacturer of punch cards and other mechanical devices, it would have foundered. Instead, it defined itself from the start as a manufacturer of business machines, in other words, any kind of machine that could provide value in the world of business. This meant machines that permitted collecting, analyzing, storing, and manipulating mountains of data and information. Despite its name, IBM evolved in the 1990s from being simply a business machine company to one that helped its customers use data and information for their business success. It saw its value and competitive advantage in more general terms as the management of information. The actual physical means of doing so, the material substrate, became of less importance. Today, IBM sees itself as using technology to generate value for its clients.

IBM is an example of how a company has consistently thrived by generating freedom of action. How did it do so? Primarily by refusing to be hemmed in to a definition of itself that would have rendered its businesses irrelevant over time. By seeing its value in more abstract and general terms, its senior managers were able to take the leaps of faith that were necessary at critical junctures in its history. IBM's example shows that freedom of action isn't just important to maintain initiative; it is vital.

Strategic Application of Seizing and Maintaining the Initiative

- Do you find yourself continually responding to competitors' actions or do you instead initiate changes that your competitors must respond to?
- Do your competitors and customers find you predictable? Is there something you could start doing that would be out of character, but that would put them on the defensive and give you back the initiative?
- How do you define your mission and business? Is it a narrow view—providing a particular category of product or service—or is it a wider view—searching for ways of fulfilling customer needs at a more general or abstract level? Could you widen the scope of your business by redefining your business and mission?
- Is it likely that you will still be serving exactly the same customers in the same way in one year, two years, five years, or even ten years? What would have to happen for this situation to remain the same at those time intervals? This will give you an indication of how realistic your forecasts are.
- Are your decisions today likely to hem you in in the short, medium, or long terms? What can you do to innovate while maintaining your freedom of action in the longer term?
- How fast can you move to implement new strategies and tactics?

Damned if You Do and Damned if You Don't: Manoeuvre for Advantage

The essence of manoeuvre is to create dilemmas for the enemy so he commits, or remains committed to, one particular course of action. This then creates vulnerabilities that can be exploited through superior intelligence, surprise and speed. Such a course of action recognizes and uses the enemy's or the competition's posture to turn it into a dilemma for the enemy or competitor.

This is extremely difficult to achieve on the battlefield, and there are only a few examples in history of an attacker creating a strategic or operational dilemma for the enemy. In fact, failures have been much more frequent than successes in this regard. For example, during the U.S. Civil War, the Confederates tried to occupy the strategic crossroads of Gettysburg to draw the Union forces into a decisive battle before the Union forces added to their material superiority. However, it led to a resounding defeat of Lee's Confederate army, and is widely acknowledged as the turning point in the war.

Brilliant Manoeuvre

The essence of manoeuvre is to create dilemmas for the opponent so he commits, or remains committed to, one particular course of action. This then creates vulnerabilities that can be exploited through superior intelligence, surprise and speed.

When the Germans invaded France and the Low Countries in May 1940, they first sent a strong armoured force into the Netherlands and northern Belgium. This played on the French and British belief that the German invasion manoeuvre would be a replica of the First World War's sweeping encirclement through the Low Countries down to Paris—the famous Schlieffen Plan. As the Germans expected, the French countered by moving their well equipped mobile divisions northward into Belgium to halt what they believed to be the main German thrust. Meanwhile, the Germans moved an even larger armoured force through the dense Ardennes Forest of northern France and south eastern Belgium between the main French force further north and the Maginot Line. This force then executed a surgical cut through northern France thereby isolating the elite French divisions and the British Expeditionary Force, leaving most of them stranded in Belgium and Northern France. Basically, the Germans won their bet because of superior strategy and not superiority of numbers or technology. They played on the French wish to avoid war on French soil at all costs, and this is what allowed them to win a resounding victory against the most powerful army in Europe. It was a risky manoeuvre that worked because it played on the mindset of the defenders. In the process, they also avoided a costly frontal assault against the Maginot Line.

Had the Germans decided to invade France by attacking the Maginot Line, this would have been a frontal attack, an example of the direct approach. Instead, the Germans attacked the French by first invading the Netherlands and Belgium, and then by punching through the Ardennes Forest, a known French vulnerability. The French had considered that possibility but saw it as too improbable. Therefore, the German attack in 1940 was an example of a successful operational manoeuvre. The Germans exploited a vulnerability, which allowed them to cut off and encircle part of the main French and British forces. This led to French capitulation and a four-year occupation by Nazi Germany, while the British had to stage an operational retreat at Dunkirk.

Is it possible in business to create a dilemma for a competitor? Is it possible to get a competitor to fall literally into a strategic trap? It is much more probable that the business trying to overtake a competitor will simply be exploiting the competitor's perceived strengths with existing customers rather than creating a dilemma out of thin air. This is because companies are not really fighting against each other but rather competing to better serve their customers and market segments. However, the principle is the same: to try to leverage the competitor's vulnerability in order to achieve a breakthrough into his market. Richard Foster called the ability to do this in a business context "the attacker's advantage."

It is interesting that not one of the vacuum tube manufacturers became a leading producer of integrated circuits and transistors. This cycle has been repeated time and again in the process of creative destruction that is modern capitalism, as Joseph Schumpeter described. This is because successful companies are usually so focused on serving their existing customers with existing or slightly modified products and services that they don't see smaller companies and other outsiders come from out of nowhere to overtake their market. We could say that the more successful a company has been in a particular segment, the more likely it will be blind to new entrants and, especially, to substitutes. The ability of a new entrant to exploit this vulnerability is what leads to the strategic dilemma for the strong incumbents. A business that is attacking an established competitor with a strong position is better to let the competition focus on existing customers and other competitors while exploiting a weakness or vulnerability in the current market coverage. This is best done by creating a new product or service to meet a need that is currently not being fulfilled. The attacker stealthily stalks the established companies, while they keep doing what they've been doing, usually quite successfully. In fact, it is this continuing focus by competitors on what has made them successful in the past that creates their critical vulnerability.

Brilliant Manoeuvre

A business that is attacking an established competitor with a strong position is better to let the competition focus on existing customers and other competitors while exploiting a weakness or vulnerability in the current market coverage.

In his bestseller on innovation, *The Innovator's Dilemma*, Clayton Christensen describes how, time and again, companies with a technical lead have failed to see the potential afforded by a disruptive technology, primarily because they are too focused on servicing the needs of their existing customers. What the new entrants and attackers did in Christensen's examples is to re-combine existing technologies and components in novel ways to serve customers that were not being served adequately, if at all, by the large, successful market leaders.

As an illustration of this cyclical pattern, Christensen describes how upstart companies with limited resources overtook leaders in hard drive technology, companies such as IBM, Seagate, and Quantum. The new hard drive models were not as technically advanced as those of the incumbents, but they combined existing components in new ways to service unmet needs in the marketplace. Once the next generation of hard drive technology would become established in a market that had not previously been served, the success would attract investment and competitors, which would expand the market for the product until it overtook the incumbents' previous markets. As Christensen points out, the large, successful incumbents actually did what was considered the right thing by focusing on their existing clients, but it is this focus—blindness even—that led to their loss of initiative. It's not as if these companies lacked the resources; rather, it was that the resources were devoted only to serving existing customers. They could often see the opportunity and even, in some cases, had their own next generation models in the works. They either didn't act on the information because they didn't see the ultimate potential of the innovation, or they were simply too focused on serving their existing customers with their existing and evolving products and services. Even more, their success hemmed them in and reduced their freedom of action, which caused them to lose the initiative against new entrants and substitutes. Conversely, the new entrants were able to exploit their outsider status by manoeuvring to exploit the leaders' strength and turn it into vulnerability. This gave them freedom of action, which led to them gaining the initiative, at least for a time.

Strategic Application of Manoeuvring for Advantage

- Regardless of the size of your current business, are you trying to penetrate a pre-existing market? If so, are there customers and market segments that are not currently well served by the competition?
- Are the existing market leaders highly successful at meeting the needs of their major customers? Are they focused almost exclusively on these customers? Do they see minor customers and un-served market segments as a nuisance or not worth the effort? If you can answer yes to any of

these questions, then there may be an excellent opportunity to create a strategic dilemma for your competitors.

- Could you recombine or combine existing components and technologies in novel ways that would meet some of the unfulfilled needs of customers or a market segment that is not currently being served?

Avoid Enemy Strengths: Use the Indirect Approach

On the night of 12 to 13 September 1759, British forces under Major General James Wolfe executed a daring manoeuvre to get around the French defences at Quebec City, commanded by the Marquis de Montcalm. This manoeuvre came at the end of a destructive though inconclusive three-month siege of the city by the British. With winter coming, Wolfe realized the need to press on with an assault against the French. However, previous attempts to engage the French without directly attacking the fortifications had failed. The French were simply too well ensconced. Wolfe decided that the solution was to sail upstream on the St-Lawrence River in order to land an infantry force of over 3,000 men approximately 3 kilometres west of the city at the base of a sheer cliff. This force then scaled the cliffs in the night, seized the small garrison that was defending the location, and then formed up on the Plains of Abraham to the immediate west of the main French fortifications on *Cap Diamant*, the highest point at Quebec. The British occupation of the position on the Plains was vital to the French, as it cut them off from reinforcements and resupply from Montreal. The French commander Montcalm felt compelled to leave the safety and strength of his fortifications and face the British in open combat on the Plains. Unfortunately for the French, the British prevailed in a whirlwind engagement that was over in about 15 minutes. The French subsequently surrendered Quebec City to the British, and were never able to recapture it. For this reason, the Battle of the Plains of Abraham is considered to be the decisive engagement during the Seven Years War in Canada. This battle is a perfect example of the use of the indirect approach in warfare.

The best way to defeat a defending enemy is to find and bypass his main defences, exposing weaknesses and gaps in the defence, and exploiting these to go deep and threaten his entire position. This also requires that the attacker avoid obstacles and be prepared to reinforce successful probes and penetrations. The indirect approach is considered far superior in military strategy because the direct approach requires attacking the enemy by frontal assault. This is usually very costly as it basically consists of doing what the enemy expects you to do, in the most obvious and direct manner possible.

Brilliant Manoeuvre

The best way to defeat a defending enemy or competitor is to find and bypass his main defences, exposing weaknesses and gaps in the defence, and exploiting these to go deep and threaten his entire position.

Over and above the fact that attacking requires more resources than defending, doing so frontally is even more costly. The enemy sees you coming and has arrayed most of his firepower and fortifications to take the brunt of your assault. In battle, an army must send waves of assault troops against the enemy's position. If it's fortified or reinforced in any way by natural or man-made obstacles, it makes the attack that much more costly. The defender also chooses favourable ground in order to canalize and surprise the attacker. At a minimum, an attacker requires a 3 to 1 advantage in numbers and firepower, but this can be even higher in the case of a frontal attack, more on the order of 5, 6, and even 10 to 1. The risks and costs of a frontal assault against an enemy or competitor's position are illustrated in Figures 2.1 and 2.2.

Figure 2.1: Direct Approach in Battle

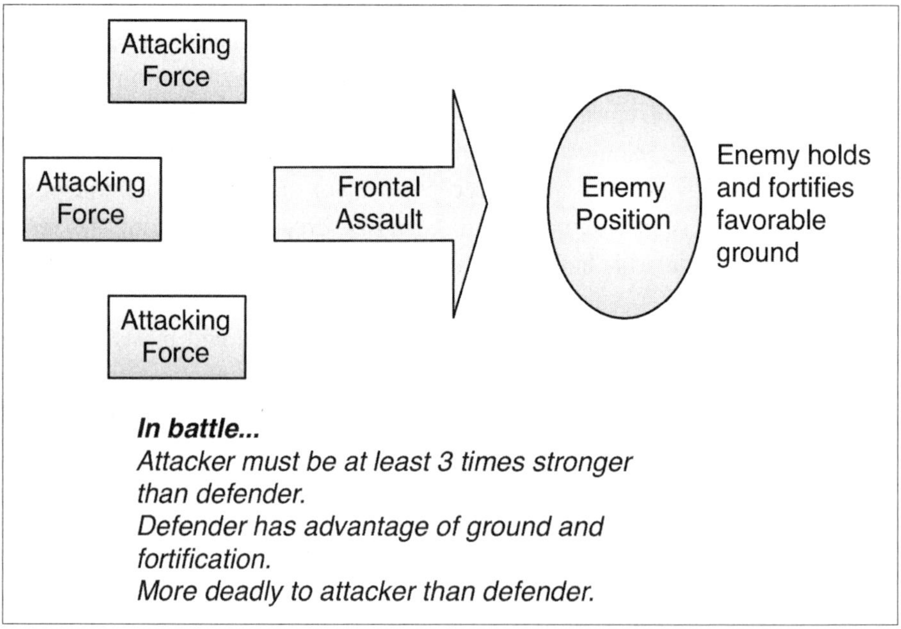

Attacking Force		
Attacking Force	Frontal Assault ⟶	Enemy Position
Attacking Force		

Enemy holds and fortifies favorable ground

In battle...
Attacker must be at least 3 times stronger than defender.
Defender has advantage of ground and fortification.
More deadly to attacker than defender.

Figure 2.2: Direct Approach in Business

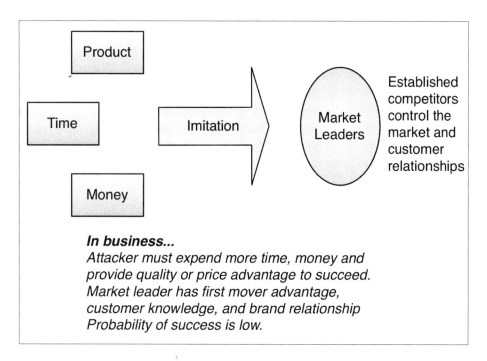

In business...
Attacker must expend more time, money and provide quality or price advantage to succeed. Market leader has first mover advantage, customer knowledge, and brand relationship Probability of success is low.

The company that wishes to attack market leaders by attacking them frontally in a direct approach faces major risks with few prospects of success. The attacker must invest considerable sums for tooling up, promotion and advertising. Established competitors, especially the market leader, have the choicest customers and the advantage of time, having ensconced themselves first in that particular segment. They have the defender's advantage of time, location, and knowledge of the ground they occupy.

Conversely, using the indirect approach, the attacker attempts to be much more subtle, mainly by creating or finding a key vulnerability and then exploiting it. The aim of the indirect approach is to go around the defender's main positions to strike him in his flank, or to go around his positions in order to attack an objective behind him. This means either hitting him with a flank attack, or bypassing him completely in order to head for open country beyond his main line of defence. As we saw in the previous section and in the example of the British manoeuvre at Quebec in 1759, this requires skill and craftiness in manoeuvring for advantage. The attacker must also show initiative, especially by creating and exploiting freedom of action. This is illustrated in Figure 2.3. By going around the enemy's prepared position, the attacker forces the defender out into the open, which negates his advantage of ground and his fortification.

Figure 2.3: Indirect Approach in Battle

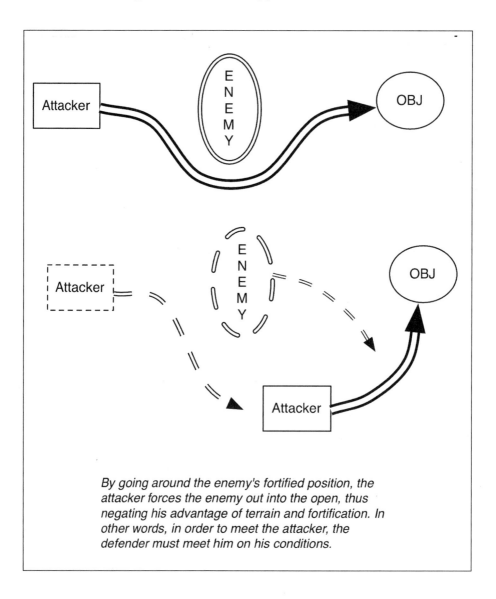

By going around the enemy's fortified position, the attacker forces the enemy out into the open, thus negating his advantage of terrain and fortification. In other words, in order to meet the attacker, the defender must meet him on his conditions.

Brilliant Manoeuvre

The aim of the indirect approach is to go around the defender's main positions to strike him in his flank, or to go around his positions in order to attack an objective behind him.

It isn't always easy to get around the enemy's defences to strike at his vulnerable flank or threaten an objective in the rear. The First World War in Western Europe started out with a huge, sweeping manoeuvre based on the famous Schlieffen Plan through the Low Countries. The French army was almost outflanked by the German Army but was able to halt the German advance and avoid encirclement at the 1st Battle of the Marne in September 1914. There then followed a "race to the sea" by both sides with repeated attempts to outflank each other. By the end of 1914, the front line ran continuously between the North Sea and Switzerland with defences arrayed in depth. This made outflanking and other indirect manoeuvres effectively impossible; it's why the war in France became associated with static trench warfare.

In business, though, the chances that there will be a continuous front of competitors with complete control of the market are extremely low. This makes the indirect approach in business much more a case of going around competitors by creating an offering for an entirely new market segment, offering new or higher quality products, or by offering the same or similar products to those of the competition for a lower price, as shown in Figures 2.4a and 2.4b.

Figure 2.4a: Indirect Approach in Business
Case 1 – Focus on New Segments

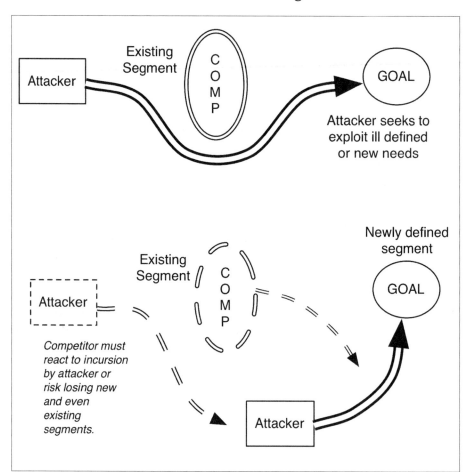

The first option (Figure 2.4a) corresponds to strategic segmentation with a view to making the competition irrelevant. The other two options (Figure 2.4b) correspond respectively to differentiation and cost leadership strategies, which have been well described in theoretical terms by Michael Porter in his seminal works, *Competitive Strategy* and *Competitive Advantage*.

We saw an example of cost leadership time and again over the decades as, first Japanese, and then Korean automakers were able to exploit their cost advantages by offering inexpensive cars that were reasonably reliable. Over the years, Japanese carmakers developed an advantage in reliability and fuel economy, and were therefore able to increase prices and compete directly with the American companies.

Figure 2.4b: Indirect Approach in Business
Case 2 – Focus on Product/Cost Leadership

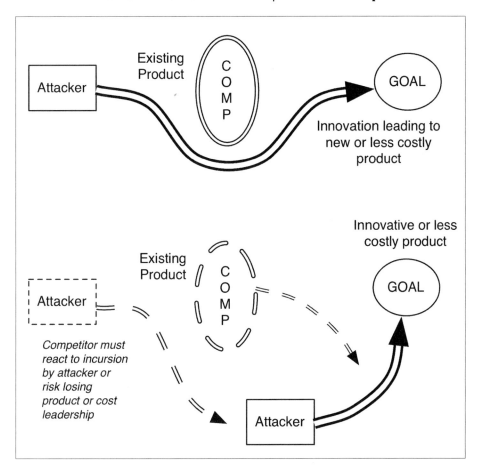

South Korean carmakers such as Kia and Hyundai are essentially repeating the same manoeuvre that their Japanese competitors did earlier, but in their case they're not only undermining the Americans' position, but also that of the Japanese.

Innovation is the key way that businesses redefine needs and markets by outflanking or encircling the competition. The more disruptive the innovation, the more it resembles a complete encirclement of the enemy. Furthermore, outflanking or encircling a competitor with an innovative product forces the competitor to expend resources in costly defensive moves. The competitor has to invest in upgrades and product differentiation to stay competitive. Even better from the standpoint of the attacker is the introduction of a disruptive product that redefines the market or customer needs, or introduces new ones.

Brilliant Manoeuvre

Innovation is the key way that businesses redefine needs and markets by outflanking or encircling the competition. The more disruptive the innovation, the more it resembles a complete encirclement of the enemy.

Apple provides the perfect illustration of this principle of the indirect approach in business. First in 2007 and then again in 2010, Apple completely re-imagined two product categories by combining their previously disparate features into single devices. The iPad and iPhone can be called breakthrough products since Apple outflanked competitors with the new product categories. They didn't bother trying to imitate others or to compete on the terms of their competitors. Instead, in the case of the iPhone, Apple modified expectations about what constituted a smart phone. This was a classic outflanking manoeuvre, and went clean around the competition. When the iPhone was first introduced in 2007, it was acknowledged immediately as a new type of product, even though many of its features already existed and its capabilities were still embryonic. In the case of the iPad, the company completed a strategic encirclement by inventing the tablet computer. In both cases, Apple introduced a breakthrough product by combining already existing technologies into a great design, which allowed it to redefine the mobile computing market.

As discussed in the section on manoeuvring for advantage, innovation can provide a steady stream of disruptive products and services that bypass the market leaders' hold on an existing market. While the market leaders and incumbents are focused on defending their turf with the best customers, attackers can swarm them by offering innovative products and services to under-served customers. These innovations often require minor capital outlays, as they are often simply re-configured, existing products or novel combinations of existing components.

Strategic Application of the Indirect Approach

- Are there customers, segments, or entire markets that are currently inadequately served or ignored by established competitors?
- Are there existing products and services that could be modified to better meet these needs?
- Are there components or technologies that could be re-combined or suitably modified to meet these needs?

- Could you effectively outflank and bypass the competition by exploiting these under-served or ignored needs?
- What competencies and resources can you bring to bear to exploit these opportunities?
- What financial, human, technical, marketing, and sales capabilities could you develop or acquire to bypass the competition?
- Can you keep the risks within acceptable bounds? What means could you use to do so?

The Path of Least Resistance: Probe for Gaps and Reinforce Successful Incursions

Let's recap the principles of offensive strategy we've explored so far. First, it is essential to both military and business success to adopt an offensive mind-set. This can be summarized as seizing and maintaining the initiative, primarily as exercised through freedom of action. The primary means of doing so is to manoeuvre for advantage, by finding and exploiting the enemy's or competition's key vulnerabilities and weaknesses. Forces are then concentrated to pit strengths against weaknesses in order to bypass the enemy's defences, and break into open country beyond his main line of defence. In business, this is done by innovating new products and services primarily aimed at markets and customers that are poorly served by the current market leaders, focused as they are on their major customers and their needs. Another approach is to fight for cost leadership or differentiate your products relative to those of the competition. However, these are more like a frontal attack. It is the indirect approach that confers the attacker's advantage, as opposed to the defender's advantage of knowledge of ground with time to prepare and fortify his position.

But here we run into a problem. How do we know the locations of the main enemy positions and gaps in the defences? Attacking forces often run headlong into the enemy's main line of defence before realizing what has happened. In other situations, they send forces directly into ambushes or miss the main opportunities to break through the enemy's defences completely.

The equivalent questions in business are: Where is the competition and what are his vulnerabilities? Where are the under-served markets and customers, and what are their needs? A key problem, in other words, is committing to a line of advance or course of action without necessarily knowing if it is going to be the right one. A business can expend considerable resources by investing in the wrong ventures at the wrong time. Igor Ansoff was one of the fathers of business strategy.

In 1965 he wrote, "Firms have shown in the recent past an unfortunate tendency to plunge rather than probe." This observation is just as relevant today as it was then. He was of course referring to the fact that many, if not most companies tend to plunge into major strategic changes without necessarily knowing what they are getting themselves into. The result can be waves of mergers and acquisitions, investment bubbles, and various other manifestations of economic, financial and business herding.

The correct way of proceeding in battle is for an attacking force to send out a vanguard of reconnaissance elements to scout for weaknesses in the defender's dispositions. Once these are identified, the main body can follow and squeeze between the defender's strong points, thus avoiding costly frontal assaults. The aim is to get around the main defences in order to threaten vital lines of communication and to reach objectives in depth. By doing so, the attacker hopes that the defender will abandon the fortifications and the advantage of holding his ground. The idea is to find the weak spots and reinforce successful penetrations of the defences.

Brilliant Manoeuvre

Send out a vanguard of reconnaissance elements to scout for weaknesses in the defender's dispositions. Once these are identified, the main body can follow and squeeze between the defender's strong points, thus avoiding costly frontal assaults.

In his book *Innovation and Entrepreneurship*, Peter Drucker identified unexpected successes and failures as rich sources of innovation. He also propounded reinforcing strengths as the road to business success. What are some of the principles for avoiding obstacles and reinforcing successes in business? Is there an equivalent in business to sending out a vanguard element to reconnoiter the enemy's defences? The answer is yes, and it involves probing for gaps in market coverage, then reinforcing successful experiments by pouring in resources to turn the incursions into breakthroughs. It is probing and following the path of success that allows a business to keep moving and innovating, without plunging recklessly into a competitor's territory.

In more recent years, Michael Raynor in *The Strategy Paradox* has proposed a more realistic and empirical reason for the success of companies. Companies that are successful are those that have happened upon successful products, services or business models then were able, either through design or blind chance, to exploit and reinforce these successes. In other words, business success is much more a question of trying many different things, then knowing enough to jump on a wave of success.

Businesses that try different things to get around established competitors and then reinforce the resulting incursions have a better chance of generating breakthroughs. None of this is foolproof of course, but there is really no alternative to taking the initiative to work your way around the competitors by offering innovative products and services. The real skill though is in identifying the successful breaches and incursions and reinforcing them. Nobody knows beforehand since no one can predict success in the marketplace. Instead, successful businesses consistently go around the competition by appealing directly to customers. They do so by making small, probing advances with new and modified products, services, capabilities, and business models. Once they see a successful penetration of a competitor's market position, they pour resources into the breach in the hope of turning the small incursion into an unmitigated breakthrough.

Brilliant Manoeuvre

Make small, probing advances with new and modified products, services, capabilities, and business models. Once there is a successful penetration of a competitor's market position, pour resources into the breach to create a breakthrough.

This has a direct parallel in the military concept of probing to find vulnerabilities in the enemy's defences rather than assaulting directly in a frontal attack. In order for this approach to work, however, the attacking force must advance on a wide front with many small probing forces. This idea of probing rather than plunging is one of the most powerful things that a company can do to remain relevant to the market over time. It's a way of merging the need for offensive strategy by seizing and maintaining the initiative, while prudently managing the risks of change and inherent uncertainty of outcomes. Figures 2.5a and 2.5b illustrate the similarities between a probing advance on the battlefield and a probing approach to innovation in business. We also see the relationship between the experimental, probing approach and the need to reinforce success by following the path of least resistance.

Figures 2.5a: Reinforcing Successful Probing Attacks in Battle

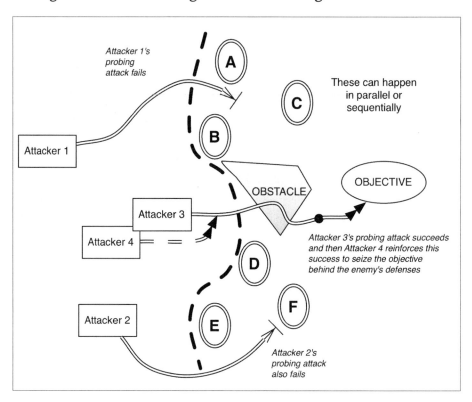

In either case, there is no certainty of success for any particular line of advance. When advancing against the enemy, the chances of finding vulnerability or weakness in the defences is much greater if you advance on a wide front and try different axes of advance. This can be done sequentially but it is better if it happens simultaneously since it generates greater surprise and speed. It also forces the enemy to spread resources because he doesn't know where the main thrust will come.

Brilliant Manoeuvre

You can't predict the outcomes of your experiments ahead of time. The objective is rather to see what works, then to reinforce that success.

Figures 2.5b: Reinforcing Successful Probing Attacks in Business

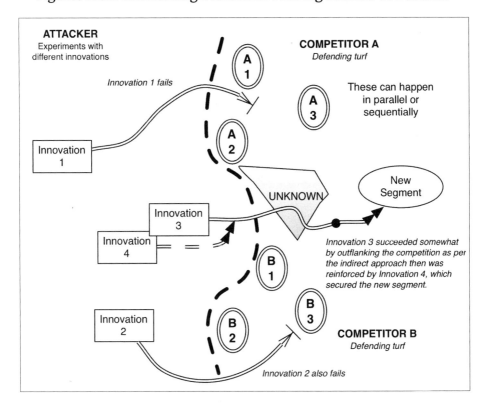

In business, the equivalent to advancing with probing attacks on a wide front is to have a number of experiments underway at the same time. These can include new or modified products, new or modified services, new internal capabilities and business processes, or even entirely new business models. The important thing, as pointed out by Raynor in *The Strategy Paradox*, is to avoid believing that you can predict the outcomes of your experiments ahead of time. The objective is rather to see what works, then to reinforce that success. You do this by identifying the successes and then reinforcing them by allocating additional resources to them. In practice, this means dropping unsuccessful, probing experiments and transferring the resources from them or from existing lines of business to the new, successful experiments. Just as on the battlefield, this takes discipline and the right information. The approach isn't perfect and foolproof—no approach is—but the alternative is trying to guess what will succeed before you have the information, then over-investing in a new and potentially unsuccessful strategy.

*King Henry III of England soundly defeated the French Army
at the Battle of Crécy in August, 1346. However, rather than
pursue the disorganized French with a view to destroying them,
he sat on his victory and this gave the French king a chance
to reconstitute his forces to fight another day. Interestingly,
the English had owed their victory to French obstinacy and the
foolhardiness of repeated, knightly charges against their center,
which allowed the English long bowmen to massacre them at a
distance from the flanks while the dismounted English knights
and infantry stood their ground in the middle. If the French had
instead gone around the English position at Crécy to attack their
lines of communication back to the Channel ports, the result
would no doubt have been very different.*

The principles of probing

- **You learn more by moving and trying things than by staying put.** The normal impulse is to stay put and defend your position when you don't know where to go or what to do. Unfortunately, this leaves you open to rapid change in the market as well as competitive threats. Moving gradually into a new market or a new product or service category gives you time to learn and adjust your approach without over-investing at the beginning. You also get to pull back if, as often happens, you've made a mistake or misjudged the situation.

- **Advance on a wide (or wider) front.** It's best to send scouting parties to report back about the lay of the land and the enemy's positions, then to follow up with more forces if you're successful. In business, this can mean trying many, small experiments with new products or markets to see what will happen, and then preserving those that succeed.

- **Don't put all your eggs into one basket.** If one can't make accurate and timely predictions to know what will succeed in the long run then it stands to reason that one needs to diversify investments and assets. This doesn't mean becoming a conglomerate. It is preferable to experiment in a controlled manner at the edges of the business while using profits in existing business lines to fuel that exploratory work.

Always cover your moves. When I was a young infantry officer, we were taught to cover our moves with a firebase that could provide support in case we came under enemy fire. The same applies in business. It's better to move gradually over time into a new market or with a new strategy by small steps. This can be done remarkably quickly if you keep up the pressure by making incremental changes in a deliberate and consistent manner.

Reinforce success with backup forces. Once you have made it through the enemy's front lines, apply resources to reinforce the initial breakthrough. The same notion applies to experimental business efforts. Success with one or some of them can be reinforced with new resources or with resources transferred from existing business lines. The result can be better positioning for the future.

Maintain reserves to exploit success. All of these principles require some level of resources, first to experiment and then to reinforce success by investing in the winners. This requires the maintenance of cash reserves or access to capital either from an existing business line, or by borrowing or by attracting new investors.

Divest from repeated failure. Trying to compete directly against a well-established competitor with a me-too product or service is analogous to attempting a frontal assault against a well-entrenched defender. It will be costly, and most probably lead to failure. Even worse is continuing to pour resources into a losing proposition such as the French did at Crécy. This is like Microsoft's repeated attempts to develop its own search engine and social networking services at a cost of billions of dollars. They work reasonably well and may even be better than the competition's, but they are attacking established services such as Google and Facebook.

Beware of complacency. An old saw in the military is that a fast advance with little enemy resistance might be a sign of an impending ambush. In other words, the enemy might be deliberately drawing you in the better to hit you when you least expect it and might possibly be over-extended. By the same token, fast progress in business can be a sign of true success, but it could also be a sign of danger. For instance, new technology will probably attract early adopters, many of whom are technophiles. They might adopt the technology enthusiastically but they might not be representative of the bulk of users, which should be the focus in most cases. It is therefore prudent to use this initial success to bolster a new product category, while remaining cognizant of the desires and needs of the wider market.

▪ **Exploit successes**. Throughout history, military commanders have been faulted for failing to exploit enemy weaknesses and reinforcing their own successes, just as the English failed to exploit their massive victory at Crécy with a pursuit. Unfortunately, this is easier said than done. The challenge is to distinguish real failure from temporary setback and, just as in the previous point, a major success from a momentary or small one. The best way is to experiment and to try different things while being careful to monitor cause and effect. This is why many companies maintain many small investments in various technologies and approaches, watching and waiting to see what will stick and what will fall by the wayside. When they see a success, they invest in it to see how far they can get, even to the point of adjusting their overall strategy and business model.

Strategic Application of the Path of Probing and Reinforcing Success

▪ Have you been failing repeatedly with a new product or market despite sustained effort and huge investment in resources? What would be the effect of withdrawing from this approach?

▪ Are you maintaining products or staying in markets because of pigheadedness, or because you can truly win with them?

▪ Do you have raging successes that you have ignored because they didn't fit your ideas of the business or strategy? What about more obscure successes within your business?

▪ What would it take to elevate these unexpected successes to replace the repeated failures? Can you transfer resources from the latter to the former?

▪ Do you have a systematic approach to experimenting with new products, markets, processes, and business models? Are you open to change or do you stick to your knitting in the face of contrary evidence?

▪ Do you reinforce successes cautiously while staying on the lookout for signs of danger and competitive threats?

Summary

- The first and most important principle of war, and the only sure road to victory, is offence. Defence should be only be used as a temporary measure before trying to regain the initiative.

- The objective—and essence—of offensive action is to seize and maintain the initiative. When you have the initiative, you can choose the time and place to strike.

- The main means of offensive action is manoeuvre, which seeks to create dilemmas for one's opponents and competitors so they commit to a course of action that enables exploitation of their vulnerabilities through one's strengths.

- A business that is attacking an established competitor is better to let that company focus on its current strong position while exploiting a weakness in its current market coverage.

- When attacking it is always better to avoid the enemy's main defences and attempt to go around them or avoid them altogether. Finding or exploiting small gaps in order to break through and go deep into enemy territory accomplishes this.

- Innovation is the main way to outflank or avoid the competition's strong defences. The more disruptive the innovation, the more it resembles a complete encirclement of the enemy.

- There is no way to know definitively at any point in time whether offensive moves are certain to work. This is why it is best to advance by probing, finding weaknesses and reinforcing successful incursions by following the path of least resistance.

- Offensive business strategy succeeds best when companies make small, probing advances, experimenting with new products, services, processes, and business models. Once they see a successful penetration of a competitor's market position, they can pour resources into the breach in the hope of turning a small incursion into a major breakthrough.

- The table on the next page provides an overview of additional applications of offensive principles in operational, organizational, tactical, and leadership terms.

Other Applications of the Principles and Concepts of Offence

Offensive Principle	Operational	Organizational	Tactical	Leadership and Influence
		Illustrative Examples		
	Implementing a major strategic change against internal opposition or resistance	Creating a new department to create a new product in a chaotic situation	Sales or business development situation with a new prospect	Getting your team to bounce back from a setback
Seize and maintain the initiative	Move fast and don't wait for perfection in the plan or the conditions.	Take advantage of enthusiasm for the project; select the best person to lead from within internal resources; staff with supporters.	Use powerful language and control the discussion by setting the agenda.	Get them together immediately to do a "lessons learned" session.
Use the indirect approach	Identify likely detractors or opponents. Try to coopt them to your approach or neutralize them by re-assigning them.	Move quickly while managing obstacles and hindrances. Only deal with them if they become manifest, because they may only be a mirage.	Ask probing questions and listen more than you speak. Respond to objections by asking why that is important to them.	Get them working on a new challenge quickly, or change the pace by doing something completely different.
Manoeuvre for advantage	Be open about the weaknesses and risks of your plan up front in order to disarm opposition. Get detractors to focus on insignificant details.	Offset weaknesses of some members with the strengths of others. Create a balanced set of capabilities.	Ask the prospect about objectives and goals rather than about what is dissatisfying or not working.	Get them looking for new challenges or initiatives so they aren't focused on the setback. Look for a quick win in something else.

Offensive Principle	Operational	Organizational	Tactical	Leadership and Influence
		Illustrative Examples		
Probe for openings and reinforce success	Experiment with different implementation approaches and then keep what is working while discontinuing what isn't.	Start small with a core team. Expand as needed with key reinforcements, or seek outside assistance without making the team too big too fast.	Look or listen for unmet or unsatisfied needs or objectives. Ask probing questions to position your products or services to meet those objectives or needs.	Celebrate small wins and successes. Recognize the work of your team members. Give the most demanding missions to your best people.

Chapter 3

Defence: Securing Position and Regaining the Initiative

But defence has a passive purpose: preservation; and attack a positive one: conquest. If defence is the stronger form of war, yet has a negative object, if follows that it should be used only so long as weakness compels, and be abandoned as soon as we are strong enough to pursue a positive object.
Defence is the stronger form of waging war.

Carl von Clausewitz

Invincibility lies in the defence; the possibility of victory in the attack.

Sun Tzu

In December 1944, Allied armies had been advancing against German forces in Northwest Europe since the Normandy landings in June. The Allies had achieved extraordinary strategic and operational success although at great cost, and had pushed the Germans back to the eastern parts of the Netherlands, Belgium and France. Despite this success, the Allies were close to exhaustion and in some cases had outpaced their ability to resupply themselves. Hitler saw an opportunity to launch a massive counterattack. This would eventually become known as the Battle of the Bulge. Hitler mustered his remaining forces in Northwest Europe for a last ditch attack through the Ardennes Forest of southeastern Belgium. In essence, he hoped to recreate the breakthrough of May 1940 so as to split the American and British Commonwealth forces. When the offensive was launched on 16 December 1944, American forces in the Ardennes, depleted, isolated and exhausted, were taken by surprise. They fell back almost along the entire front. Recognizing the critical nature of the situation, Eisenhower deployed the 101st Airborne Division to the area and ordered them to hold the city of Bastogne at all costs. This was vital ground because it was a major regional crossroads, the control of which would give the Germans the opportunity to continue their advance. The siege of Bastogne and the defensive battle fought by the American and British Commonwealth forces allowed the Allies to halt the German offensive and eventually stabilize the situation. This set the conditions for an Allied counteroffensive, launched on December 24th, which lasted well into January 1945. This eventually led to a major though costly Allied victory. The Battle of the Bulge proved to be the last major German counteroffensive of the war on the Western front. The reality of the situation had forced the Allies to go on the defensive, but it was defensive success that set the conditions for the renewal of offensive operations that lasted to the end of the war.

Defence is the fighting posture of a force that has relinquished the initiative, either deliberately or owing to the actions of the enemy. It is not decisive in and of itself but judiciously combined with offensive action can lead to ultimate victory. With that said, even if one is in an overall strategic or operational level offensive posture, one must still play defence at the tactical level in order to secure and protect the gains already achieved. No matter what the circumstances, it is always a good idea to maintain some level of defence as a precautionary measure.

Brilliant Manoeuvre

Defence is the fighting posture of a force that has relinquished the initiative, either deliberately or owing to the actions of the enemy. It is not decisive in and of itself but judiciously combined with offensive action can lead to ultimate victory.

Steve Jobs returned to the helm of Apple Computer in July 1997, after having been forced out the company he co-founded in the mid-1980s. As detailed by Leander Kahney in his book about Jobs, *Inside Steve's Brain* (p. 15): "Apple was in a death spiral. The company was six months from bankruptcy. In just a couple of years, Apple had declined from one of the biggest computer companies in the world to an also-ran. It was bleeding cash and market share. No one was buying its computers, the stock was in the toilet, and the press was predicting its imminent passing." The first six months or so after his return, Jobs spent reviewing every single product line and all the R&D projects in the pipeline. After this period, he realized that the main problem with Apple was that the company had lost sight of its driving force, which was to create and market cutting-edge, user-friendly products. There were more than three dozen products in different categories, everything from high-end graphics design workstations, to printers, and the Newton handheld computer (an early attempt at an iPad-like device). Moreover, the company and its products had lost their cachet. They were perceived as expensive and not worth the premium price. Jobs decided that a partial retrenchment was in order. Intuitively understanding that the company needed focus, he decided to cancel most of the development projects, and to withdraw or phase out most of the company's products. This included discontinuing printers, the Newton, and the plethora of computer types that had multiplied over the years. He decided that Apple would pull back to basically four types of computer. Henceforth, there would be two types of desktop computer, a high-end one for designers and technical users, and a less capable one for the average user. The same positioning would be implemented for laptops. It is this positioning that led to the introduction of the iMac, PowerMac, iBook, and PowerBook lines. The company's financial situation improved slowly at first, and only returned to profitability in early 2001. However, it is this defensive retrenchment and focus on a strong position that set the conditions for the company's resurgence in the early 2000's and the introduction in 2001 of the iPod, which revolutionized the music industry.

Sometimes, defence is required by circumstances or as a result of an opponent's actions. This is what happened to the Allies, and especially the American forces in Belgium during the Battle of the Bulge. At other times, though, defence is a conscious choice that fits into a wider strategy. This is the course that Steve Jobs adopted in early 1998 after he returned to the leadership of Apple Computer. He had to stop the company's slide; anchoring the company on the solid position of a few quality products was the way to do it.

There are five main reasons to adopt a defensive posture in business, and they all have corollaries in military operations:

- **To stabilize the situation with a view to regaining the initiative.** This implies that you've lost the initiative and need to anchor on a secure piece of ground so you can stop the enemy's advance.

- **To recover and reconstitute your forces.** Any advance or attack eventually exhausts itself. An attacking force needs time to rest and resupply, and also to consolidate its gains.

- **To delay the enemy's advance.** The object is to force the enemy to concentrate and deploy for attack. Once they've done this, the defender withdraws in a controlled manner, leaving empty positions. This can only work for a limited time, but it can be effective in buying time.

- **To deny advantage or ground to the enemy.** Sometimes even on an offensive operation one has to be on the defensive in certain areas. This often happens to secure a line of departure or an assembly area against a pre-emptive enemy attack.

- **To wear down an opponent.** Sometimes a force has the strength to go on the offensive immediately, but instead deliberately waits for the enemy to attack so as to meet them on favourable ground with a sturdy defence. This takes advantage of the attacker's propensity to become exhausted in the attack. It allows the defender to counterattack at an opportune moment or even to launch a counteroffensive.

This listing provides goals of defensive actions. However, to carry them out successfully requires an understanding of the principles of defence, and an ability to implement them in actuality as a situation unfolds. The remainder of this chapter will discuss each of these principles, how they are implemented in military practice, the interaction of these principles, and the best means of applying them in business.

Principles of defence

- **Positioning.** Defensive manoeuvres depend above all on the selection and preparation of strong positions from which to repulse enemy assaults. As the opening quotes show, defence is inherently stronger than offence; this is largely because the defender usually gets to choose his ground and fortify it.

- **Preparation.** The more time to prepare, the better. This is because you can carefully select your position on ground that the enemy must conquer, or that allows you to control an approach to such ground. You can then take the time to get to know the approaches, the nature of the terrain, and to fortify your position.

- **Depth.** Thin defences are too easily breached. As we saw in the chapter on offence, the objective of an attacker is to find a weakness in the defences so as to penetrate deeply and disrupt the defending force. To be truly effective, defences must be arrayed in depth, with successive lines of obstacles and fortifications. It also helps if the position is located with an obstacle such as a river so as to canalize and delay the attacking force.

All Around Defence. As noted in the chapter on offence, the attacker tries to go around the enemy's main defences to strike in his flank, his rear, or to completely outflank him and capture an objective behind him. This hits him in a vulnerable area and forces him to abandon his strong positions to fight in the open. As a result, the defender must always be on the lookout for an attack from any quarter. The most successful assaults are usually the ones least expected from the most unexpected direction.

Mutual Support. Defences must be arrayed to support each other synergistically. That way, if the attacker tries to assault one position, there is another position nearby that can engage the attacking enemy, or from which to launch a counterattack. The attacker not only has to face a defence in depth with positions capable of sustaining an assault from any direction, but he also has to assume that another position will block his way or launch a counterattack.

Active Defence. It should be apparent by now that defence doesn't imply passivity or inactivity. Just because one has lost or temporarily given up the initiative to the attacker does not mean not reacting to his moves. In fact, a strong defence requires counterattacks and other countermoves to fully exploit its inherent advantage.

Figure 3.1: A Battalion Defensive Position on the Town of Smallville

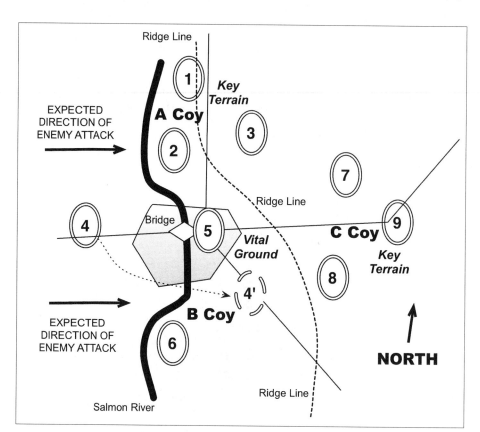

These principles are illustrated in Figure 3.1 above, which depicts a defensive deployment for an infantry battalion. The town of Smallville represents vital ground for both the attacker and the defender, as it sits astride a major crossroads (see straight lines leading out of the town) and the main bridge over the Salmon River. The enemy is expected to attack from the west. There is a ridgeline that runs in a north-south orientation to the east of the town. It is essential that this ridge be occupied by part of the defending force to the north of the town, as it is key terrain. In other words, if A Company ("A Coy" on the diagram) loses control of the high ground to the north of town, the enemy will be able to outflank the town to the north and come into the defences from behind. The battalion as a whole is arrayed in a standard triangular formation, with two companies defending up along the major obstacle that is the river, and C Company in depth occupying key terrain to the east of the town. Overall this position is well positioned to make use of the river as an obstacle. A Company is deployed to deny the key high ground to the north of town. B Company is deployed to control access to the crossroads and to protect the bridge river crossing. B Company's 4th platoon is also deployed forward of the main positions to delay and canalize the enemy, thus buying additional time to prepare the fortifications. This platoon also has an alternate position behind 5th and 6th platoons (shown as 4'). C Company's location is critical to the defence of the town because it allows reinforcements to be brought forward if needed. Conversely, its loss would make the rest of the defensive position irrelevant, and the ability to maintain control of the vital ground would be compromised. Each of the platoons (numbered ovals on the diagram) is also deployed in an approximate, triangular formation within each of the companies. Each of the platoons is arrayed in all around defence and in mutual support. In other words, they can sustain an attack from any direction, while also covering each other. In addition, the battalion commander has some flexibility to counterattack with either 7th or 8th platoons, should it be necessary to re-establish one of the forward positions. This affords some potential for active defence.

Effective Positioning and Preparation

On July 1st to 3rd, 1863, the Confederate and Union armies fought the greatest battle of the U.S. Civil War. In just three days, approximately 50,000 men were killed or wounded in a battle that is widely acknowledged as the turning point in the Civil War. Lee's Confederate army had advanced throughout the month of June into Pennsylvania, intending to disrupt and dislocate the Union army and put pressure on Washington, while simultaneously relieving the pressure on Northern Virginia. The Confederate forces were drawn to the town of Gettysburg, a busy crossroads in southern Pennsylvania. In and of itself, the manoeuvre was an excellent example of the offensive principles of warfare. As the Confederate forces pressed on the town from the north and west on July 1st, a Union cavalry division under Buford fought a rear guard action to the north of town with a view to delaying the Confederate advance. This bought time for the Union infantry to occupy defensive positions to the south of the town centred on Cemetery Hill and Cemetery Ridge. As the battle wore on over the next three days, the Union infantry and artillery eventually extended their positions to the south on Little Round Top Hill. The Union army repulsed a final desperate charge by the Confederate forces of Pickett against the Union's centre on the 3rd of July. The successful defence of Gettysburg by the Union army led to the retreat of Lee's Confederate army on July 4th after he had ordered a hasty defence be organized to the north of the town. The Union commander

Meade, however, only pursued the Confederate army half-heartedly. Had he been more aggressive, he may have routed the retreating southern army, which might possibly have led to a quicker end to the Civil War.

The Battle of Gettysburg is an almost perfect example of the successful application of the principles of defence, particularly that of the selection and active defence of a strong position. Gettysburg was vital ground for the Confederate army; the town's crossroads were the key to controlling Pennsylvania and threatening Maryland and Washington. In military terms, Gettysburg was vital ground for both sides. However, as with most built up areas, the best way to defend it was not in the town itself, as this would have left the surrounding countryside in the control of the Confederates. Rather, the successful defence of the vital ground required the occupation and defence of the key terrain around the town, specifically the hills and ridges to its south, as these dominated the southern approaches of the town. Moreover, this high ground, running from Cemetery Hill to Cemetery Ridge to Little Round Top to the south, was extremely difficult ground to attack. The ground was rocky and steep in many areas, making it easier for its defenders to fortify. Conversely, in the areas that were easier for an attacker to cross, visibility was relatively unrestricted and afforded open fields of fire to the defenders on the ridge and hills. A defending force has rarely occupied such a favourable position in the history of modern warfare. When combined with the judicious use of active defence, counterattack and manoeuvre, the Union army was in an extremely strong position.

As with military defence, effective business defence requires the selection, preparation and fortification of strong positions. In fact, it's a bit striking to think that business strategists have used the term positioning for years to refer to the act of selecting and defending a strong competitive advantage. This is the domain of competitive strategy, also known as business strategy. It has offensive and defensive components. Offensive business strategy is the theory and practice of using a business' strengths and advantages to select or create a strong position in a product market segment. It does so by outflanking the competition to occupy vital ground and key terrain beyond the competition's immediate defences. By analogy, we can consider the market to be the ground, and the particular product or service and the way it is positioned as the actual, geographic position. By extension, defensive business strategy is the theory and practice of defending those advantages and positions once the ground has been conquered, or seized without a fight. This dynamic of offence and defence is the essence of business strategy. The resemblance to military strategy, operational art and tactics is indeed fortuitous.

Brilliant Manoeuvre

Effective business defence requires the selection, preparation and fortification of strong strategic positions.

Like a good defensive position, a business position must occupy or control vital ground. As mentioned above, this is a location that both sides in a battle or war must control to have a chance at victory. In business, this is a product market segment that is so valuable that its control will bring a large and sustainable stream of highly profitable revenue to whichever company controls it. The danger is in relying too much on such a strong position that you ignore the signs that you're being outflanked by the competition, as noted in the chapter on offence.

Research In Motion (RIM), the Canadian developer and manufacturer of the BlackBerry series of smart phones, had that kind of sustainable competitive advantage when it first came out with the BlackBerry. The vital ground was the lucrative corporate and government market. The key terrain or key competitive advantage was security. To be used by governments and large corporations, data communications devices must be highly reliable, centrally controlled, and allow secure encryption of messages and data. No government or Fortune 500 company would allow classified email and messaging unless they felt that the communications system could provide a high level of security and reliability. RIM was able to provide these through its proprietary encryption processes and communications servers. These conferred an almost insurmountable advantage to the BlackBerry system over the course of the mid-1990s to about 2010.

Brilliant Manoeuvre

A business position must occupy or control vital ground while keeping an eye for signs of being outflanked by the competition.

The potential revenue and profit of a product market segment is analogous to the relative value of a military location or objective. For instance, Gettysburg was a valuable location for both sides since it stood at a major, strategic crossroads. This made it vital ground. By the same token, some product market segments are so valuable that they can be considered vital ground in business terms. This was the case with the mobile communications segment in the corporate and government markets. However, in order to control this vital ground, RIM had to occupy a position that would give it a commanding competitive advantage and leadership. This is akin to the way the Union and Confederate forces fought over the key terrain on the ridges to the south of Gettysburg. For RIM, the key terrain in the corporate and government markets has been security. This is RIM's positioning in that particular market.

The BlackBerry became something of a status symbol to professionals and business executives in the public and private sectors. Many of them literally became addicted to their "crackberries." Strong position in the corporate and government sectors translated to strong brand loyalty and dependence in users, simply because the BlackBerry devices were provided by employers and were ubiquitous. Interestingly, the BlackBerry never really caught on as a consumer smart phone. That only happened when Apple introduced the iPhone in 2007. Furthermore, Apple has never openly attacked RIM in the corporate and government markets, especially in terms of security of communications. Apple CEO Steve Jobs knew he couldn't win that battle or didn't think it was worthwhile. Either way, he chose not to compete in that space, choosing instead to go around RIM and to appeal directly to smart phone users on the basis of chic, brand, and usability within a wider consumer-type ecosystem.

Any business position is ephemeral, even one seemingly as strong and unassailable as that of RIM with its BlackBerry in the corporate and government markets. This is why defence can only succeed as a temporary competitive posture. It can be used to protect an advance once it's achieved, as RIM did initially, but in the long run a company must be on the offensive. The key is to use the strong defensive position of a successful product market mix to build reserves to go on the offensive as soon as possible. This can be achieved tactically within an existing product market mix, or strategically, with a new one.

Brilliant Manoeuvre

Defence can only succeed as a temporary competitive posture. It can be used to protect an advance once it's achieved but in the long run a company must be on the offensive.

The remaining sections of this chapter represent a distillation of the most useful defensive principles for use in business. As long as we keep in mind that defence is only a temporary measure, and that offensive action must prevail overall, then there is much to be learned by applying these military concepts to business.

Strategic Application of the Principles of Effective Positioning and Preparation

- Do you occupy product market segments that represent large streams of highly profitable revenue for your business? If you're not occupying these segments, why not? Are others likely to be interested in one or more of these segments? Are you at least trying to battle for vital, strategic ground?
- What is your position relative to your strategic product market segments? Are you on key terrain or is it likely to be occupied by a competitor?
- Can a competitor threaten your existing position? Could they wrest it away from you in some way? Is there an alternative position in the particular strategic segment under consideration that would allow a competitor to dominate?
- Can you prevent or delay competitors from occupying alternative positions that threaten your vital ground?

Depth

Defences should be arrayed in as much depth as possible, in order to slow and wear down the enemy's assault. Depth is enhanced by placing positions on or in the vicinity of natural or artificial obstacles such as woods, watercourses, hills and ridges, minefields, and ditches.

In the summer of 1943, the Germans prepared a major offensive to breach a massive bulge in the Soviet line. This bulge was centred on the city of Kursk. The Germans hoped to pinch off this bulge, then resume the offensive operations that had been stalled since the spring. Uncharacteristically, the Soviet commander Zhukov was able to convince Stalin to delay the Soviets' summer offensive until the Germans had launched their attack on the bulge at Kursk. Zhukov argued that the Soviet forces could be arrayed in great depth in multiple lines of defence. He knew that the Germans had limited resources to exploit any initial successes, and that they would get caught in a quagmire as they probed deeper and deeper into the Soviet positions. When they finally launched their offensive in early July, the

Germans were initially able to penetrate the Soviet defensive array with two major thrusts. However, this was only against Soviet outposts and lightly defended lines. The Soviets were able to canalize the German thrusts and lead them to their main lines of defence. Even when the Germans were able to get past a line of fortifications, there was another one a few hundred metres beyond. Natural or artificial obstacles such as rivers and minefields strengthened many of the fortifications. The German offensive ground to a halt and was called off by Hitler on the 13th of July. The Soviets then launched a massive counteroffensive, which pushed the Germans back hundreds of kilometres.

By the same token, a company can create depth in its defences by occupying more than one position in a product market segment. This is common in many sectors. Many car manufacturers have consistently occupied all or most of the positions in a hierarchy of value within the automobile market. For instance, General Motors was originally created to occupy all of the possible niches in the car market, everything from entry-level compacts to family sedans to luxury models. The idea was that as a person's income and functional needs changed, they would be able to change cars while staying with GM. That way the company would get the revenues no matter what the purchase, though profitability obviously varied. The approach was so successful in the 1940s that most of the American manufacturers had emulated the GM business model by the end of the 1950s, presenting a range of options to buyers of all stripes. Many also diversified outside of personal automobiles into other forms of transportation. The main impetus was to maximize revenues from any set of buyers, effectively creating and then leveraging brand loyalty over the buyer's lifetime.

Brilliant Manoeuvre

A business can create depth in its defences by occupying more than one position in a product market segment.

This essentially defensive strategy has been emulated in most industries. Procter and Gamble offers high, middle and low range household and personal hygiene products of all types. In fact, this practice is now the rule in most consumer products industries, where manufacturers offer a full range of products so they can prevent competitors from luring away their customers with higher or lower-range products as their needs and ability to spend change. This can be done laterally or vertically. In the first instance, the object is to occupy the entire value hierarchy.

Products and services with higher perceived value and quality tend to be much more profitable than ones that are at the lower end of the scale. This is one of the reasons why companies are consistently trying to move up the value hierarchy in terms of positioning. In the second instance, it means offering related or similar products so that the full spectrum of different functional needs is covered, not just different quality or value levels. This is why Procter and Gamble is present across the household products market, not just in one area. They don't want Church and Dwight (e.g. Arm and Hammer products) edging them out of their customer base. This can be done on the basis of common branding, but more often it is through specific branding. There are Arm and Hammer cleaning products and Arm and Hammer toothpaste. The commonality is apparently in the baking soda in the mix. On the other hand, there is Tide laundry detergent but not Tide toothpaste.

Brilliant Manoeuvre

Occupying multiple positions in a particular product market segment as well as related product market segments is therefore analogous to depth of defences. It forces competitors to mobilize and deploy many more resources than would otherwise be needed to be competitive, and confers a marked strategic advantage to the company that can be more things to more people.

Sometimes greater depth can be used to create a delay and buy time to react to competition. We saw how Buford's cavalry division was able to delay the advance of Confederate forces on July 1st north of Gettysburg by fighting from hastily chosen positions. This bought time for the Union infantry forces to make it to the high ground south of the town and therefore dig in for the expected Confederate assault. Had Buford not been effective in his delaying tactics, the outcome of the battle and war may have been considerably different.

The same type of manoeuvre can be used in business. Returning to RIM, its overall dominance of the smart phone market started to erode with the introduction of the iPhone by Apple in 2007. Although there was originally no threat to RIM's dominance in the corporate and government sectors, the situation changed greatly with Apple's introduction of the iPad in April 2010. By offering a device that corporate users found useful, Apple made its first inroads into RIM's traditional institutional strongholds. RIM only launched a version of its Play Book tablet computer in April 2011, but it was clearly not ready for prime time. RIM went ahead anyway because it felt it had to offer a tablet to corporate users, or at least reassure them of the prospect of having a workable solution within a reasonable time frame. This was clearly a defensive manoeuvre designed to buy time, although with few positive results for RIM. However, we can see how a delaying action can be used in business.

Strategic Application of the Principle of Depth

- Are there alternative positions to yours in your chosen product market segments?
- Could you create products or services that would allow you to occupy them provisionally or for a longer term?
- What is the full range of vertical positions in terms of product or service quality or perceived value?
- Are there product market segments adjacent to or otherwise related to your key position(s) that are likely to attract competitors onto your vital ground? Could you occupy some or all of this ground?
- Are there positions nearby that you should or could deny to competitors simply so they don't get a toehold on your vital ground? What key terrain must you occupy to prevent them from encroaching on your position(s)?
- Is there a position you must occupy provisionally to buy time for reinforcements, i.e., so you can develop a full-blown product or service to occupy that or a related product or service category?

All Around Defence

When I was a young infantry officer in the mid-1980s, I commanded a platoon on a joint Canadian-Norwegian exercise in northern Norway as part of Canada's NATO commitment. As part of our manoeuvres, we had to prepare a series of simulated defensive positions along what we expected to be the main Soviet axes of advance if they were to invade northern Norway. Our commanding officer kept reminding us that a putative Soviet attack in our sector could come from any direction using any means. This meant we had to be arrayed in a number of isolated positions that would have been able to face threats from all directions. The Soviets had mechanized ground troops, bombers, helicopter-borne troops, paratroopers, and amphibious forces so as to cross the numerous fjords. In addition, we expected that they were able to deploy commandos for reconnaissance and sabotage purposes as well as secret agents, and that they could listen to our radio communications. This is what is called a multidirectional threat, and we had to prepare for all of these eventualities.

You never really know where the main enemy attack can come from. For that matter, you often can't distinguish between the main attack and a supporting attack or probing incursion. In fact, as explained in Chapter 2 on offence, the whole point of offensive operations is to go around enemy defences to strike at vulnerable objectives in the enemy rear, or to hit the main positions in their flanks or rear where they are assumed to be most vulnerable.

Brilliant Manoeuvre

You never really know where the main enemy attack can come from. For that matter, you often can't distinguish between the main attack and a supporting attacking or probing incursion.

A client of mine, a mid-sized corporate and institutional service business, was facing increasing competition from all sides. Traditional suppliers were moving downstream into their market, luring away part of their clientele. Traditional intermediaries who distributed their services to customers were moving upstream into their business. Users were doing more and more of the work internally. Technology, especially the Internet, was making data and information important for customer decision-making, and that had heretofore been mostly proprietary, widely available for free on the Internet. Simultaneously, an increasing number of individuals who had been laid off or sought early retirement in the recession had started up their own mom-and-pop businesses offering similar services at lower fees. We worked to develop strategies to seek out and defend novel positions in existing segments or even completely new segments. This has proven to be an intensive process of trial and error reinforcing successful initiatives. No company can ever cease to be on the lookout for threats from all quarters, even those that are considered highly improbable or even impossible. In the case of my client, the combined effect of the recession and the availability of information through the Internet have made competition extremely cutthroat in their chosen sectors. In the short term, they can buy time by defending increasingly precarious positions but over the longer term, the only solution is to go on the offensive.

Brilliant Manoeuvre

No company can ever cease to be on the lookout for threats from all quarters, even those that are considered highly improbable or even impossible.

Strategic Application of All Around Defence

- Are you able to detect threats from any direction? These could be suppliers moving downstream, customers or distributors moving upstream, new technologies or products as substitutes, or completely new competitors who are entering your sector.
- Could you buy time by occupying some of these alternative positions? This ties back to the questions on depth.
- What competitive threat(s) could completely undermine your current position? What can you do to counter them?
- What countermoves can you make to occupy a position or to deny it to a competitor before he moves?
- Do you have a reserve to counter unexpected threats or moves by competitors? Could you reassign resources to do so?

Mutual Support

As depicted in the diagram of a defensive position, defending forces must be arrayed to be mutually supporting. If an enemy unit attacks one of the smaller positions, there has to another one close by that can fire at the attacker, preferably in its flank or rear. When combined with effective selection of positions, depth, and all-around defence, a defensive position should present a quagmire for an attacker. As the attacker advances into the defensive array, he should be fired at from all directions and many positions, thus making any further advance extremely costly. This is what the Germans experienced as they advanced against Soviet forces in the Battle of Kursk. As they attempted to outflank a position, they would come under withering fire from an adjacent position, thus making the attacks extremely costly.

The equivalent to mutual support in business is when a company is able to create an entire ecosystem that builds on its main products or services. This is when it has multiple products and services that are synergistic, or that are required for the whole system to work effectively and efficiently. For instance, Gillette was able to do this right from the start by creating a man's razor with replacement razor blades. The Gillette razor only worked with Gillette blades, and vice versa. Gillette could literally give away the razor, because it was the blades that were the main source of revenue, and very profitable at that. Neither product on its own made sense. Cable and telecom companies have also managed to create a synergistic effect and *de facto* customer loyalty through the lock-in effect. They do this by offering lower pricing over long-term contracts for cell phones, landlines, TV, and Internet services. They also offer package pricing which is meant to entice customers to acquire more than one product or service, and thus benefit from economies of scale. In some cases, unique products and services can give a telecom company a strong competitive position. This is what AT&T accomplished for a time in the U.S. through its exclusive distribution and user license with Apple for the iPhone, although the company's seeming inability to offer stable network access in many locations undermined the brand and the exclusive relationship with Apple.

Brilliant Manoeuvre

The equivalent to mutual support in business is when a company is able to create an entire ecosystem that builds on its main products or services. It has multiple products and services that work in synergy.

That paragon of business strategy, Apple, has also created a powerful ecosystem for its products and services. It was initially built on iTunes and the distribution agreements with various music publishers. iTunes can only work with the iPod and vice versa. When the iPhone was introduced, it included a virtual iPod, and was activated and updated through iTunes, thus further solidifying the defences through mutual product support. The App Store followed, and with the network effect, it created further synergies, which were then reinforced through the introduction of the iPad. This is only a rapid analysis of the synergies Apple has created through mutual support. There are many others with Mac computers and operating system, applications software, the Apple Store, Apple TV, and iBooks. This is truly the best example of depth and mutual support to create business synergies.

Strategic Application of Mutual Support

- Do you offer products and services that are mutually supporting, or are they disjointed and uncoordinated? Worse, are some of them in competition?
- Could you create an ecosystem that would generate customer loyalty and reduce the probability of a competitor luring away your customers with similar products and services?
- Do your customers have needs that are currently unfulfilled and that you could meet by creating new offerings?
- Do you see a competitor that is feeding off of your success with a complementary or synergistic offering? Could you acquire that competitor or its product, or otherwise develop your own offering to meet that need?

Active Defence

Active defence completes the picture of effective defensive manoeuvres. It also provides a link back to offensive strategy. One of the principles of war is the need for offensive operations to secure victory. Active defence is the principle that allows a defender to maintain an offensive mindset, even in the face of overwhelming odds. Active defence involves the judicious use of counterattacks, spoiling attacks, and blocking manoeuvres to keep the attacker off balance and to give hope to the defenders.

Colonel Joshua Chamberlain was in command of the 20th Maine Regiment at the Battle of Gettysburg. Chamberlain and his men had the vital task of securing the Union army's left flank on Little Round Top, which was at the south end of the ridgeline occupied by the Union infantry. On July 2nd, after repulsing multiple Confederate assaults and attempts to outflank their position, Chamberlain and the 20th Maine's men were exhausted and nearly out of ammunition. Rather than stay on the defensive and wait for another assault, Chamberlain took the initiative by launching a bayonet charge down the hill. This spoiling attack so surprised the enemy that the 20th Maine was able to capture many of the Confederate soldiers and secure the vital left flank of the Union army. Even though the Union army was on the defensive overall, Chamberlain's leadership stole the initiative from the Confederates at a critical juncture in the battle.

I recall a NATO exercise when I was a young platoon commander in Germany. We were preparing to launch a mock attack on a German army position, as we were involved in force on force manoeuvres in the German countryside. Unbeknownst to us, part of the German forces defending the objective we were meant to attack decided to attack our forces as we were lining up in the assault position. Needless to say the Germans took us completely by surprise, as we were not expecting that kind of offensive action on their part. Had it been a real battle, the enemy would have indeed spoiled our day. In the event, the exercise umpires declared our unit 'combat ineffective,' meaning that we had been notionally defeated by the Germans. It was a very valuable lesson for me, as it showed the importance of keeping an offensive mindset to surprise an attacking force.

Active defence is highly applicable in business. There are a number of ways that a company can counter a competitor's moves. One of the most common is to undertake legal action. This is extremely common in the technology sector, as companies are continually introducing similar devices and services. Once an innovation comes out, it seems that competitors can't help but be inspired to come out with a similar competing one. According to the *New York Times* and *Guardian* websites, at one point in 2010, just about every major telecom company in the world was suing at least one other company in the sector, either for patent infringement or for price fixing.

Although this is aggressive behaviour, it is probably ultimately not that effective in the long run. Much more powerful is to continually improve existing products and services by innovation. This is analogous to a spoiling attack or a blocking manoeuvre. The former involves attacking a competitor who is about to introduce a similar product by raising the bar through product or service improvements. The latter involves moving into a position in order to deny it to a competitor.

Brilliant Manoeuvre

Innovating by continually improving existing products and services is analogous to a spoiling attack or a blocking manoeuvre.

As noted previously, Gillette originally came up with the idea of the razor with disposable blades. At some point, however, there were generic replacement blades as well as other companies with competing products, which meant that Gillette would lose a significant proportion of its highly profitable revenue stream. Instead of focusing on a legal approach, Gillette has maintained its technological advantage for decades by positioning itself as the creator of innovative shaving products for men. First came the Trac II with its two blades. Then there was a triple blade razor. The company also added shaped razor handles, tiny cushions to make the shave smoother and at last count, a five-bladed razor.

This isn't really an offensive strategy, as it doesn't involve searching out new or radically different product market segments. Instead, it requires letting the competition imitate one's previous products, while staying a step ahead by continually introducing modifications and improvements. This has the effect of pre-empting innovations by competitors, who must be truly innovative to completely outflank one's dominant position. The ability to stay one step ahead of the competition, and to continually conduct these types of spoiling attacks or blocking manoeuvres is reinforced through the application of depth and mutually supporting products and services. Once a customer is in your circle of influence, they have less incentive to seek out competing products and services.

Brilliant Manoeuvre

The ability to stay one step ahead of the competition is reinforced through the application of depth and mutually supporting products and services.

Strategic Application of Active Defence

- Have you been passive in the face of challenges and threats from competitors? If yes, why do you think this is?
- How could you become more aggressive in the face of competitors trying to take away your business?
- What means are available to you to counterattack your competitors' incursions?
- What opportunities are there for you to occupy a position preemptively in order to limit incursions by competitors before they occur?
- Could you conduct a spoiling attack on a competitor that is fixing to enter your market or outflank you by offering improved products or services?

Summary

- Defence is the stronger form of battle in both war and business because the defender usually has the choice of position and time to prepare a well-developed defensive system characterized by depth, all-around defence, mutual support, and active defence.

- On the other hand, defence is only a temporary expedient, appropriate to stabilize the situation with a view to regaining the initiative; recovering and reconstituting forces; delaying the enemy's advance; denying advantage or ground to the enemy; or wearing down an opponent.

- Defence and offence are complementary and synergistic approaches to strategy, operational art, tactics, and any other competitive interactions. Moreover, just as there is an ebb and flow in war and battle, there is a rhythm of attack and defence, advance and security, required to be successful in business in the long term.

- Defensive manoeuvres depend above all on the selection and preparation of strong positions from which to repulse enemy assaults. Business defence requires the selection, development, and fortification of strong market positions.

- Thin defences are too easily breached. To be truly effective, defences must be arrayed in depth, with successive lines of obstacles and fortifications. A company can create depth in its defences by occupying adjacent market segments with a range of products and services. This forces competitors to mobilize and deploy many more resources in order to attack the defender's position.

- A defender must always be on the lookout for an attack from any quarter. The most successful assaults are usually the least expected. No company can ever cease to be on the lookout for threats from all quarters, even those that are considered as highly improbable.

- Defences must be arrayed to support each other synergistically. That way, if the attacker tries to assault one position, there is another position nearby that can engage the attacking enemy, or from which to launch a counterattack. A company that creates an entire ecosystem that builds on its main products and services generates massive mutual support and synergy between each of these components.

- Strong defence requires counterattacks and other countermoves to fully exploit its inherent advantage. The most powerful form of active defence in business is to continually improve existing products and services through innovation. This principle also acts in synergy with mutual support and depth of defences.

- The table below provides a summary of other applications at the operational, organizational, tactical, and personal leadership levels. This provides an overview and illustrations of how the principles of defence can be useful in all aspects of business management and leadership, not just corporate and competitive strategy.

Other Applications of the Principles and Concepts of Defence

Defensive Principle	Operational	Technical	Tactical	Leadership and Influence
	Illustrative Examples			
	Product line milked for maximum revenue as a retrenchment in that business area	Introduction of a new pay and accounting system	Client has complained about a product	New manager must be counselled for poor performance
Positioning	Maintain existing positions within product market segment.	Position as a means of achieving greater performance at a reasonable investment.	Empower front line client reps and sales people to resolve client complaints as quickly as possible with minimal fuss.	Present the counselling as a means of improving his/her performance, and not as a punishment.
Preparation	Plan and prepare for retrenchment and defence as carefully as for a product or market offensive.	Brief all stakeholders and keep them informed of the changes; provide training and logistic support as required.	Train sales and client reps to resolve client issues; develop protocols that support low level empowerment and initiative.	Research situation beforehand; rehearse if needed; anticipate objections and extreme reactions; select environment for feedback.

Other Applications of the Principles and Concepts of Defence (cont.)

Defensive Principle	Operational	Technical	Tactical	Leadership and Influence
	Illustrative Examples			
Depth	Within limits of resources, modify or transfer existing products to occupy as many positions within product market segment as feasible.	Keep old system functioning until new one is online; develop contingency plans for disruptions and to ensure business continuity.	Keep on lookout for recurring problems and complaints; ensure proper supervision and coaching of reps.	Ensure higher support beforehand; use concrete examples; focus on observed behaviour; keep coercive measures only for backup.
All around defence	Watch for competitors penetrating market with improved products or services.	Assess risks and threats to system implementation and project success and prepare contingency plans to deal with these or mitigate them.	Assume problems can come from anywhere and don't assume client is damaged.	Anticipate objections, excuses, accusations, extreme reactions; prepare contingency plans to deal with these.
Mutual support	Within limit of resources, create a product ecosystem that maximizes synergy between existing products and services.	Create a comprehensive project implementation plan that covers all aspects of the transition.	Ensure HR, IT, compensation, and other support is fully in line with policies and protocols supporting empowerment.	Create organizational support systems; provide coaching and mentoring; review progress frequently; provide training if needed.

Other Applications of the Principles and Concepts of Defence (cont.

Defensive Principle	Operational	Technical	Tactical	Leadership and Influence
	Illustrative Examples			
Active defence	Launch legal challenges against suspected product copying; improve products and services within limit of resources; remain as aggressive as possible to support other company initiatives in other areas.	Implement contingency plans as problems and hindrances arise; review progress often and compare against plans; adjust plans as needed to maintain focus on project objectives.	Actively search for recurring problems and patterns of complaint; modify products and services to pre-empt further complaints and problems; provide feedback to sales and marketing.	Be firm but fair; counter ad hominem attacks and emotional reactions; stay calm and focused on observed behaviour rather than assumed motivation and intent.

Chapter 4

Selection and Maintenance of the Aim: The Principle of the Objective

Direct every military operation toward a clearly defined, decisive and attainable objective.

US Army Field Manual FM 3-0

Every military operation must have a single, attainable, and clearly defined aim that remains the focus of the operation.

Canadian Military Doctrine (CFJP 01), 2011

A single, unambiguous aim is the keystone of successful military operations. Selection and maintenance of the aim is regarded as the master principle of war.

British Defence Doctrine, 3rd Edition, 2008

The Master Principle of War (and Business)

As we can see from the opening quotes, selection and maintenance of the aim or, as the U.S. military puts it, "the principle of the objective," is the most important principle of war. At first one must select the proper aim, then one must maintain it. Both steps are crucial, as there is no point in selecting an aim if one can't actually achieve it.

This chapter is pivotal since it articulates this master principle of war and how it relates to business. This is essential for reaching the full potential of an organization and achieving its objectives. I have deliberately chosen to introduce it at this point after first discussing the concepts of offence and defence because the objectives, in combination with the strategic posture of the force or organization, whether it has the initiative or not, sets the conditions for a realistic determination of ends, ways and means. First, we examine why the principle of the objective is critical to achieving success both on the battlefield and in business. We then discuss how to select the overarching, strategic objective as opposed to the immediate aim. As we will see, this involves the careful balancing of ends, ways, and means. It is never enough, however, simply to select an objective. It is also critical that it be translated into action throughout the entire organization, from the boardroom or national headquarters all the way down to the individual employee or private soldier, sailor, or airman. This is achieved through the application of top-down, nested, hierarchical planning. It is a structured approach ensures that the entire organization is mobilized to achieve one clear, overarching objective. At every level of the organization, from the top all the way to the smallest team or work group, leaders are required to clearly articulate their objectives and how they will be achieved in the broadest sense. This then frames the planning and action of the next lowest level in the organizational structure. It also ensures that leaders at all levels set objectives and create plans that are fully aligned with the objectives and plans of the whole organization, as well as the next highest level in the organizational structure. This is 'mission analysis,' a step-by-step process of analyzing the tasks an organization has received through the process of nested, hierarchical planning, as defined above, as well as the overall purpose of the organization, so that objectives can be developed that merge with those of the entire organization. Mission analysis is about finding purpose within the wider objectives of the organization. The final section of this chapter will show that this overall approach, what in the military is referred to as 'mission command,' empowers everyone in an organization to achieve its objectives by exercising personal initiative at all levels, even that of individual employees or soldiers.

Is it an objective, a goal, or an aim?

Whenever people get together to strategize and plan, they end discussing whether an objective is the same as a goal, or whether a goal is the same as an aim. In the military, an objective has traditionally been construed as a physical location that a force must capture. However, with the evolution toward counter-insurgency and other operations other than war, the term objective has come to designate any goal or outcome to be achieved. For the sake of simplicity, I will use the following terms as synonyms for objective: goal, aim, target, and outcome. On the other hand, the terms mission, vision, and end state have specific meanings in the worlds of military and business strategy. I will define these terms in due course as I introduce them, and I trust that the nuances of meaning will be evident from the discussion. I also trust that the equivalencies I present between business and military terms will be clear from the discussion.

Objectives allow us to focus our energies and resources. They allow us to channel our efforts and actions towards a predetermined outcome. They must be achievable with reasonable levels of risk, but be also sufficiently challenging so as to motivate individuals, teams, organizations, and even countries to outstanding levels of achievement. I've listed the five main characteristics of objectives in the following text box. We've already seen how the selection and maintenance of appropriate objectives is critical to success. In the remainder of this chapter, we'll learn how to select a single, overriding objective and develop it into a hierarchy of nested objectives that encourages individual initiative and aligns the entire organization to its overarching objective.

Brilliant Manoeuvre

Objectives allow us to focus our energies and resources. They allow us to channel our efforts and actions towards a predetermined outcome.

The Principle of the Objective

- Objectives provide focus to allow individuals and organizations to say yes or no to activities, while channelling actions and resources towards their accomplishment.
- Carefully selected objectives must balance ends, ways, and means. The key questions are: What (ends) is to be achieved and why? How (ways) should it be achieved? What resources (means) are needed to achieve it?
- Ends, ways, and means provide a framework to generate a nested hierarchy of subordinate goals that must be accomplished by elements of the organization in order to meet overarching objectives.
- Leaders and teams at all levels of an organization, from the top to the bottom, develop their own objectives through a process of mission analysis.
- The nested hierarchy of objectives and mission analysis channel individual initiative and align the entire organization toward the achievement of its overarching goals through mission command.

The Art of Saying No

When Iraq invaded Kuwait in August of 1990, the consensus throughout the world was that Saddam Hussein's forces had to be expelled from Kuwait. US president George Bush rallied much of the world around this objective, obtained UN Security Council approval for the strategy and operation, then assembled a coalition of the willing to carry out the mission. There was a clear objective, limited in time and space, and easy to determine when it would be completed. When the ground campaign started on February 23rd, 1991, everyone held their breath, expecting massive coalition casualties. However, the US-led ground forces didn't just move to invade Kuwait from the south. They instead carried out a huge sweeping manoeuvre through the Iraqi desert to the west of Kuwait and surrounded most of the Iraqi forces deployed in Kuwait and southern Iraq. The manoeuvre, a brilliant application of the indirect approach described in Chapter 2, led to the rout of the Iraqi Army, with tens of thousands of casualties and the parallel loss of only a few hundred coalition troops. President Bush declared a ceasefire on February 28th, only 100 hours after the beginning of the ground battle. At the time, some media commentators and politicians, as well as military officers, felt that it was a mistake to stop in southern Iraq, and that the opportunity that had been afforded by the rout of the Iraqi army and air force should have been exploited to drive on to Baghdad in order to oust Saddam Hussein and install a less threatening regime. Saddam's subsequent defiance of the UN Security Council and Western powers, particularly the United States, may be seen as vindicating that view, but it's easy to forget just how great a feat of diplomacy it had been to build the coalition in the first place. Though the Berlin Wall had fallen and Germany was striving toward reunification, the Cold War was still not officially over. The wisest course of action in early 1991 was to end the military campaign as soon as its objective was reached. The objective was unambiguous, clearly articulated and agreed by all participants in the campaign, so success was easy to measure. When it was achieved, there was no need to continue the war. People who complained afterwards that the objective should have been changed did so only with the benefit of hindsight. It was Monday morning quarterbacking. The aim of Operation Desert Storm in 1991 was the expulsion of Iraqi forces from occupied Kuwait, not the overthrow of the Saddam regime nor the democratization of Iraq. A massive air campaign followed by a lightning land offensive was the way to achieve this end after diplomacy failed to achieve the required objective.

Contrast the first Gulf War of 1990-91 with the entire period of the 1990s and early 2000s and the eventual invasion of Iraq in March 2003. Never was there any broad agreement on objectives nor a sense of the ultimate outcome. The United States and its closest allies, Britain, Canada, and Australia, were in favour of disarming Saddam and keeping him disarmed. Russia, France, and China, each with a UN Security Council veto, variously endorsed, opposed, obfuscated, and obstructed the intentions of the UN, the US, and its allies. There was no clearly articulated international goal, such as containment of Iraq, continued disarmament, or a return to normal participation in international relations. It is this situation of uncertainty and lack of resolve in dealing with Saddam Hussein that eventually led the second Bush Administration to use the war against terror and the claims of continued, Iraqi development of weapons of mass destruction as reasons to invade Iraq. With the Iraqi war, the war against the Taliban in Afghanistan then became a sideshow, even though it was arguably a greater source of global instability. The lack of clear objectives led to nearly a decade of war and occupation and tens of thousands of casualties, and still counting, in both Afghanistan and Iraq.

These examples of clear and unclear objectives concerning Iraq and the Saddam regime show why the principle of selection and maintenance of the aim is considered to be the master principle of war, which applies to actual war, peacekeeping, or pacification of an occupied country. It also applies in all other fields of endeavour, and business is no different. Selection and maintenance of the aim applies to all levels of business: strategic, operational, and tactical. Just as the objective and the mission statement are fundamental to success in war and conflict, a company's vision and mission provide the fundamental orientation and impetus to all action within that enterprise. Every individual and team in the organization must contribute to the accomplishment of the mission. In war and conflict, failure to select and adhere to the objective can lead to defeat, death, and destruction. Even in business where a failure to identify and stick to the right mission and objectives will not lead to loss of lives or anything as dramatic and final, such a failure, however, can lead to the disappearance of the enterprise.

Brilliant Manoeuvre

Every individual and team in the organization must contribute to the accomplishment of the mission.

The unfolding of the international financial crisis since 2008 demonstrates the vital importance of selecting and maintaining proper business objectives. Canadian banks in particular have been able to weather the storm relatively unscathed. The major Canadian banks—RBC, Bank of Nova Scotia, Bank of Montreal, Toronto Dominion Bank, and CIBC—have been able to remain profitable and even grow through the turmoil because of their prudent lending and investing practices. Media pundits in Canada, the US, and elsewhere have attributed this approach to Canadian bankers' alleged phlegmatic conservatism. In actuality, it results from a combination of prudent government regulation and the banks' focus on long-term preservation of capital as an overriding objective. Canadian banks and the Canadian financial regulation system never lost sight of their main mission: to provide a safe haven for capital. In other words, a bank that doesn't preserve capital isn't a bank but rather a glorified investment fund. Many of the largest banks in the world forgot this most important fact, particularly those based in Europe and the US. They relied more and more on lending to fundamentally unsound clients, many of who were unable to pay back the loans. Many of these shaky borrowers were consumers who never should have qualified for loans, especially to buy overpriced houses. Some of these borrowers have been sovereign states with profligate spending habits, such as Greece, Italy, and Spain. This is why, even as I write, a huge financial crisis is unfolding throughout Europe. Through most of the period that led to the crisis, during the late 1990s and first decade of the 21st century, the major Canadian banks for the most part refused to gamble in a significant way on high-risk lending, especially in the US sub-prime mortgage market. It is instructive that the Canadian bank with the highest sub-prime exposure, CIBC, has also been the one with the greatest financial difficulties. It would have been easy for the leadership of the major Canadian banks to seek faster growth in the US and other international markets, but the ability to stay focused on long-term profitable growth and prudent lending practices has contributed greatly to their financial stability throughout the global financial crisis of 2008-2011. The Canadian banks were able to say no to imprudent expansion of business, and this is what allowed them to thrive during the unfolding crisis.

One of the hardest decisions in business is to say no. It can be a new product, a new market, a new competitor, or an acquisition. Business leaders are often led astray by failing to identify and adhere to a clear business objective. As a result, when threats and opportunities arise, they fail to put them in the right context, i.e. within the framework of their mission and objectives.

Brilliant Manoeuvre

One of the hardest decisions in business is to say no.

In his latest book co-authored with Morten Hansen, *Great by Choice*, Jim Collins shows how Dallas-based Southwest Airlines established itself as the only consistently profitable US airline by initially copying the business model of California-based Pacific Southwest Airlines (PSA) in the late 1960s. Southwest imitated everything, even down to creating operating manuals by observing PSA in action and inferring its processes and procedures. Southwest then stuck relentlessly with the model, making minor tweaks and improvements over the decades. Southwest stayed true to its mission and objectives. It selected the right objective and maintained it through thick and thin, becoming the only consistently profitable airline and one of the most successful companies in the US. Meanwhile, what did PSA do? It decided to diversify into the car rental business and hotels because it perceived that it could build a business model to provide end-to-end travel and accommodation services for busy business travellers. This wasn't necessarily a bad idea as all companies must experiment with new products, markets, and business models, as pointed out in Chapters 2 and 3. However, PSA went overboard and invested heavily in hotels and car rentals without first probing to learn and see where the market gaps were. Instead, the company launched simultaneous assaults on two new fronts. The result? None of the new fronts worked, so that the company meandered for years before it was sold to US Air.

Developing Strategic Objectives: Ends, Ways, and Means

Military strategy requires a balancing of ends, ways, and means. Ends are the objectives to be achieved. They are the 'what' and the 'why' of the strategy. Ends are often expressed as an end state. This is a succinct description of the state of affairs to be achieved to consider the strategy a success. Ways are the strategy, stratagem, or plan that aims to achieve the end state. Ways answers the question,

Figure 4.1: Ends, Ways and Means

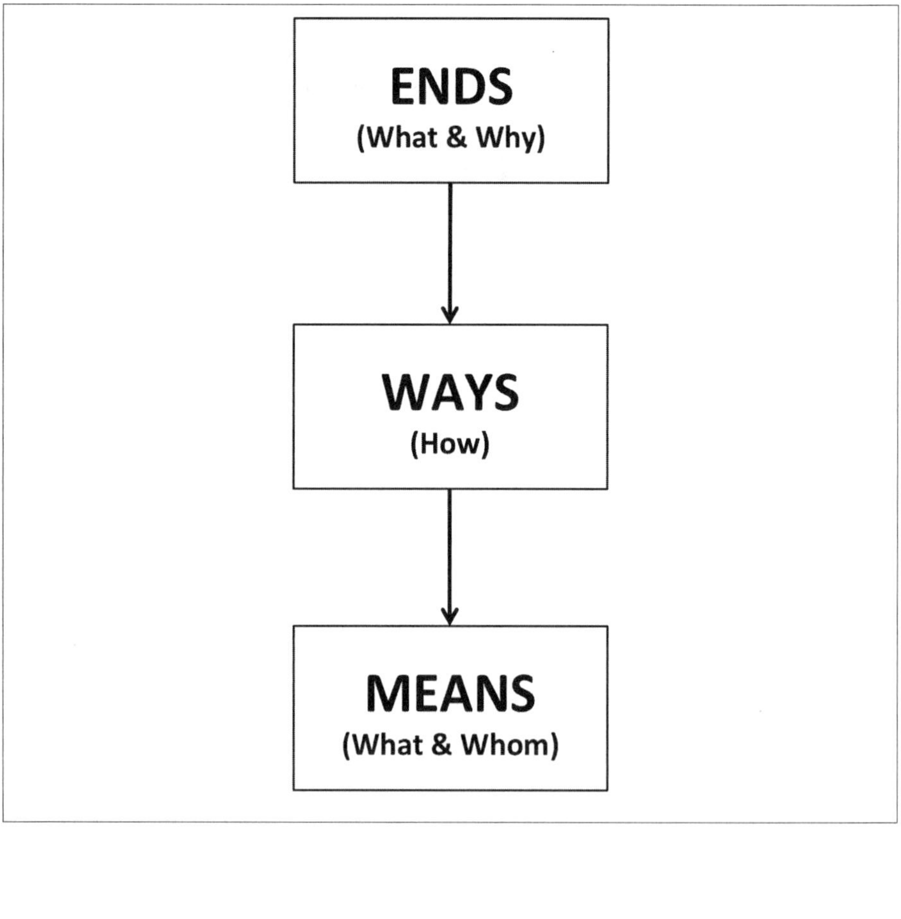

"How will we achieve this end state?" Means are the resources that are used to implement the ways that will achieve the ends. Considering means answers the question, "With what and with whom shall we carry out this plan of action?" In the military, these terms are usually used in strategic and campaign planning, but I have found throughout my military career and in my practice as a consultant that the concepts are applicable no matter what the organizational level, time horizon, or field of endeavour. Military doctrine tends to picture the relationship between these three elements as in Figure 4.1.

This looks very clean and rational, with a sequential progression from ends through to ways to means. In reality though, these three steps for selecting an overall aim are more intricate and involved. Figure 4.2 shows that the relationship between ends, ways and means is really more of a triad and that they must be kept in dynamic equilibrium.

Figure 4.2: Interaction of Ends, Ways and Means

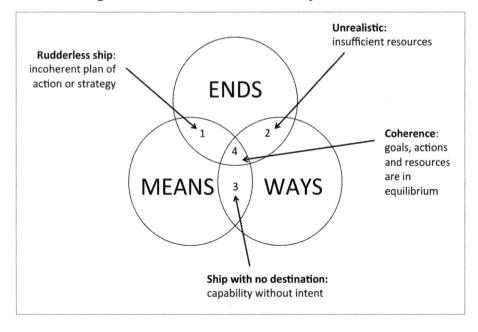

The selection and maintenance of the ultimate aim (ENDS) must be in equilibrium with the plan of action (WAYS) for achieving it and the resources (MEANS) this requires. I use the term equilibrium because the process is never static. It is really more of a constant balancing act, where the evolving situation must be continually re-evaluated so that aim, plans, and resources are kept in dynamic balance. By extension, lack of one of these components creates a situation of imbalance, which can lead to mission failure. In situation 1 shown in Figure 4.2, there is an objective and the resources to attain it, but without an effective strategy or plan of action, the organization will be like a rudderless ship. There is a destination but no mechanism to get there. In situation 2, there is an end and a brilliant stratagem to achieve it, but without sufficient or appropriate resources—the actual means to carry out the plan—the goal will be unrealistic and therefore unattainable. Situation 3 reminds us of a tramp steamer, going from port of call to port of call, but with no final destination. Situation 4 is the ideal, where the ends, ways, and means are finely balanced and kept in dynamic equilibrium through constant attention to the environment, the evolving situation, and the interplay of these three components of goal setting.

The best military illustration is the oft-misunderstood subject of guerrilla warfare, because it exposes the interaction of ends, ways, and means in a transparent way. Guerrilla warfare is the strategy of the weak even though it is often depicted otherwise. Recourse to guerrilla strategy and its associated tactics such as small unit raids, ambushes, terror bombings, kidnappings, torture, summary justice, political propaganda, psychological warfare, etc. stem from a realization that the force one is commanding is incapable of highly coordinated, and highly damaging offensive action. It's an extreme form of strategic defence that completely concedes the ground to the enemy—usually the government side or an occupying army—while simultaneously adopting selected offensive tactics at the level of small teams and units. This semblance of offensive action is intended as a means of maintaining morale and disrupting the much stronger enemy until the guerrilla force can regain the initiative and go on a major offensive. Alternatively, it can be successful if the enemy simply gives up and withdraws. The end state is the withdrawal of the occupier or the downfall of the government. The way to achieve this is to avoid defeat by continuing the fight even if the physical effects on the enemy are initially minor. The key intent is to operate on the moral plane: to create the perception in the mind of the stronger side that continuation of the struggle is not worth the effort in lives and treasure. The means of effecting guerrilla warfare are usually poorly trained, lightly armed and equipped peasants living in austere conditions, and operating from remote bases. Organizational structures are fluid, leadership is heavily politicized, and ideology pervades the guerrilla or insurgent force from top to bottom. This is warfare almost exclusively on the moral or psychological plane. It is effective to the extent that insurgent forces can maintain morale and, little by little, establish their dominance of the country. The image of Viet Minh fighters in Vietnam operating from rice paddies and in mountainous areas and living on a bowl of rice a day springs to mind. It has been the strategy of the Taliban and its allies in Afghanistan since the overthrow of the Taliban regime in late 2001 and early 2002.

Guerrilla warfare shows how critical it is for a military commander to set goals that are achievable given the resources and capabilities at his command. An insurgent force in an occupied country is seldom able to achieve its stated aim of freedom from occupation by going on a strategic offensive. By the same token, the occupying force must set an objective that is realistic given the limited resources its government and population are willing to devote to the occupation and pacification of another country. As intimated above, this is exactly what we've seen in Afghanistan since the overthrow of the Taliban government in late 2001. What would be a realistic end state for US and NATO forces and the current Afghan government? Is it to completely defeat the Taliban and other anti-government elements? Or is it simply to make the country inhospitable to Al Qaida? What about Afghanistan itself? Should it continue to be a semi-feudal theocracy, or evolve into a Western-style democracy? Selecting and maintaining the aim is more a question of working within the realm of the possible and the expedient rather than lofty ideals.

This illustrates the weightiness of goal setting, at least in the realm of conflict, geopolitics, and global diplomacy. But what about business? How does this logic apply to the setting of business goals? Business is, of course, an economic endeavour. Business executives, entrepreneurs, and investors are constantly operating under the assumption of limited resources, at least over their relevant time horizon of 2 to 5 years. They must also contend with extreme uncertainty, competitive threats, changing tastes, and important risk. Nothing is given. Business leaders must therefore also seek a dynamic balance between their business goals (ends), their strategies and plans (ways), and the resources they can realistically assign to achieve them (means).

Brilliant Manoeuvre

Business leaders must seek a dynamic balance between their business goals, their strategies and plans, and the resources they can realistically assign to achieve them.

The same balancing act applies in the case of business as in war and conflict. You can set the lofty goal of becoming the world's leading company in your particular sector or market, but if you can't even meet the needs of your current customers, then you may have to set your sights on a more attainable goal in the near term. The same could be said about the capabilities of the organization. If you want to operate globally but only have a national distribution and supply network, then you might have to put in place a global network first, either on your own, or working with strategic partners. Alternatively, you could take a gradual approach, building your network sequentially as you expand from country to country, continent to continent. Once again, everything must be in dynamic equilibrium, with the ideal being congruence of ends, ways, and means, as depicted in Figure 4.3

Figure 4.3: Congruence of Ends, Ways and Means

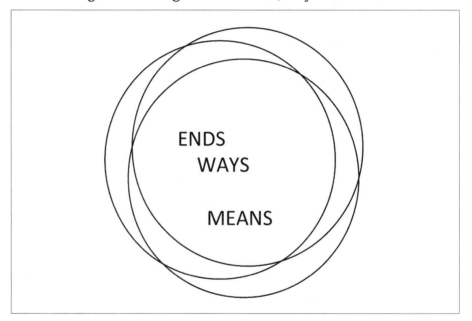

One of my consulting clients was a municipally owned and operated transit service in a small city with a population of about 120,000. After analyzing the service's strategic situation, particularly the potential transit requirements over the next 10 to 15 years, it became apparent that the bus company did not have the management capability to properly estimate future demand. We noted that commuters and other riders use public transit only if there is sufficient supply. We also realized that the driving force of any transit system is its network of stations, routes, and stops. Transit depends on sufficient buses and they must go where people want to go at the most convenient times. If those conditions aren't met, people don't ride the bus. The city had previously spent several hundred thousand dollars on a branding campaign to get people to take the bus, to no effect. The ultimate vision was also to change what's known as the modal split between public and private means of transportation during rush hour. This would alleviate future road and parking requirements, especially downtown, and also contribute to a reduction of greenhouse gas emissions. Some people will go to great lengths to take the bus because they believe in public transit, don't want a car, and want to contribute to reducing greenhouse gas emissions. Others have to take the buses because they can't afford private transportation; for example, the poor, elderly, handicapped, and students. Most people, however, choose their mode of travel on the basis of comfort, convenience, and speed. A city transit service that can't meet those demands can have a lofty green vision but it can't force people to take the bus if the bus doesn't reach them and take them where they want to go in a timely and efficient manner.

Working with management, we developed an initial action plan that would position the transit service for the long-term vision while also setting more realistic short-term goals for three to five years. The city committed itself to investing in developing the transit network and infrastructure, but to do that first required operational research to determine travel patterns. In parallel with this, the city committed itself to enhancing the management of the transit service while creating an operating structure that would be more business-oriented. The ultimate vision of efficient green transit that alleviates traffic in the downtown core was translated into the more realistic mid-term goal of building an efficient and comprehensive transit network with better management. The focus then shifted from considering advertising campaigns or which type of greener bus was needed, to technical considerations of travel patterns, user needs, and the infrastructure that would support that goal. In the terms of our strategic goal-setting framework, the end was the creation of an efficient and effective transit service that people would actually want to use; there were four ways this would be done: by building a better network, focusing on real customer needs, improving day-to-day management and operations, and creating a high-performance organization. The means or necessary resources would be requested as the city was able to invest according to the priorities determined from the operational research and the infrastructure plan in order to support the network build-up of buses, shelters, buildings, and road upgrades.

Strategic Application of Ends, Ways, and Means

- What is your ultimate vision and objective?
- What would be the best way to achieve this vision or goal?
- Do you have the means to achieve this objective in the manner you've defined?
- Do you need to change the way you intend to achieve your objective? If so, would this lead to the attainment of your goal or vision?

- Do you need to break up your ultimate vision into sub-goals and to sequence these over time?
- Given all of this, are your objectives still realistic? If not, what means or ways would you need to change? Are these changes realistic? If not, how can you make your objectives more realistic?

Translating Objectives Into Action: Nested Hierarchical Planning

The previous section detailed how to develop objectives that balance the ends with the ways of achieving them and the means that are available to do so. The discussion implied that the composition of the organization that will work toward the goal must be taken into consideration. This is where the determination of ends meets the structural and resource realities of the organization. Goals are only achievable if they can be articulated into workable plans that build on the organization's capabilities, structure, and resources.

> ### Brilliant Manoeuvre
>
> **Goals are only achievable if they can be articulated into workable plans that build on the organization's capabilities, structure, and resources.**

Military planners have developed a method for translating ends, ways, and means into well-articulated and coherent statements of the end to be achieved, the organization's mission, and the plans for executing the mission to achieve the objective. This process can also be mapped onto business planning processes to show a rough equivalency between the two. The military processes provide insight into the business processes, and show how they can be applied for business success.

We can see in Figure 4.4 the parallel mapping of concepts that change the abstract discussion of ends, ways, and means in the previous section into a method for transforming objectives into results. In military terms, the end state is a succinct articulation of the situation as it should be from the perspective of the commander of the force at the end of that particular operation. The end state can and usually does evolve with the situation, although the ultimate end state at the strategic level provides the vision for the end of the conflict. For instance, the end state for

Figure 4.4: Nested Hierarchical Planning

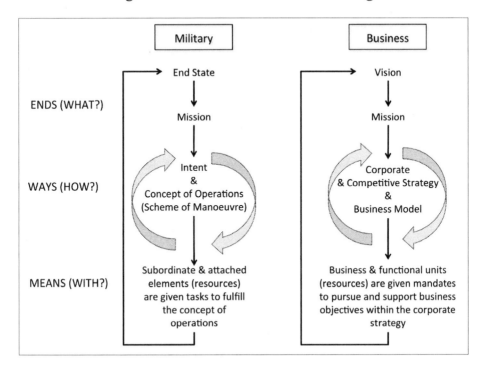

the Allies during World War II was the unconditional surrender of Nazi Germany, fascist Italy, and imperial Japan. Nothing less would be accepted. The mission is an articulation of that particular organization's role in achieving the end state. For the Allied forces in the northwestern Europe theatre of operations in World War II, the mission was to establish a foothold in northwest Europe, and to fight Germany to its surrender. Thus, the mission of the forces involved in Operation Overlord, including the Normandy invasion and the campaign to defeat Germany, was "*Following the establishment of strong Allied forces in France, operations designed to strike at the heart of Germany and to destroy her military forces will be undertaken.*" The objective was crystal clear, as was the Allied forces' role in achieving that objective.

But Operation Overlord was a highly elaborate plan, involving many sub-components. The intent was to land a strong army in Normandy, while pinning down German forces elsewhere and keeping Hitler and the German High Command guessing as to the main thrust. The Germans believed that the most likely landing place was at the Pas de Calais in Northern France, near the Belgian border, as this was the closest point to England. The Allies chose Normandy for a number of reasons but mainly because it would create surprise. The Allied concept of operations was to create doubt in the Germans as to the main thrust while putting nearly all of the Allied eggs into the Normandy basket. This required an elaborate hierarchy of plans and sub-plans. Each of these plans was intended for and executed by a different organization within the combined Allied naval, air, and land forces. For instance, while Operation Overlord was the overall plan of attack, there was an amphibious landing operation, Operation Jubilee, and a naval operation to support it, Operation Neptune. There was also a huge deception campaign called Operation Fortitude, which was designed to keep the Germans guessing about the main thrust. The Allies even created a fake army under command of George Patton, the First US Army Group, supposedly positioned in southeastern England to create the impression that the landing force would disembark in the Pas de Calais. Instead, the main forces left from southern England headed for Normandy, a much more treacherous undertaking.

Once the main landing force had established a beachhead on D-Day, there was a series of linked ground and air operations by Allied forces consisting of nested structures of army groups, armies, corps, divisions, brigades, battalions, companies, and platoons to expand the bridgehead, and then breakout into the open French countryside. After that, there would be a series of offensives to reach into the heart of the German homeland, while Allied air forces bombed its industrial heartland and the Soviet Army hammered the Germans in the east. Each of these operations had a different objective within the overall intent and mission to drive the German forces back to Germany and then eventually to defeat them, with total capitulation as the end state. The whole campaign plan consisted of a series of nested objectives, missions, and plans, all articulated according to an overarching intent coordinated through detailed planning, intelligence, and effective field command. This is how military forces take the most general and high-level strategic objectives and translate them into successful action on the ground.

Top-down, nested hierarchical planning is critical for the full articulation of the organization's mission and for translation into purposeful action. This is what most leaders in non-military fields intuitively understand the most about military leadership: the ability to translate abstract goals into specific and measurable concrete actions that an entire organization can execute in a coherent manner. Moreover, modern military forces, at least in Western countries, can no longer rely on rote patterns of action and iron discipline. Nested hierarchical planning, while initiated from the top-down, is the first part of the process that leads to concerted action toward a single, overriding outcome that also leverages individual initiative. People have to understand what the aim is, why they are working toward it, and how it is to be achieved in the broadest terms possible. They can then motivate themselves and inspire their collaborators and followers to put their collective brains together to resolve the inevitable problems that will crop up, but also to break down their own particular part of the equation into manageable bits, so that their own team members can then work on their respective pieces of the puzzle. When combined with mission analysis in an overall philosophy of mission command, organizations can achieve remarkable outcomes.

Brilliant Manoeuvre

Top-down, nested hierarchical planning is critical for the full articulation of the organization's mission and for translation into purposeful action.

Think of any major or minor undertaking in business, government, society or even the domestic environment. How can you get anything done without fully articulating what you are trying to achieve, identifying the resources you need and that are reasonably available, and then coming up with a coherent plan of action? Think of Boeing setting a strategic objective to develop a radically new type of jetliner, the 787 Dreamliner, which makes minimal use of metal in its design. Airbus also had to articulate and break down into manageable bits its goal of developing a radically new type of jetliner, the double decker A380. The same applies to Bombardier Aerospace which is working on a new small jetliner, the C Series, that will fit between the small, regional jets and the smallest of the current jetliners, Boeing's 737 and Airbus's A320. These projects are huge in scope, requiring armies of engineers, designers, financial experts, marketing and sales people from many different countries, all working toward the development and integration of one of the most complex artifacts of modernity, the commercial jetliner. This isn't just a simple matter of creating a work breakdown structure and applying project management principles. It requires careful analysis and a balancing of the ends, ways, and means of the organizations involved at all levels.

The end state is simple: a fully functioning, safe, efficient, and effective commercial jetliner airlines are willing and able to purchase and operate at a profit. The mission for the companies involved is to develop and build these jetliners. The intent is to do so within a set time frame to exacting standards of design, safety, innovation, efficiency, and effectiveness, so that customers will want to purchase and operate these aircraft for 20, 30, 40 years or more. The aircraft companies must also create plans based on their concept of operations, and require a business model to design, build, integrate, market, and sell these planes. Moreover, these plans must be based on realistic assessments of the resources required, and the means to marshal them in a sustainable manner. The various teams, sub-contractors, suppliers, distributors and organizational groupings will then have a clear framework of action aligned on the overarching goal of developing and producing airliners that will last for decades.

Brilliant Manoeuvre

People have to understand what the aim is, why they are working toward it, and how it is to be achieved in the broadest terms possible.

This is a very concrete business example, one which can apply to R&D, academic institutions, government projects, healthcare, charity work, community action, any endeavour that requires a complex analysis, breakdown, and synthesis of thought and action towards a common goal. What about the more abstract strategic business goals, such as becoming the market leader, repositioning a company, expanding from a domestic presence to becoming a global player? What about creating a business in the first place? This discipline of nested hierarchical planning is crucial to the achievement of these more abstract goals. In fact, it is most applicable in these cases because people need to aim at a real-world target. For instance, the owner of the small company I mentioned in Chapter 3 wants to grow significantly over the next five years. Working with the entire management team and not just the owner, we articulated a clear vision of what the company would have to look like and act like in order to achieve the owner's overarching objective of massive growth. We articulated the company's mission, one that leverages its unique positioning and value proposition while executing the vision. We then broke down the vision and mission into more manageable bits, which we've called major thrusts. There are six of these designed to build on that company's particular strengths and past successes, while minimizing the competitive threats it faces and overcoming the weaknesses identified in our strategic profiling. Two of these strategic thrusts represent major axes of advance over the coming years for the business. Three others represent new or expanding lines of business. The final thrust is the development of the organizational wherewithal, the structures, systems, processes, and resources that the company needs in its organization and people to actually execute on the mission and plan. So, much like the municipal transit service strategy described in the previous section, this company must develop its organizational and human capabilities in full alignment with its business goals. Each of the thrusts has been assigned to a specific manager for execution, and these managers have clear marching orders with financial and business objectives they must achieve in order to accomplish their role in the overarching strategy. Moreover, each of these thrusts will have its own business model, and these can intersect to produce a company-level business model as they are developed, integrated, and supported by the thrust with respect to organizational capabilities.

Strategic Application of Nested, Hierarchical Planning

- What is the vision or end state for which you are aiming, one that balances ends, ways, and means?
- What mission would allow you to realize that vision or end state?
- What is your broad intent in that regard, such as your positioning and posture? Do you wish your products and services to be highly differentiated, constantly innovating to stay ahead of the pack, or do you prefer instead to be the cost leader? Is your overall posture offensive or defensive? Are you seeking to defend your position, or to go on the attack to overtake your competitors by staking out your position in virgin territory?
- What is the broad scheme of manoeuvre and concept of operations that will transform your vision into action and results? How does this translate into a functioning business model that can succeed over time and that supports your mission?
- What resources are required? Who will execute the plan and what roles are they expected to play? What specific tasks and responsibilities are required of the subordinate elements and leaders in your organization? How do these tasks fit together and how are they sequenced in time and space to produce the effects you're seeking?

Determining Your Role: Mission Analysis

Let's recap so we know where we've been and where we're going. The organization has its overall strategic goal, expressed as an end state or vision. The organization's leadership has articulated its mission so that its members know where they're going and the organization's particular role in getting there. There is a high level plan of action, expressed as an overall intent with a concept of operations that articulates the scheme of manoeuvre, or business model. Responsibilities have been assigned at the highest level. The question now is how to ensure that every leader and team in the organization can articulate his or her goals and create plans that fit into the larger intent, and so they aren't going off on tangents or creating empires that aren't fully aligned to the organization's vision and mission. This is where mission analysis comes into play, and it is crucial for ensuring that managers and leaders at lower levels of the organization can plan and act in accordance with the overall strategic intent.

In standard military terms, a mission is a clear, concise statement of the task of the unit and its purpose. The interesting thing though is that the mission doesn't come directly from the superior commander's orders, but rather as the result of a process of analysis by the subordinate commander. There are many variations on this approach in military doctrine, but the one I learned as a young officer and the easiest to apply outside the military setting is to answer the following questions in sequence.

Steps in Mission Analysis

1. What are the vision (end state), mission, and intent of the whole organization?

2. What are my immediate superior's vision, mission, intent, and concept of operations for our part of the organization?

3. What explicit tasks, roles, and functions within the greater concept of operations has my immediate superior given me?

4. Are there implied tasks that are required to support these assigned tasks?

5. What are the limitations on my freedom of action? In other words, are there constraints (musts) and restraints (must not's) I must follow?

6. What can I observe, infer, and assume from the foregoing?

7. What is the most concise statement of my mission?

8. How has the situation evolved since the last time I answered these questions? Has it changed, or is it similar to the previous round of analysis?

From these questions, it should be possible to formulate a mission that fits into the bigger picture of the organization of which you and your team are a constituent element. In other words, you can't formulate your mission statement and make your own plan of action, statement of intent and end state, without first determining how you fit into the puzzle. As an illustration, I will delve deeper into the thought process I followed during my command in Bosnia. I give the background situation at the start of Chapter 1, so I won't repeat it here. The following table gives the answers I gave to the mission analysis questions listed in the text box. By carefully answering and analyzing these questions, I was able to develop a mission statement for my unit: a reinforced infantry company responsible for maintaining the peace and enforcing the provisions of the Dayton Peace Accords in Drvar and Bosansko Grahovo, Bosnia-Herzegovina, from mid-August 1999 to early March 2000.

Mission Analysis Steps	My Answers and Analysis
Division commander's intent and concept of operations	From the division commander's orders: "The purpose of our deep operations (i.e. psychological and information operations) is to persuade the belligerent forces (in Drvar this was the so called HVO, or Croatian Defence Militia) and the population of Bosnia that they should implement the Dayton Peace Accords fully and that they should not support those who obstruct these. Conditionality (we will only support those whose motives and actions are sound) will be applied wherever it is necessary to obtain leverage. Civil-military cooperation operations will broaden and deepen the peace. *While wishing to avoid an overbearing attitude, our own force posture and training will be designed to demonstrate our capability to deter unacceptable behaviour by the belligerents.*" (I've edited for clarity.) My deductions: We must operate simultaneously on the moral and physical planes by demonstrating our strength and willingness to use force to deter those who would break the peace. We must provide factual information to the population and persuade them that the best long-term strategy is to support the peace accords and those who want peace and stability.
My Commanding Officer's (CO) intent and concept of operations	Battalion's Area of Operations: The Canadian battle group was one of four battalion-sized units within our division and was deployed in the extreme northwest corner of Bosnia near the Croatian border and the Serb borderlands, where the population mix was Serb, Muslim, and Croatian.

Mission Analysis Steps	My Answers and Analysis
My Commanding Officer's (CO) intent and concept of operations (continued)	CO's Intent and Mission: Essentially the same as the division commander's. CO's Concept of Operations: The three reinforced infantry companies, of which I had command of one, would have broad responsibilities to execute the division commander's and the CO's intent and mission within our respective areas of operations. We would not, as a rule, be deployed outside of these so we could become intimately familiar with our areas and populations, and build networks of information and trust with the locals. The light armoured reconnaissance squadron would patrol the Croatian border area and conduct mobile patrols. It would also be a mobile reserve in case of need in any company area. The CO also maintained a strong reserve element consisting of the mortar platoon, antitank platoon, and pioneer platoon, to reinforce any company with additional firepower or infantry if needed. The helicopter detachment would be ready to ferry troops and equipment if needed. The CO would only send reinforcements to the infantry companies and would request reinforcement from the division and higher headquarters upon request from the company commanders, because they would be in the best position to make that judgment. The aim was to achieve security without antagonizing the population or provoking hostility by an overbearing military presence.
My assigned and implied tasks	I was given responsibility to enforce the Dayton Peace Accords in the northern part of Croat-dominated Canton 10, particularly the towns of Drvar and Bosansko Grahovo, and surrounding countryside. This included ensuring that the HVO (Croatian Defence Militia) unit under Brigadier Drazan Milic would stay docile and in their barracks. We also had a wide mandate to conduct patrolling, support the international community workers of the various UN and European bodies, cooperate with allied forces present in our area, and keep the population informed of what was really happening to counter the constant barrage of propaganda they received from the Serb and Croatian political apparatuses. We also had to provide physical protection to the dozens of international aid and reconstruction workers. It was implied that this level of protection would extend to any Bosnian civilian that would be under threat of violence, whether criminally or politically motivated.

Mission Analysis Steps	My Answers and Analysis
Constraints and restraints	We could support humanitarian relief and reconstruction efforts only if they would not detract from our primary peacekeeping functions. We had to fully respect our rules of engagement, which had been approved by National Defence Headquarters for the overall deployment to the Balkan theatre. My company could not operate outside the assigned area of operations without the CO's approval and detailed coordination with our other sub-units.
Observations, inferences, and assumptions	My area of responsibility had a population of approximately 11 to 12,000 people, about 60% of which were Croats who had been displaced from other areas in Bosnia during the war, primarily from central Bosnia and the Sarajevo area. The remaining 40% or so were Serbs who had originally lived in Drvar and Bos Grahovo prior to 1995 but had been expelled by a Croat offensive. My area had been overwhelmingly Serb prior to the war (97% Serb out of a population of 17,000). There were no Muslims. There was a Croatian militia unit based in Drvar, pompously designated 1st Guards Brigade, even though they were only the size of a small infantry battalion. There had been numerous incidents of anti-Serb violence since 1996, and the previous two summers (1998 and 1999) had seen major riots by Croats against Serb returns. I assumed that any small incident or perception could be used by the Croats against us and the international community. I also assumed that anything could be blown out of proportion, and that espionage by the Croats would be a major concern. All of these assumptions proved to be correct as the mission unfolded.
Mission statement	C Company group to maintain security within our area of responsibility in order to support the civil aspects of the Dayton Peace Accords, particularly the return of displaced persons. We will uphold the military provisions of the accords with the Bosnian Croat 1st Guards Brigade, while at the same time contributing to the undermining of the political and social elements that continued to cause instability, fear, and insecurity in the area of responsibility.

Mission Analysis Steps	My Answers and Analysis
Has the situation changed?	I conducted an abbreviated mission analysis regularly throughout the deployment for the numerous tactical operations we conducted in support of our overall mission. In other words, every time we wanted to achieve a specific effect in our area of operations, I went through this process to ensure that the mission statement was clear and precise, and that we were staying within the bounds of our roles and mandate.

Brilliant Manoeuvre

Mission analysis is a powerful tool to determine how a leader and organizational element are meant to fit into the wider organization's mission and plans.

In Drvar and Bosansko Grahovo, this meant specifically that our actions would more often than not be perceived with animosity and even enmity by members of the Bosnian Croat community while being welcomed by Bosnian Serbs, especially those that were seeking to re-establish themselves in the two towns. My intent was to get close to the civilian population, both Serb and Croat, in order to identify and deal with the criminal and extreme nationalist elements (often one and the same) that threatened the peace. This would also allow us to get our message, the NATO message, to all the civilian population, no matter what their ethnic background. I judged this to be critical to our effectiveness, as our message would counter any false information and propaganda that I knew would be spread by hardliners, especially the Croat nationalists who controlled Canton 10 politically. Consequently, I directed that the core message of information and security patrolling would be that it was up to the civilian population to report the crimes and intimidation that were rampant in both ethnic camps. We would insist that it is a citizen's responsibility to demand accountability from government and law enforcement agencies. I assigned specific responsibilities to each of my company's three platoons, with special planning and executive responsibilities for the respective platoon commanders, all three of who were bright and energetic young infantry lieutenants. My most experienced platoon commander was given the responsibility of conducting inspections of the 1st Guards Brigade of the Croat HVO to ensure they remained compliant with the military provisions of the peace accords. The platoon was based in the main camp in Drvar and alternated camp security and patrol responsibilities of the town and Drvar sector with the platoon of one of the other lieutenants. To the latter, I also assigned the responsibility of conducting information operations including the weekly "SFOR Radio Show" on the civilian Radio Drvar station. The third platoon commander was responsible for patrolling and maintaining security in the remote Bosansko Grahovo area. This platoon lived in a 'platoon house' in that town and had to be fairly autonomous owing to the distance and remoteness from our main operations. Consequently, I gave a wide mandate to this lieutenant similar in many respects to my own mandate and operations in Drvar proper.

We see from this that mission analysis is a powerful tool to determine how a leader and his or her team or organizational element are meant to fit into a wider organization's mission and scheme of manoeuvre. The key is that mission analysis is a bottom-up activity. In the military, the superior commander conducts his mission analysis, situational estimate, and mission planning then issues his direction to his subordinate commanders, so they know what is expected of them. From there, the subordinate commanders can analyze their role and the expectations that have been laid on them, and formulate their own end state, mission statement, intent, scheme of manoeuvre, and plan of action. Their subordinate commanders then do the same thing. On it goes all the way down the organization. Furthermore, as the direction and planning trickle down to all levels of the organization, the mission analysis and planning that is conducted by the subordinate commanders and their staff officers can lead to questions and issues requiring co-ordination. These get reported to the higher commanders and their respective staffs for resolution and selection of priorities. The system works well in the demanding and dangerous conditions of modern warfare and peacekeeping.

So how does all this apply to business? The company's board, CEO, and senior executives determine the broad outlines of its corporate strategy including: vision, mission, and objectives; which businesses the company will operate; performance goals and indicators for the businesses; whether each of the businesses plays a key or supporting role, and whether that role be offensive or defensive. The leaders of each business must then conduct their mission analyses to see how they fit into the bigger picture of the company's corporate strategy. Within the successive levels of each business, managers must repeat this process of mission analysis, so they can determine for themselves how their part of the organization fits into the larger strategy.

The leaders of the business lines and functional areas must conduct their mission analysis to see how they fit into the bigger company picture, and how they must support each element of the its strategy and positioning.

This is a process that is best seen from the inside, as the executives, managers, and members of each successively smaller organization and team within a company create its vision, mission, and plans to fit into the greater scheme of things. However, this type of information is competitively sensitive, so I will create a completely notional example to illustrate how the process applies in a business setting. Moreover, based on my experience with consulting clients, this process is hardly ever applied outside a military setting. It's one of those well-kept secrets of military wisdom that needs to be applied more frequently in a business setting.

To illustrate the application of mission analysis to business, let's imagine that you are a sales manager with a small manufacturer of custom packaging for cosmetics and generic pharmaceuticals. The packaging is similar for both types of products as are the suppliers, production, and warehousing. The sales and distribution channels are completely different as are the nature of the buyers, marketing, merchandising, and promotion. The CEO, also the company's majority shareholder, wants to double the company's size within four years, expanding the customer base to all of North America from its current concentration in eastern Canada and New England. The vision is to become a leading producer of quality packaging for the entire pharmaceuticals and cosmetics industries in all of North America. The new strategy entails an expansion from generic pharmaceuticals manufacturers to all pharmaceuticals companies, particularly those providing over-the-counter drugs because it's felt that the packaging is similar to that of cosmetics. There are also many similarities in distribution and merchandising. The company's mission, therefore, is to provide integrated, quality packaging solutions at reasonable cost for the pharmaceuticals and cosmetics manufacturers in all of North America. It will do this by providing a complete packaging solution. All the pharmaceutical or cosmetic manufacturer needs to do is ship the product to the company's facilities and it will do the rest, including sourcing inputs, designing the packaging and instructions, doing the packing and warehousing, shipping to distributors, etc. In other words, they are aiming to provide an end-to-end solution for manufacturers of generic pharmaceuticals and cosmetics.

The senior team has developed a strategy based on three major business thrusts: grow the pharmaceuticals business; grow the cosmetics business; grow the capabilities to provide end-to-end packaging solutions to these customer groups. The company has traditionally had only one sales team, but with the new strategy, the CEO decided to split the company into three groups to focus on each thrust. There is therefore a VP for each of Pharmaceuticals, Cosmetics, and Operations, and each has been given wide freedom of action to execute the strategy within his or her area. You are now part of the pharmaceuticals group, responsible for developing the over-the-counter (OTC) drug segment. VP Pharmaceuticals' intent and concept are shown in the table below, as is your mission analysis.

Mission Analysis Steps	Answers and Analysis
CEO's vision and intent	Vision: Become a leading producer of high quality packaging for pharmaceuticals and cosmetics manufacturers in all of North America. Objective: Double size within four years and expand customer base to all of North America from current concentration in Eastern Canada and New England. Mission: Provide integrated high quality packaging solutions at reasonable cost for both markets. Concept: Provide an end-to-end solution for manufacturers of pharmaceuticals and cosmetics. Separate sales groups with one production and operations group servicing sales in both markets. Use mass customization approach for tailored customer solutions while optimizing efficiencies and economies of scale.
VP Pharma's intent and concept of operations	Vision: Preferred supplier of integrated packaging solutions for all major pharma manufacturers in North America wanting high quality packaging. Objectives: Maintain generic pharma clients; reach all OTC drugs manufacturers as customers within 2 years; reach all other pharma manufacturers within 4 years. Mission/Intent: Provide integrated packaging solutions so the pharma manufacturers can focus on developing and marketing their products, and not worry about packaging logistics. Concept: Three sales teams focusing on three distinct client groups; generic sales team to expand to North America; create OTC sales team and build on existing client relationships in current clients to offer OTC packaging solutions, then extend to other companies; expand from OTC clients into other areas of pharma manufacturers and build sales team for proprietary pharma manufacturers as required.

Mission Analysis Steps	Answers and Analysis
Assigned and implied tasks	Assigned: Develop the OTC manufacturers clientele. Implied: Build a sales team; leverage existing relationships in generic pharma companies that also have OTC products; lay the groundwork to extend the same model to pharma companies that focus on proprietary drugs.
Constraints and restraints	Must reach all OTC manufacturers within 2 years and all other pharma companies with OTC products within 4 years. Can go faster as opportunities arise.
Observations, inferences, and assumptions	I infer from the foregoing analysis that the OTC sales effort is the critical one for the company, because it provides the bridge from existing relationships in current generic drug manufacturers to all other pharma companies. While OTC clients will be a major revenue source in and other themselves, the companies with proprietary pharmaceuticals form the bulk of the sector and that is where our company's major future growth will come from. I therefore assume that the OTC sales team will be a priority for growth and resourcing over the next 2 years.
Mission statement	Our mission is to expand existing client relationships in generic pharma to OTC drugs with a view to transferring this expertise to the proprietary pharmaceuticals manufacturers, first through OTC products, and then in support of all their other pharmaceutical products.
Has the situation changed?	As the situation evolves in the next few years, you sit down with your team on a regular basis, or as needed, and redo this mission analysis to confirm that you're still on the right track.

This notional illustration of mission analysis leads to a few critical observations. The first is that mission analysis is a dynamic process. Whether it is at the corporate, divisional, or team levels, the situation must be constantly assessed to determine whether the mission and goals are still relevant and, more importantly, still within the bounds of the superior manager's intent and concept of operations. The second point is that the mission statement for any particular executive and sub-organization tends to flow of necessity from the analysis. Once the first five steps of the process have been done, the mission statement tends to be obvious. The final and most important point is that mission analysis is the glue that holds the whole framework of nested hierarchical planning together. Mission analysis enables managers and employees at all levels of the organization, no matter what their role or tasks, to fit into the big picture and know their mission. In other words, everyone knows what he or she has to do and how everyone relies on him or her. This empowers everyone to exercise initiative to achieve the vision and mission of the organization. In the military, this is known as mission command, and we turn to this in the final part of this chapter.

Brilliant Manoeuvre

Regardless of organizational level, the situation must be constantly assessed to determine whether the mission and goals are still relevant and, more importantly, still within the bounds of the superior manager's intent and plans.

Applying Mission Analysis to Your Business

- What are the vision, end state, mission, and intent of the whole organization?
- What are the vision, mission, and intent of my superior's superior?
- What are my immediate superior's vision, mission, intent, and concept of operations for our part of the organization?
- What explicit tasks, roles, and functions within the greater concept of operations has my immediate superior given me?
- Are there implied tasks that are required to support these assigned tasks?
- What are the limitations on my freedom of action? In other words, are there constraints (musts) and restraints (must not's) that I must follow?
- What can I observe, infer, and assume from the foregoing?
- What is the most clear and concise statement of my mission?
- How has the situation evolved since the last time I answered these questions? Has it changed or is it similar to the previous round of analysis?

Mission Command Is Focused Initiative

Mission command is the philosophy of focused initiative. In the military, no commander can foresee every possible variation of execution and outcome in his planning. What's more, friction, uncertainty, and the enemy's actions can play havoc with the best-laid plans. This is why it is necessary to provide as much information as possible to subordinate commanders, and even front-line soldiers, so that they can think and act in a manner that is commensurate with the overarching intent and mission in order to achieve the desired end state. With everyone free to exercise their initiative within a well-defined framework, military forces evolve from the traditional image of rows of automatons following orders to the letter, to one of a swarm of intelligent agents thinking and acting in a coherent but somewhat unpredictable manner. The high-level commanders gain the advantage of all these thinking minds acting in concert, whereas the enemy has to face an army of strategic thinkers and master tacticians. There is no better way to execute Sun Tzu's dictum to "adopt formlessness," meaning that the enemy (or competition) find it difficult or impossible to infer your intentions from your apparent actions.

The key in mission command is that commanders define the 'what' but not the 'how' of any operation or mission. By providing the end state, objectives, and intent, the superior commander sets the broad parameters for the planning and execution at successively lower levels of the organization. There are certainly strictures on how things get done, and all military forces are highly focused on standardized problem solving and operational systems. However, these only form a backdrop for the thought process that leads to strategic, operational, and tactical decision-making. If a platoon commander knows what the company commander wants to achieve with a particular mission, say the securing of a crossroads so that another company in the battalion can pass through to conduct its own mission, then when the plan goes awry after the enemy ambushes the company commander, that platoon commander can continue with the mission and improvise a new plan on the fly. This is wonderfully illustrated by a scene in the first episode of the HBO series *Band of Brothers*. The company is on exercise in the English countryside and the incompetent company commander gets lost with the platoon that was supposed to secure an objective. Second Lieutenant Dick Winters (this is all based on real events) takes over the operation and successfully captures the objective. His improvisation succeeds because he understands the whole sweep of the company's plan, and can execute it despite the company commander's inability to carry out his part.

Brilliant Manoeuvre

Mission command—the exercise of focused initiative—is only possible when everyone in a company is aware of and completely understands its vision, mission, and concept of operations; when everyone is keyed to the CEO's intent and the objectives that have been set for the next year, the year following, the next decade, etc.

This philosophy of mission command is highly applicable in business. Plans rarely go the way they are expected to. As soldiers are fond of saying, "a plan is only good until you cross the line of departure." We can say the same about any business strategy or plan. Customers get to choose whether they actually like your products or not. Governments introduce new legislation. A key executive departs. A competitor launches a hostile takeover. An obscure company comes out of nowhere and launches a completely new service that takes you by surprise and undermines your existing market leadership. Mission command—the exercise of focused initiative—is only possible when everyone in a company is aware of and completely understands its vision, mission, and concept of operations; when everyone is keyed to the CEO's intent and the objectives that have been set for the next year, the year following, the next decade, etc. Nested hierarchical planning and mission analysis create a culture of alignment and empowerment, which enable everyone to be on the lookout for changes in the internal and external environment so they can react in a timely and effective manner that employs their knowledge and skills to achieve the aim in spite of resistance, competition, miscalculations, and miscommunications.

Applying Mission Command to Your Business

- Does everyone in your company or organization know its vision, mission, and basic operating concepts?
- Has every executive, manager, and team leader developed a plan of action that fits within the next higher leader's intent and concept of operations?
- Have they thought long and hard about their own mission, about how they fit into the bigger picture of the organization, the division, the team?

- Do your people have the freedom to exercise their initiative within the strategic, operational, and tactical frameworks that have been determined?
- Are your people afraid to take initiative for fear of upsetting their manager or of rocking the boat?
- Can you genuinely say that you and everyone in your organization are fully aligned on the higher intent and objectives, or are you pursuing your own private agenda?

Summary

- Selection and maintenance of the aim is the master principle of war and business. It provides the impetus and framework for action for the entire organization.
- The real skill is in selecting an objective that can be achieved. It is good to set stretch goals, but they must not be so lofty as to be nearly impossible. An unrealistic goal can be seen as unachievable and can undermine morale and cohesion.
- Objectives must balance ends, ways, and means. The key questions are: What (ends) is to be achieved and why? How (ways) should it be achieved? What resources (means) are needed to achieve it?
- Ends, ways, and means provide a framework to generate a nested hierarchy of subordinate goals that must be accomplished by elements of the organization in order to meet the overarching organizational objectives.
- Organizational objectives must be translated into a detailed and tailored roadmap for action at successively lower levels of the organization. It is not enough, however, to simply set an objective and develop a plan. Everyone at every level must analyze the direction they've been given and identify how they are meant to fit into the bigger puzzle.
- The process of mission analysis is therefore critical to success because it is how leaders and employees of an organization come up with mission statements and objectives appropriate to their respective roles and functions within the organization, and consequently can make a plan to execute their role in the greater scheme while having the understanding to adapt to inevitable changes and difficulties with initiative and resolve.
- Initiative, properly channelled through nested hierarchical planning and mission analysis, enables mission command, where leaders at all levels

are not told how to do their jobs, but rather what outcomes they are expected to achieve.

- The philosophy of mission command demands that leaders at all levels contribute to the development of their own objectives through the process of mission analysis, while framing decision-making and using the initiative of their own followers.

Chapter 5

You Can't Be Everywhere at Once: Exploiting Limited Resources

*Just as the center of gravity is always found where the mass
is most concentrated, and just as every blow directed against
the body's center of gravity yields the greatest effect, and—
moreover—the strongest blow is the one achieved by the center
of gravity, the same is true in war.*

Carl von Clausewitz

*In war, then, let your great object be victory, not lengthy
campaigns.*

Sun Tzu

*The pertinent question is not how to do things right but how
to find the right things to do, and to concentrate resources and
effort on them.*

Peter Drucker, **Managing for Results**

Business and war are both economic activities. They are concerned with the
allocation of scarce resources to achieve desired outcomes. Estimates are often
incorrect or incomplete, and the actions of opponents and other stakeholders can
be miscalculated or unknown until it is too late. Leaders, therefore, must continually
evaluate the resources at their disposal, marshal new ones, and allocate them in a
timely manner so their organizations can carry out their functions and attain their
objectives. The picture painted in Chapter 4 is of a static, once-only planning and

decision-making process, but this is only a starting point. The reality is that war and business are dynamic undertakings. No sooner has one side decided on a plan, and started to act upon it that the other side reacts to these actions, and does something unexpected or disruptive that derails the best-laid plans. This interplay of move, countermove, and counter-countermove is the substance of conflict and competition.

The aim of this chapter is to describe the principles that underpin the dynamic aspects of war and business so that leaders can continually assess, act and adjust their plans and execution to achieve their desired objectives. These principles are described in the following text box.

Dynamic Principles of Action

- **Centre of Gravity.** The centre of gravity is what gives a body its power, balance, and strength. We can extend this by analogy to any organization. The key to effective prioritization of resources is to understand the centre of gravity of one's own side, while estimating that of the opponent.

- **Main Effort.** The main effort is the activity, function, or part of the organization that gets priority access to resources and senior leadership attention. The main effort channels and focuses the organization's resources by the understanding of both the organization's and the opponent's centres of gravity.

- **Economy and Mass.** Economy and mass are two sides of the main effort coin. Decisive action comes from mass applied to the main effort, which aims to destroy or disrupt the opponent's centre of gravity. To achieve mass, resources must be concentrated in time and space. Concentration creates weaknesses and gaps elsewhere, which must be compensated to some degree through economy of force.

- **Speed and Agility.** Time is the ultimate resource. Brute speed can compensate for time and resource limitations. If you can assess, act, and adjust faster and more often than your opponent, then you can present him with a continuous stream of dilemmas. Agility can also compensate for limited resources and can contribute to speed of decision-making, reaction, and execution.

- **Flexibility.** Organizations need flexibility to respond to threats and opportunities. This can be achieved by giving multiple roles and tasks to organizational elements.

Recognize Your Own and Your Competitors' Centres of Gravity

The centre of gravity of a military force is the wellspring of its power and strength. For instance, the military centre of gravity of the United States is its material strength and the country's ability to generate and move massive quantities of materiel, manpower, and weaponry in relatively short periods of time anywhere in the world. American military commanders simply assume material superiority no matter where or against whom they are fighting. The enemy can confront American forces on their terms, but this would require the ability to destroy or otherwise neutralize this material superiority. During the Cold War, western countries believed that only the Soviet Union had the capability to confront the United States on such a level. Alternatively, the enemy can attempt to make American superiority irrelevant by attacking the country's will to fight. The enemy does this by acting on the moral plane of war, with the physical plane in support. The wars in Afghanistan and Iraq illustrate this principle well. Insurgents usually avoided direct clashes with American ground forces because they couldn't match them in mobility, protection, and firepower. Instead, they worked on the moral plane, using psychological warfare, the media, propaganda, and ideological attacks. The insurgents used military engagements to the extent needed to generate opportunities for psychological warfare. Their objective was to create doubt in the minds of the American people about the wisdom and even the morality of continuing the struggle.

Similarly, every business has a center of gravity, although the concept tends to be couched in synonymous terms such as strengths, unique capabilities, fundamental value proposition, key differentiators and the like. A business's centre of gravity is its source of strength. It is that which differentiates it in the minds of customers, investors, competitors, executives, and employees. Managers at all levels of a business must understand and accept this centre of gravity. Moreover, they must recognize the centres of gravity of established and up-and-coming competitors. This is so they can neutralize them more effectively, while maintaining the ability to leverage their own unique attributes. Intimate knowledge of one's own centre of gravity plus an estimation of that of competitors provide the logical framework for analyzing objectives and strategy. When you recognize your centre of gravity, you can focus your mental and material efforts on what's important, and discard or reallocate inefficient activities and resources.

Brilliant Manoeuvre

A business's centre of gravity is its source of strength. It is that which differentiates it in the minds of customers, investors, competitors, executives, and employees.

Apple's centre of gravity is its ability to combine or re-combine existing technologies into novel products that people feel compelled to buy for reasons of utility certainly but also for reasons of cachet and status. Apple's products are as much works of art as highly effective and efficient instruments. Steve Jobs often said that Apple was at the juncture of art and science, design and functionality. Jobs's every waking minute was oriented to the creation and refinement of highly integrated, powerfully effective work and communication tools. He built a company around the ethos that electronic devices must not only be functional and well-designed but also works of art that rest delicately in the hand, while conferring power and status to their users. This focus on artful design and functional precision led to a certain type of minimalism, which guided almost all product and marketing decisions.

The most successful companies over the long term are those that have a clear recognition and understanding of their centre of gravity. They know what makes them unique, and why it confers power and strength to their activities. ExxonMobil is the largest oil company in the world because it understands the critical importance of finding and exploiting reliable, secure, long-term sources of oil. That is what is needed to be successful in any kind of natural resource business, but ExxonMobil is better at it than anyone else. BP also has a clear understanding of the need to secure sources of oil, but its self-image of risk-taking has led it to become involved in ventures that are much riskier than other oil companies. In fact, no matter what happens in the world competition for new sources of oil, it always seems that BP is involved in the riskiest and most dangerous parts of the world. This has led to major financial and business disasters for BP, such as its investments in Russia and its continuous wrangling with Russian oil companies and the Russian government. This risk-focused centre of gravity is what led to BP's less-than-stellar safety practices over the years, culminating in the massive disaster of the Gulf of Mexico in early 2010. With ExxonMobil having access to some of the best and most secure sources of oil in the world, the driving force of access to resources leads BP to consider riskier sources. The company must therefore build its centre of gravity as the best risk-taker in the oil business. Whether it is or not is certainly open to discussion, but one can't deny that BP has turned taking risks to secure oil supplies into a continuous way of doing business. With ExxonMobil's strong position, BP and other oil companies have really no other choice but to go for broke in the hope of making big finds that will supply them for years. This draws them to countries with large oil reserves but with governmental and business practices that leave companies open to threats of graft, expropriation, and political manipulation.

Brilliant Manoeuvre

The most successful companies over the long term are those that have a clear recognition and understanding of their centre of gravity. They know what makes them unique, and why it confers power and strength to their activities.

This discussion, and the example of the United States' centre of gravity highlight the fact that an organization's centre of gravity, while being the wellspring of its strength and power and the source of its uniqueness, is also inevitably its most glaring vulnerability. This is why it mustn't just be exploited and leveraged to achieve desired objectives but also protected. This realization also provides the conceptual underpinnings to decide how to attack and undermine a competitor or opponent. If you're Apple, you don't go after Microsoft or RIM by trying to do what they do. You go after them by undermining their particular centre of gravity. In both cases, this has meant leaving the corporate and institutional markets to them and focusing instead on consumers, who are much more likely to respond to brand uniqueness and the coolness factor of Apple's products than are clients in a corporate setting. Apple's campaign against Microsoft's dominance of computing is a case in point, illustrated in Figure 5.1.

Figure 5.1: Apple Crossing the 'T' of Microsoft

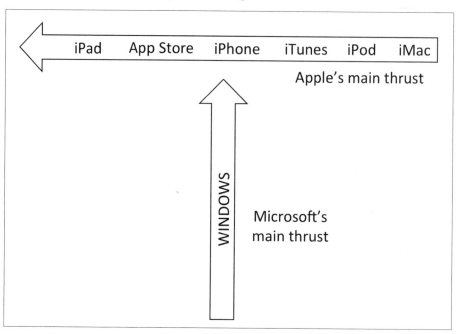

The diagram shows Apple 'crossing Microsoft's T.'[1] This was the pinnacle of naval manoeuvring in the late nineteenth and early twentieth centuries. Battleships would follow each other in single file with the object to fire successive broadsides as each ship in the line passed the enemy's formation. The ideal manoeuvre was to do so by 'crossing the T,' which required crossing ahead of the enemy's main line at a 90-degree angle. By this manoeuvre, it was possible to bring each successive ship's guns to bear in a broadside against the enemy ships while the latter could only bring their forward facing guns to bear. As only the first ship in the line could fire, the line whose T was crossed would receive the enemy's broadsides with little ability to respond in kind.

During Steve Jobs's tenure as CEO, Apple was able to consistently bring new products to bear against Microsoft. Microsoft's centre of gravity was its dominance

---

[1]   I am grateful to Dr Alan Weiss of Summit Consulting Group for this example.

of the personal computing platform through its Windows operating system. Bill Gates and Microsoft did everything they could in the 1980s and 1990s to dominate the computing world by putting Windows on as many computers as possible and, by the late 1990s, most PCs were delivered with a Windows operating system. This gave Microsoft the ability to integrate its application software, and to set the standard for competitors' products and services. While Microsoft developed myriad products and services for PCs, its dominance was almost entirely due to the ubiquity of the original Windows 3.1 and Windows 95 operating systems and their successors. Gates's strategy was to make Windows dominant as a computing platform without controlling the hardware, and to exploit this to the greatest extent possible. The strategy was designed to leverage and protect Microsoft's centre of gravity, which was the ability to develop and exploit the Windows platform.

Microsoft's centre of gravity was simultaneously its greatest vulnerability. Everything in Microsoft depended on its Windows dominance, especially in the corporate, institutional, and government markets. The company had to maintain almost complete backward compatibility with previous versions of Windows, both in desktop and server versions. The need to be compatible with many different variants of the basic PC platform also drove design and marketing. This made Microsoft vulnerable to new product and service categories, and Apple was the main beneficiary of this vulnerability from about the year 2001.

We can see this with Apple's successive introduction of novel products and services since the late 1990s. Apple's strategy entailed the successive development and marketing of unique products and services that built on each other's strengths, while being able to function independently. The key was a relentless focus on design and quality of user experience, achieved by sticking to a closed platform that closely integrated hardware and software. All Apple products were developed and sold as fully integrated appliances and devices. This gave the company the freedom of action to create products and services that fit perfectly together, and also kept out unauthorized competitors or companies that couldn't exploit the Apple platforms without prior approval. In broad strokes, this was how Steve Jobs and Apple crossed Microsoft's T. First, came the iMac in 1998, an innovative all-in-one computer design. Then in 2001 came the iPod, which launched Apple into non-computing markets and, especially, opened up the world of content. iTunes gave the company entry into the music business, and Apple is now the largest music retailer in the world. The iPhone, as discussed in previous chapters, continued the onslaught against Microsoft while adding another potential victim, Research in Motion's Blackberry.

The key point is that Apple was relentless in introducing game-changing products and services that were figuratively at right angles to Microsoft's main business line. Microsoft still controls the major institutional, governmental, and corporate markets in early 2012, and will probably continue to do so for quite some time. Apple's crossing of Microsoft's T, however, has made the latter a minor player and, therefore, a non-threat in most non-organizational and non-desktop computing markets. Apple has fired successive broadsides at Microsoft, while Microsoft has only been able to fire a few of its guns against Apple. We therefore see two companies in competition with two very different centres of gravity and, consequently, two different strategies.

Strategic Application of Centre of Gravity

- What is the driving force of your business?
- How can you best exploit this driving force? What unique capabilities and strengths do you bring to its exploitation?
- Can you identify or build a centre of gravity around this driving force and these unique capabilities and strengths?
- What is the centre of gravity of your principal competitors? Can you undermine or neutralize their respective centres of gravity while exploiting your own?
- How does your own centre of gravity make you vulnerable? How can you reduce that vulnerability to protect your own centre of gravity?
- How can you cross the T of your main competitors?

Designate Your Main Effort

The reason for emphasizing the centre of gravity is that it is crucial to the prioritization of resources. As already mentioned, resources are always in short supply, so a military commander must plan for and designate a main effort. The main effort of a military operation is usually a designated unit or formation that is carrying out the commander's plan. During World War II, the Western Allies designated the forces that were assigned to defeat Nazi Germany as the main war effort because Germany was deemed the more dangerous of the Axis members from the Western perspective. As a result, the US and Great Britain assigned many more resources to fighting Germany than to fighting Japan, at least until Germany had been defeated. Within the European theatre of the war, the main effort was northwest Europe, because the quickest, most effective way to defeat Nazi Germany was to destroy the German armed forces—Germany's strategic centre of gravity—and strike at its industrial heart. Consequently, massive resources were devoted to equipping the Soviet Union, to the strategic bombing of Germany, and to the ground offensive to liberate northwest Europe and invade Germany. Meanwhile, the Mediterranean theatre received fewer resources. Allied operations in the Mediterranean and Italy were designed to siphon off German forces from the Allied main effort while achieving secondary strategic objectives in North Africa, the Middle East, and the Balkans. The concept of the main effort is illustrated in Figure 5.2.

Figure 5.2: Main Effort

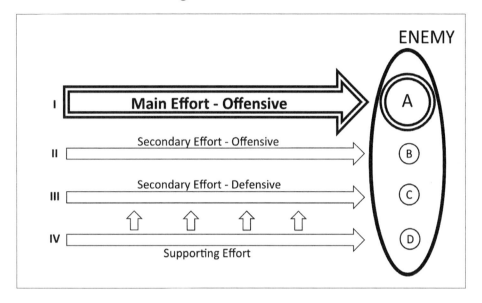

We see in this diagram that each of the four elements in this organization has received a distinct task and objective. Element I has been designated as the main effort, with the mission to achieve objective A. Elements II and III have been designated as secondary efforts, and must achieve respectively objectives B and C. Element IV has the role of supporting the manoeuvre elements. This could involve logistics and supply, preliminary reconnaissance operations, training, or any other type of supporting function. The scheme of manoeuvre is reflected in the   main effort being an offensive posture as is one of the secondary efforts, whereas the third element has a defensive role. Moreover, the main effort is intended to exploit the centre of gravity, and its objective is the destruction or neutralization of the enemy's centre of gravity, both shown as double lines. In terms of the example above, the forces assigned by the Allies to invade and liberate northwest Europe and defeat Nazi Germany were on the offensive, and were focused entirely on the German centre of gravity, its armed forces. The forces in the Mediterranean and the strategic bombing forces were in secondary, offensive roles, whereas all of the Allied logistics, intelligence, and political efforts were supporting functions to facilitate the success of the strategy. There were other defensive efforts, such as ensuring the air defence of Great Britain and the defence of the convoys at sea against Germany U-boat attacks.

The same concept can and should be applied to companies as they seek to achieve their vision and objectives, as we described in Chapter 4. As a matter of fact, the principles of centre of gravity and main effort apply to all endeavours where there are limitations on resources available to achieve an objective. We've already given some examples of how business leaders have used the concept of main effort to pare away the unessential in order to focus on what will achieve the biggest bang for the buck. One was Steve Jobs's decision to eliminate most of Apple's products in order to focus on only a few major items, such as the iMac. Another was Southwest Airlines' relentless focus on direct flights between secondary cities using only one aircraft type, thus simplifying maintenance, training, and logistics, and allowing specialization on one particular type of customer. This model has been successfully reproduced in Canada with WestJet—even down to relying on the same aircraft as Southwest, the Boeing 737—as well as Porter Airlines, which concentrates on first-class service on short-haul routes for business travellers between major Canadian and American cities in the northeast using Bombardier Q400 turboprops. In all these examples, company leadership has decided that some things can't and shouldn't be done. This frees time and resources to focus on the main effort, with secondary and supporting roles for lesser areas of the company.

Brilliant Manoeuvre

Company executives must decide that some things can't and shouldn't be done. This frees time and resources to focus on the main effort, with secondary and supporting roles for lesser areas of the company.

We can see the effects of not focusing effectively by considering Sony's struggle to adapt to changing realities in consumer electronics and technology. Sony was built on the belief that its engineers and designers could achieve anything they could imagine. Sony used to be associated with leading-edge products that allowed users to have unique and compelling entertainment experiences. Whether it was transistor radios, colour TVs, or video-cassette recorders, Sony used to be at the forefront of innovative design and marketing. This is the company that designed and introduced the Walkman. Company president Akio Morita went against the advice of his marketing executives when he decided to go ahead with the Walkman because he felt that it met a need for customers which even they didn't know they had. Sony has been struggling for years because of the company's inability to concentrate its forces on a main offensive effort, one that would protect and exploit its unique centre of gravity. In fact, Sony provides an interesting contrast to Apple. Both have built their brand on developing and marketing great consumer electronic devices for entertainment. Both have access to great content, Sony through its control of CBS and Apple through iTunes. But Apple has become the most valuable technology company, while Sony has languished owing to lack of focus.

General Electric is a company that exemplifies the principle of centre of gravity and main effort even more clearly than Apple. GE has been around for over a century. Though initially a manufacturer of electrical generation and distribution equipment, GE has evolved to become an industrial and financial conglomerate. Its centre of gravity is superb management. The company excels at attracting, developing, retaining, and promoting excellent managers and leaders at all levels. The succession to Jack Welch in the late 1990s revealed just how much depth of senior management there was. Though Jeffrey Immelt was ultimately selected to replace Jack Welch in 2001, most of the runners-up were selected to run other Fortune 500 corporations in the same time period. GE has developed the reputation as an incubator of top management talent. Researchers at the Richard Ivey School of Business at the University of Western Ontario tested this hypothesis in a 2009 study, and found that not only do other companies seek GE executives, but the former GE executives generate above-average results in the companies that hire them. GE's main effort over the decades, therefore, has been to reallocate their superb, managerial talent and capital from under-performing businesses to ones with more potential. When a decision is made to enter a new business line, the company allocates the resources to buy an existing business, or to start one from scratch. This is the offensive component. Businesses that are designated for divestiture are either milked for cash or sold off, or both. This is the supporting, defensive component. The important point is that GE focuses its managerial talent and capital on high-growth businesses, while low-growth businesses are exploited, then eventually sold.

Strategic Application of Main Effort

- From your analysis of your centre of gravity, where should your main effort lie?

- Can you design your main effort to undermine those of your competitors? In other words, can you use your centre of gravity and main effort to cross your competitors' Ts?
- What resources and capabilities are required to implement your main effort?
- What secondary and supporting efforts are required to make your main effort work?
- How can you free resources from secondary and supporting efforts to reallocate them to your main effort?
- Who will you designate to lead your main effort?

Economy and Mass

The principles of centre of gravity and main effort lead naturally to decisions about mass and economy. These are the two sides of the main effort coin. In order to have sufficient resources for the main effort, they must be taken from lower priority activities and objectives. In military terms, forces must be concentrated or amassed to achieve the desired outcomes with the main effort. These resources come from other areas and the units that are providing the reinforcements to the main effort have fewer resources at their command. Though they are somewhat denuded, they must still achieve their objectives, so they do this through economy of force methods. Ultimately, though, economy of effort can result in a decision to stop doing certain things, and to accept risk in those areas.

> ## Brilliant Manoeuvre
>
> **In order to have sufficient resources for the main effort, they must be taken from lower priority activities and objectives.**

The scheme of manoeuvre should exploit one's centre of gravity to destroy or neutralize the enemy's centre of gravity by using the principles of main effort, economy, and concentration to achieve the needed mass against the enemy's forces so that the mission can be achieved as quickly as possible with the least effort. Just as the strategist must balance ends, ways, and means, as described in Chapter 4, the operational planner and tactician must balance considerations of main effort, economy, and mass, to concentrate forces for full effect at the right time and the right place, whether on defence or on offence. Moreover, defensive and offensive postures of subordinate elements can be combined to achieve an overall force posture. For instance, a commander of a division, a formation consisting of approximately 20,000 troops, may designate two of his three brigades as the main effort of his attack plan with a view to breaking through the enemy's defenses and capturing an objective in his rear area. In the meantime, he may designate the third of his brigades to protect the flanks of the attacking brigades. The third brigade, therefore, would be in a defensive posture, and thus would not need as many resources as the brigades that are attacking, since we already know that defence is stronger than offence. The division commander is, therefore, likely to take one of that third brigade's tank battalions and re-assign it to reinforce one of the brigades in the main effort. This is how military commanders concentrate forces for the main effort, by figuratively robbing Peter to pay Paul, and accepting the risk that Peter may not have enough resources to carry out his full functions.

Brilliant Manoeuvre

Balance considerations of main effort, economy, and mass, to concentrate forces for full effect at the right time and the right place, whether on defence or on offence.

How does this apply in business? The closest analogue is the decision to launch a new business line. A company experimenting with new products or markets is likely to uncover opportunities. However, the company may not have all the resources necessary at that particular point in time to exploit the opportunity unless the decision is made to take resources from other areas of the company. This can be from support functions but a more productive use of resources would be to take them from areas that are either not as productive as the new opportunity is likely to be, or those that are highly successful and that are producing a lot of cash. This is similar in some respects to a Growth-Market Share matrix, as shown in Figure 5.3.

This model was originally developed for General Electric to serve as a means of assessing its various businesses for decisions concerning investment and divestment. While the model has been challenged over the years by strategy theorists, it nonetheless provides a useful way to discuss the principles of mass and economy and their application to corporate strategy. The point is that a company's current and future business ventures can be assessed for their growth potential.

Figure 5.3: Growth-Market Share Matrix

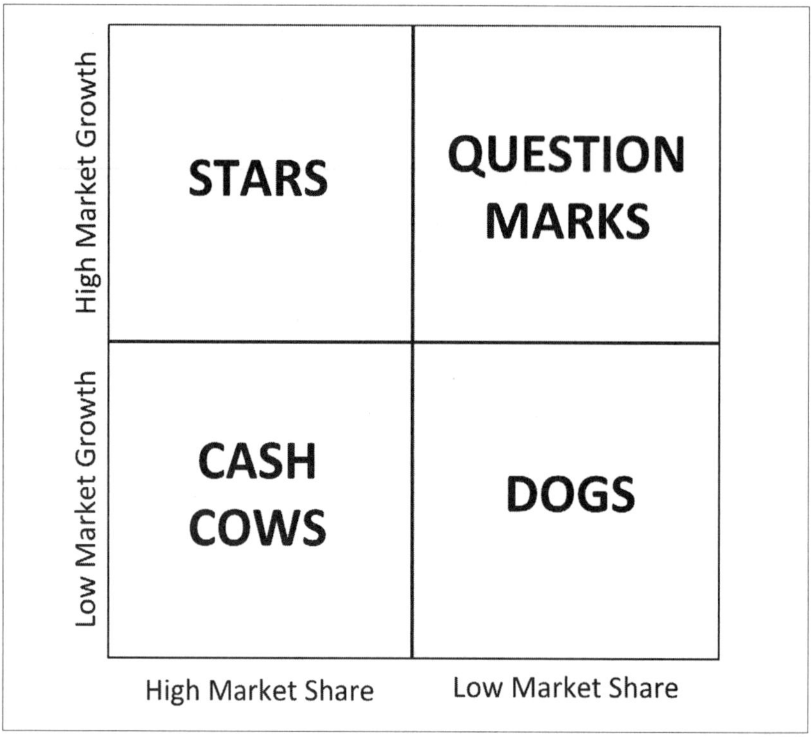

	High Market Share	Low Market Share
High Market Growth	STARS	QUESTION MARKS
Low Market Growth	CASH COWS	DOGS

The model also provides a way to determine which businesses are likely to be candidates for divestiture or to provide much needed resources to exploit opportunities. The 'Question Marks' are the company's experiments. This is the first part of the probing approach to offensive operations that I described in the final section of Chapter 2. The second part concerns selecting high growth potential candidates from among the question marks so they can eventually become 'Stars.' 'Dogs' are experiments that will not pan out or formerly great businesses that have lost their revenue generation capability and profitability. Dogs are the most evident source of resources for reallocation to high potential Question Marks so they have a chance of becoming Stars. In other words, the decision about Dogs corresponds to a military commander who deliberately chooses to withdraw from one area in order to reallocate the forces to another higher priority area or mission. The other obvious source of resources for investment in potential Stars is to milk the company's 'Cash Cows.' These are the highly successful businesses that generate plenty of cash with little effort or investment on the part of the company. They can be past their prime, but not necessarily. Cash Cows are kept on the defensive, because they don't need the resources that the offensive growth strategy requires. They are not the main effort of the company, but they are critical to its success in turning its high potential Question Marks into future Stars, because they can generate the cash to finance internal growth.

The best example of the application of this approach is the pharmaceutical industry. Few industries provide such a clear-cut example of the principles of mass and economy in support of a main effort that exploits the company's centre of gravity. The centre of gravity of these companies is their ability to generate novel, successful drugs in a continuing stream over decades. Their main effort is R&D, but this requires a massive, sustained effort over time. The hope of every pharmaceutical CEO is to discover a blockbuster drug, such as Lipitor or Viagra, a Star product or business line that can become a Cash Cow that will generate massive revenues over decades in order to fuel R&D. Unsuccessful experiments and poorly performing drugs—the Dogs of the pharmaceutical business—must be eliminated quickly in order to free resources for continued development of new, successful drugs which, it is hoped, will in turn become the future Stars and eventual Cash Cows of the company.

So, in the same way, a company must have a grasp of how its main effort protects and exploits its centre of gravity while, at the same time, undermining those of its competitors. The next, key step is the identification of which activities support the main effort, and the way in which they do it. The company should derive experiments in order to generate Question Marks. These experiments should be in areas related to the company's existing products and markets, but there should also be a certain number of experiments in unrelated areas since it is impossible to know how success will be attained in the future. Similarly, some of the company's Stars and Cash Cows may no longer be relevant to the company's future growth as its main effort evolves.

Brilliant Manoeuvre

A company must have a grasp of how its main effort protects and exploits its centre of gravity, while undermining that of its competitors.

Business strategy is a dynamic process of continually assessing and re-assessing what is working and what isn't, so that resources can be marshalled and concentrated on those activities that will generate the greatest chances of success rather than squandering efforts and resources on uncoordinated activities and businesses. Economy of effort in secondary areas is essential to free resources and to provide managerial focus on concentrating forces for an offensive in an area that has a greater likelihood of succeeding. By concentrating forces for the main effort, a company can create the needed mass to make a strategic breakthrough and to pour forces into the breach.

Strategic Application of Mass and Economy

- What are your Question Marks, the experiments that have potential to become future Stars and even Cash Cows?
- Are your Question Marks only in areas related to your centre of gravity and your current, main effort, or have you ventured somewhat outside the safe confines of your existing customers, products, and markets?
- Are all of your Stars focused on the main effort?
- Are all of your Cash Cows part of the main effort or of secondary efforts?
- Could you divest some of your Stars or Cash Cows even if they are part of the main effort? Do you have some that are not part of the main effort, but that could generate considerable cash for re-investment in the main effort?
- Has the situation evolved to the point where you are re-evaluating your main effort, and possibly even your centre of gravity?
- Do you have businesses now that you would be willing and able to divest in order to free resources to invest in experiments that appear to be succeeding?
- Can you generate cash from your highly successful businesses to invest in creating Question Marks, and to transform those with potential into Stars?

Speed and Agility

During the Battle of the Bulge in late 1944, General Patton, commander of the 3rd US Army, turned his forces from their west-east orientation in response to a surprise German counter-offensive through the Ardennes Forest of southeastern Belgium. He then force-marched his army at great speed north to counter-attack into the German flank. The speed and agility that were demonstrated in this manoeuvre were instrumental in stabilizing the Allied front and contributed to the eventual defeat of the German offensive.

Brilliant Manoeuvre

Offensively, speed and agility allow us to recognize opportunities quickly in order to seize the initiative. Defensively, speed and agility enable us to react adequately to competitive threats, before competitors can exploit them.

Speed and agility are vital for offensive and defensive success in military strategy, operations, and tactics. Moreover, they are essential in decision-making and execution. There is little point in executing quickly if you can't come to a hasty decision in the heat of battle. Conversely, agility and velocity of decision-making are wasted if the force can't execute efficiently with speed. Speed contributes to mass and economy by enabling the rapid marshalling and concentration of forces at key decision points from lower priority or less critical areas. Agility is the ability of forces to re-configure and to re-orient quickly and with relative ease so the forces can move from one mission to another or change direction in the event of a new situation such as when a contingency plan is put into effect. Both speed and agility can compensate to a certain extent for limitations in resources because forces can be 'double-hatted.' This means that a force in a secondary effort can be given a backup mission to reinforce another unit on a higher priority effort should the enemy do something unexpected. This allows the commander to make contingency plans in case the initial plan goes awry, as often happens in battle.

Speed and agility are also essential in business for both offence and defence. Offensively, speed and agility allow us to recognize opportunities quickly in order to seize the initiative, and to execute before the competition does. Defensively, speed and agility enable us to react adequately to competitive threats, before competitors can exploit them, in order to protect existing positions. Speed and agility are applicable at all business levels, strategic, operational, and tactical. When we combine these two dimensions, we get a two-by-three matrix that shows potential decision-making and execution applications of speed and agility. The following table gives some examples of these applications.

	Offensive	Defensive
Strategic	*Decision*: Don't dither over experiments that show promise; decide quickly to reinforce them. *Execution*: Reallocate assets and capital quickly and efficiently to high potential areas.	*Decision*: Decide quickly on whether to imitate or simply monitor a competitor's new product. *Execution*: Imitate success; don't reinvent the wheel by trying to reinvent a successful product by a competitor; reverse engineer competing products and services.
Operational	*Decision*: Ensure all managers and employees fully understand the strategy and intent, and empower them to formulate their own missions within the wider mandate. *Execution*: Create processes and systems that empower and enable rapid and repeatable tactical decisions and outcomes.	*Decision*: Kill Dogs and failed experiments, whether they are products or processes, quickly and without fuss. *Execution*: Implement changes and new systems and processes quickly to avoid resistance and dithering.
Tactical	*Decision*: Salespeople qualifying leads quickly and efficiently so they focus on high potential prospects. *Execution*: Creating client proposals quickly and efficiently once conceptual agreement has been reached.	*Decision*: Customer service agents are empowered to respond and correct reasonable complaints. *Execution*: Errors are corrected quickly and without fuss once the decision is made to make them right.

These examples show some of the applications, but how is it possible to actually create speed and agility? Speed and agility in decision-making come from resolve, realism, common understanding, relevance, empowerment, risk acceptance, and standardized decision-making processes. Speed and agility in execution come from common systems, predetermined routines, contingency planning and accepting risks. These elements form the principles of speed and agility. Let's look at each one.

Resolve

Resolve is the readiness to make a decision, and to stick to it when the going gets tough. All great leaders and teams have resolve, and it ultimately depends on the confidence that things will actually turn out as anticipated even if they don't go exactly as planned.

Realism

This is the ability to match beliefs with the real world, to come to terms with things as they are as opposed to how we wish they were. Obviously, there is a balance to be struck between resolve and realism. Too much resolve can be like attacking an enemy in a fortress where one wastes forces on frontal assaults. Sometimes, you have to realize that your plans just aren't working, and that it's better to withdraw with your forces relatively intact in order to fight another day. On the other hand, plans can take time to come to fruition, so this is also part of realism.

Common Understanding

When everyone in the organization understands its vision, mission, and objectives, and knows where they fit into the overall plan of manoeuvre and what vital role they play, they can apply their own initiative and reasoning to resolving the inevitable problems and dilemmas that arise as a result of friction, uncertainty, error, and competitors' actions. This is the entire point of mission command as described in Chapter 4. A service technician that understands the company's strategy and goals can spot new opportunities when he or she visits customers, and then feed the opportunities to sales and marketing. Silo and NIMBY mentalities are antithetical to speed and agility. Mission command is the cure, as described in chapter 4.

Relevance

The overall objectives and strategy provide the framework for decision-making, for determining what is relevant, and what is not. The centre of gravity and the main effort are particularly important in this regard. In this chapter, we've described these two concepts in largely strategic terms, but they apply at all levels of the organization and decision-making. If an opportunity arises, the key question that needs to be asked to permit a decision is whether it might strengthen or weaken the organization's or a competitor's centre of gravity. The second question is whether it is likely to reinforce the main effort, or take resources away from it. If the responses are affirmative, then a hasty decision to go ahead with the opportunity is probably warranted. If the responses are negative, then the opportunity probably warrants immediate dismissal.

Empowerment

This is the natural corollary of common understanding and relevance. If managers and employees know something to be true or right, and it fits within the stated objectives and strategy, they should be empowered to use their initiative to exploit the resulting opportunity, to defend against the threat, or to correct the mistake. Once again, this is the whole point about mission command as described in Chapter 4.

Risk Acceptance

This, in turn, is the corollary of empowerment. You can't expect people to take quick decisions and act upon them with speed and agility if they fear reprisals or punishment when the inevitable mistakes are made or when problems of execution occur. In a culture where risk is recognized and accepted, decisions will tend to be quicker and more effective than in an organization where everyone is covering their behind.

Standard Decision Processes

Speed and agility are enhanced by standard decision processes, where everyone in the chain of command knows what is expected and how to go about collecting and weighing information, determining potential courses of action and responses by competitors, judging their relative effectiveness, and selecting optimal courses of action. The mission analysis process described in Chapter 4 is one example of such a process. I will describe a few more in Chapters 6 and 7. The important thing is that companies must have well-understood decision processes that are applied consistently by everyone at all levels of the organization. It also helps to follow the military practice of adopting hasty decision-making and planning processes, as these accelerate decision-making and execution considerably.

Common Systems

This principle should be blindingly obvious, but it isn't always followed. One of the companies I consult for had many systems for managing customer relationships, which slowed information processing, decision-making, and execution. They also lacked standard templates for developing and submitting proposals. On some occasions, senior management would discover that two different divisions of the company were talking to the same client about the same project without coordination.

Predetermined Routines

This is similar to the previous point but whereas common systems are actually physical, routines are common procedures for responding to events and situation changes that are predictable in form but not necessarily in content. For instance, all companies know that there are likely to be customer complaints, but they don't necessarily know what the nature of the complaints will be. In that case, routines should be developed which allow for quick and efficient decision-making and execution. It follows that these routines can be automated and built into common systems for everyone to use.

Contingency Planning

This principle relates directly to the notion of risk and uncertainty. All organizations require contingency plans to deal with unexpected threats and opportunities. This is because assessment of risk is only based on probabilities. Decision-makers never know for sure whether their assessments of probabilities will be borne out in reality. In addition, some possibilities are inherently uncertain such that no amount of risk assessment can give us an idea of its probability and impact. Contingency plans give the assurance of being able to react, at least quickly enough to buy time to reallocate resources or to withdraw to fight another day. Chapter 6 will go into much greater detail on this matter. There is also a corollary of contingency planning which entails giving many, alternative tasks and roles to certain groups within an organization. I will address this in the final section of this chapter.

Application of Speed and Agility

- Use the offensive and defensive applications table to determine ways to increase speed and agility within your own business.
- Evaluate your organizational and personal speed and agility using the list of principles just discussed.

Flexibility Through Multiple Roles

How does flexibility differ from agility? Agility is the ability to change direction and tasks without re-configuring or re-structuring the organization, whereas flexibility is the ability to re-configure and re-organize quickly in response to operational needs. In the previous section, we saw that contingency planning is one of the ways that a military force or a business can increase speed and agility. Contingency plans are a function of the organization's flexibility. They are developed in advance, and can be activated in case the situation changes drastically, either when a new threat materializes or an opportunity suddenly presents itself. However, units aren't just waiting in the wings to come into action. Consequently, military commanders usually designate some of their units to carry out alternate functions in case of implementation of contingency plans.

Brilliant Manoeuvre

Contingency plans are developed in advance and can be activated when a new threat materializes or an opportunity suddenly appears.

For instance, if a unit is given the task of pursuing the enemy when the main effort is successful and there is a breakthrough of the enemy's main, defensive zone, that same unit can also be given an alternative task in the eventuality that the enemy counter-attacks the main force in its flank, and the latter needs reinforcement to secure its position. The primary task of this unit would be exploitation of the breakthrough and pursuit of the enemy, and its alternate task would be to protect the main effort's flanks in the event of an enemy counter-attack. This type of contingency plan is known as a 'be prepared' task. The intent isn't to put as much planning and preparation into the alternate task as the primary one, but there should be a minimum of preparation in case it is needed.

A variant of multiple tasking is to assign successive tasks or roles to units as the plan unfolds. The operation is divided into distinct phases, and units can be given different roles in each phase. For instance, unit A may be given the role in phase 1 of providing covering fire for the main assault force, unit B, while the latter is conducting the assault. During phase 2, unit B would then have the more defensive role of securing the objective they have captured, while unit A pursues the retreating enemy.

Alternate tasks and time-phasing are secondary ways of working with limited resources but they don't achieve the same payoff as exploiting the centre of gravity, designating a main effort, concentrating mass in one area by economizing effort and force elsewhere, and deciding and executing with speed and agility. However, they do amplify these principles because they increase the flexibility of resources that can be employed in more than one area, and on more than one type of task.

Flexibility is challenging for military forces, and it is all the more so for business organizations because managers, employees, and business systems are usually highly specialized to execute a certain function under specified constraints with carefully assigned resources. For instance, a production facility is configured to produce one or a few different types of manufactured products. Any change in product configuration can require significant production re-configuring and re-tooling. This is why approaches such as mass customization and flexible manufacturing have become more common in the past few decades. Services and discontinuous operations, such as managing projects, are more amenable to the principles of flexibility, but the challenge remains creating high levels of adaptability as the situation and needs evolve. One of my consulting clients wanted to generate additional revenue from existing clients. We determined that the project managers who managed the client projects after the deal closed were in a position to deliver additional value on the projects as they saw opportunities to do so. We also estimated that they would be able to manage repeat, routine business from existing clients, thus freeing up the sales staff to focus on bringing in new business from current or new clients. In both cases, the project managers required additional flexibility so they could do their original project management function, while adding the ability to suggest additional, revenue-generating opportunities to clients, and to manage routine client relationships of a repetitive nature.

Generating Additional Flexibility

- Can your organizational elements and selected managers and employees carry out more than one function?
- Can they be given the tools to identify and react to new opportunities and threats as they arise, or does the entire system require re-configuring?
- Can people and teams be designated as backups as a way of increasing speed and agility and to create additional depth in case of increased demand for certain services?
- Can projects and initiatives be broken into phases so that resources and people can be assigned to different tasks and roles in succession,

rather than keeping elements idle while waiting to be used as the project advances?

Summary

- Developing manoeuvres and plans isn't a one-off activity. Competitors are continually countering our moves, which means we must be constantly seeking to counter their counter-moves.
- The dynamic nature of conflict and competition require an understanding of both sides' centres of gravity; the designation of a main effort; the ability to concentrate mass on the main effort while economizing in other areas; speed and agility; and flexibility.
- The centre of gravity is the wellspring of strength and vitality of an organization. It provides its sense of balance and power. It must be exploited, but it must also be protected, as it is also the greatest source of vulnerability.
- The main effort is a designated organizational element, task, or function that channels and focuses its resources to achieve breakthrough results. It usually leverages the centre of gravity, while attacking the competition's.
- Economy and mass are the twin sides of the main effort coin. It is these principles which allow an organization to free up resources to concentrate them on the main effort.
- Speed and agility provide additional options to a business for allocating and reallocating resources quickly in response to competitive threats and opportunities.
- Flexibility is needed throughout an organization to enhance economy, mass, speed, and agility in support of the main effort.

Chapter 6

No Plan Survives Contact with the Enemy: Planning, Friction, and the Fog of War

Everything in war is very simple, but the simplest thing is difficult.

Clausewitz

Failure is our most important product.
R.W. Johnson, Jr., Former CEO, Johnson & Johnson[2]

Unforeseeable events derailed a strategy that any reasonable person would have given an excellent chance of succeeding and very little chance of failing as completely as it actually did.
Michael E. Raynor, The Strategy Paradox

If something fails despite being carefully planned, carefully designed, and conscientiously executed, that failure often bespeaks underlying change and, with it, opportunity.
Peter Drucker, Innovation and Entrepreneurship

One might surmise from those opening quotes that this chapter is all about failure. In a way it is, but it is in fact much more about turning failure, friction, and uncertainty to one's advantage. As Drucker said, failure is often a sign of opportunity—if you're open to seeing it that way. To do this, one must recognize the essential unpredictability of any competitive or conflict-based undertaking, such as war or business. One must also have the tools to properly assess and mitigate these uncertainties and to turn them to one's advantage.

---

[2] As quoted in *Built to Last*, by Jim Collins and Jerry Porras.

I had occasion to experience this phenomenon myself on numerous occasions during my military career. But it's not just failure that can lead to opportunity. Sometimes it's just plain luck. One incident in particular sticks in my mind. As already described, I commanded a company-sized peacekeeping unit in Bosnia in 1999-2000. At one point during our deployment we got word from the division headquarters that we had to conduct random searches of Croat military vehicles to check for illegal weapons. We were also expected to search the personal vehicles of Croat soldiers from the 1st Guards Brigade stationed in Drvar. Random vehicle searches are best conducted through vehicle checkpoints. I developed a deliberate plan for the operation and on the appointed day we deployed our checkpoints around the town to conduct the surprise searches. Unbeknownst to me at the time, this operation disrupted a demonstration that had ostensibly been planned by the Bosnian Croat nationalists to protest the closure of their radio station in Drvar, which had been shut down for broadcasting anti-Serb propaganda. Apparently, by setting up our vehicle checkpoints in town, we had spooked the local hardliners into believing that we had heard about their plans. The UN Resident Envoy, Peter Chappell, claimed that we had made a brilliant move to disrupt the demonstration. This was critical, because demonstrations tended to deteriorate quickly into riots in Bosnia. I never told him that it was blind chance that we struck when we did. I felt that the less said, the better. That way I turned plain luck into an opportunity to send a message about our intelligence capabilities and responsiveness to threats to the peace.

Brilliant Manoeuvre

We must recognize the essential unpredictability of any competitive or conflict-based undertaking, such as war or business.

Business can be viewed as a succession of unforeseen events, some fortuitous, others less so. The important thing is to be on the lookout for opportunities, rather than seeing uncertainty, failure, and friction as the kiss of death for your plans. A pharmaceutical company was test marketing a new drug with doctors in the city of Chicoutimi in the province of Quebec. The response to the drug for its intended purpose was fairly inconclusive, but the company did notice that it was being prescribed with greater frequency by obstetricians. Upon investigation, it turned out that doctors had been prescribing it to women who had gone into labour because one of its side effects was to slow down, or even stop, labour. Apparently, exhausted doctors who were on duty were prescribing it in order to give themselves some rest before going back into action. The company did the proper testing and rebranded the drug for that express purpose. This is just one example of many of companies seizing opportunity. This apparently happens quite frequently in the pharmaceutical industry: everyone knows the origins of Viagra® as a heart medication with, shall we say, remarkable side effects.

Brilliant Manoeuvre

Business can be viewed as a succession of unforeseen events, some fortuitous, others less so. The important thing is to be on the lookout for opportunities, rather than seeing uncertainty, failure, and friction as the kiss of death.

Peter Drucker's book on *Innovation and Entrepreneurship* shows that most sources of innovation are the result of seizing opportunities from unexpected failures, unforeseen successes, and uncontrollable outside events. My intent is not to reproduce that excellent book's work, but instead to see what elements of military wisdom and practice in regard to friction, uncertainty, and failure can be applied to business, and how to turn these inevitabilities into opportunities for success. Consequently, this chapter builds on the discussion on probing and reinforcing success that we first presented in Chapter 2. In a way, this discussion provides the theoretical and practical underpinnings to the philosophy of trial and error, of experimenting, reinforcing success, withdrawing from failure, reallocating resources, and harnessing of personal initiative through mission command. We'll start by examining what I call 'the four horsemen of the apocalypse' that derail the best laid plans. Then we'll look at five practices for dealing with these obstacles to success, and for turning them into potential opportunities.

Tools for Turning Uncertainty Into Opportunity

- **The Four Horsemen of the Apocalypse:** Recognize and accept the fundamental uncertainty, friction, and incompleteness of our knowledge as the first step to formulating more realistic plans and more effective actions.

- **Assumptions:** Assumptions provide a framework to advance planning in the absence of certainty and knowledge.

- **Scenarios:** These are descriptions of future events and situations that are designed to reflect extremes and to consider possible actions and intentions of opponents so that decision-makers can consider the unexpected and prepare for it.

- **Options:** We often paint ourselves into a corner by neglecting the full range of possible courses of action. There is always more than one option at any decision point.

- **Simplicity:** Simple plans and processes are better understood and easier to implement than complicated ones.

- **Opportunism:** As US General Gordon R. Sullivan said, "Hope is not a method." How one sees failure and opportunity is essentially a question of attitude and perspective. When the unexpected happens, you have to assess the situation quickly and determine how to use it to your advantage.

The Four Horsemen of the Apocalypse

The Planner's Four Horsemen of the Apocalypse

- **Friction:** As Clausewitz put it, "Everything in war is very simple, but the simplest thing is difficult." Friction is the natural tendency for our plans to go off the rails through miscommunication, misunderstanding, and just plain difficulty and complication.

- **Uncertainty:** This is the good old 'fog of war.' The business equivalent is the notion of risk, which is the potential for loss or failure. It is the product of probability of occurrence of a disruptive event multiplied by its potential negative consequences.

- **Lack of Knowledge:** The things we don't know are often those that hurt us the most. However, they are in principle knowable and the condition of ignorance can be eliminated by acquiring the requisite knowledge and information.

- **Opponents' Intentions and Actions:** Soldiers are fond of saying that "the enemy gets a vote." Simply put, you can have the most exquisite plans, but your opponent or competition will usually find a way to counter at least some part of them. In some cases they can completely preempt your plans.

Friction

The Allied landings on Omaha Beach on D-Day, June 6th, 1944 highlight the effects of friction on military operations. The US 29th and 1st Infantry Divisions had meticulously planned and rehearsed the landings. Battalions, companies, platoons, squads, and even individual soldiers knew exactly what they had to do, why they had to do it, and when they had to do it. There was only one problem. The fog, wind, and waves on the morning of the assault caused most of the initial assault groups to bifurcate wildly from their planned routes and to land in the wrong locations. The assaulting troops were as prepared as they could ever be when the landings went ahead, but no amount of planning and practice can eliminate the friction of actual combat, much less the effects of climate and weather. It was only their competence, resolve, and initiative that enabled these forces to gain a toehold and expand it into a proper beachhead.

Most accidents and man-made disasters are the result of friction. The explosion of the Columbia space shuttle after launch in 1986 resulted from a chain of events and miscalculations. Most of these were preventable, and many mid-level managers and engineers just assumed that higher-level authorities were aware of all of the problems and risks that they themselves could see, and that there were safeguards in place. There was also a perceived need to stick to the launch schedule, even though the effect of cold weather on the launch vehicle was considered a major threat to the success and safety of mission and crew.

Friction is the wear and tear, the wasted heat and energy, which result when two physical objects or surfaces rub against each other. There is no better metaphor for the mechanical waste and fumbling that occurs in complex undertakings and organizations. In fact, the more complex and risky the undertaking, the more likely that friction will wreak havoc. It's important to realize that friction is not the same thing as risk. Risk is the result of identifiable events and occurrences. The probabilities and impacts of risks can be assessed and quantified, and treatment measures can be put in place to mitigate risks. Friction is different. You just know it will occur, but you don't where or when. Consequently, one compensates by designing robustness and resiliency into systems, building in redundancy, and contingency planning. These practices can be viewed as wasteful, in a sense, but this is the only known way to deal effectively with friction.

Brilliant Manoeuvre

The more complex and risky the undertaking, the more likely that friction will wreak havoc. We must compensate by building robustness, resiliency and redundancy into our plans and systems.

There are multiple examples of friction in business. Ford's development and introduction of the Edsel shows that a company can do just about everything right, yet the project can fail for reasons that are still hotly debated by business theorists. In *The Strategy Paradox*, Michael Raynor describes how Sony did just about everything right to develop and introduce the Beta video standard, but it still lost that battle, simply because of the near simultaneous introduction of the VHS standard by Panasonic. A few years ago, an industrial sawmill burned down in a Northern Ontario town, throwing the few hundred employees out of work, turning it into a ghost town. The company decided that the investment to rebuild the facility was unwarranted given the downturn in the global market for wood products. A known risk (fire) turned into a major disaster for the inhabitants of that small northern town through the friction of the international markets.

Military commanders compensate for friction by constituting a reserve and only committing it in dire circumstances. Military forces also train relentlessly, rehearse difficult manoeuvres, and develop processes, drills, and procedures for just about every possible situation that can occur in battle. And even then, there is still friction. The same philosophy must be applied in business even though the costs come out in financial and economic terms rather than in human lives.

Uncertainty

Uncertainty arises when we make assumptions or hold beliefs about the future that frame our plans and actions within a particular context. For instance, uncertainty about exchange rates is less relevant to a company that doesn't export than to one that does. When the US-led coalition invaded Iraq in early 2003 to eliminate the weapons of mass destruction (WMD) it was claimed to be developing, there was uncertainty about their existence and location. Consequently, the military invasion plans had to take this into consideration. I was sent to Kuwait in early 2003 as the Canadian liaison officer to the coalition headquarters leading the assault. Once the war began, every time an Iraqi missile was launched at a target somewhere in Kuwait, it was assumed that it carried a chemical or biological warhead. As a result, there were elaborate measures in place to counter this threat, some of them very complex and demanding. The coalition military leaders were simply not ready to accept the risk of getting hit by a chemical or biological attack without putting in place all necessary measures to mitigate that risk. It was uncertainty about the exact Iraqi capabilities and intentions with respect to WMD that led to these measures.

No one can predict the future, much to the chagrin of many economists and financial theorists and their media acolytes, who prefer assumptions of perfect knowledge and rational decision-making.

To say that uncertainty permeates economic life and business is an understatement. You wouldn't know that from reading most business journalists and even most business books though. Many commentators apparently assume that business executives and entrepreneurs have perfect knowledge before launching a new business line, acquiring a competitor, or entering a new market. That's why the tone of much business journalism and 'theory' is accusative rather than seeking to understand the real uncertainties and risks of business. Why did company A enter that market at that time? Didn't management know there was a recession just around the corner? Why did company X not acquire company Y? Didn't they see that they had a great product that would be a massive future success? Well, no, they didn't know this! Why? Because no one can predict the future, much to the chagrin of many economists and financial theorists and their media acolytes, who prefer assumptions of perfect knowledge and rational decision-making. As Phil Rosenzweig has shown in *The Halo Effect*, many, if not most, theories about business success are based on examining successful companies at a particular point in time then abstracting their purported success characteristics. The problem with this approach is that it is based largely on selection bias. Companies that are identified as highly successful at any point in time are likely to exhibit similar characteristics simply because the companies have been arbitrarily grouped together and the researcher has abstracted what appear to be commonalities. It's tautological. So we get exhortations to "stick to your knitting" and follow the 'hedgehog' strategy (be a specialist and do one thing really well) alongside claims that it's better to diversify and to follow the 'fox' strategy (be a clever generalist). Both sides have evidence to uphold their claims. Both sides could be right, both could be wrong, or one or the other could be right, depending on the external and internal circumstances, the economics of the business, and the business models themselves. To that we must add the quality of the ownership, the management, and the strategy. In consumer toiletries, over-the-counter drugs, and household products, can anyone doubt that Procter and Gamble or Johnson & Johnson have been successful by diversifying their products and businesses? On the other hand, how successful have oil companies been in diversifying out of the oil business? In fact, we can argue that success and strength in oil, and natural resources in general, comes from specialization. The commonality comes from the recognition of the ubiquity of uncertainty, risk, and friction, not from stock answers to complex questions.

Lack of Knowledge

What is the difference between uncertainty and lack of knowledge (or information)? Uncertainty is characteristic of events and their causes and consequences that are fundamentally unpredictable or unknowable. On the other hand, lack of knowledge it is the condition of ignorance, i.e., not knowing something that is in principle knowable and certain. Uncertainty can be mitigated or reduced through trial and error or risk management, whereas simply seeking or asking for information can eliminate the condition of ignorance. The difficulties of dealing with uncertainty are understandable, but staying ignorant is inexcusable when the means of acquiring information and knowledge are readily available, especially in the age of Wikipedia and the Internet. As an illustration of this, when I was in Bosnia some things were basically uncertain. We could estimate possibilities and probabilities of certain events, causes, and outcomes, but we never had certainty about them. What the true intentions of any of the former belligerents were or when or if they were considering disruptive activities, such as demonstrations, riots, and other acts of violence, were fundamentally unpredictable, although there were potentially signs of these, without any certainty though. On the other hand, we had to protect civilian and uniformed members of the international community that were resident in our area of responsibility in the event of violent outbursts. Not knowing the exact living locations and usual whereabouts of the international workers under our protection would have been inexcusable. This was information that was readily available, and we would have been remiss not to acquire it and keep it up to date.

Brilliant Manoeuvre

The difficulties of dealing with uncertainty are understandable, but staying ignorant is inexcusable when the means of acquiring information and knowledge are readily available.

The same distinctions apply in business. Back in the early 1990s, Walmart made its entry into the Canadian market by buying Woolworth's Canadian stores and opening a number of new ones. At the time, I was living in Gatineau in the province of Quebec, an overwhelmingly French-speaking community of almost a quarter million people. Walmart had just opened one of its superstores in that city. However, almost all of the signs in the parking lot and the store were in English. Not only did this contravene the laws in the province of Quebec concerning French language signage, it also irritated the store's clients and created a media controversy. Walmart couldn't know how successful its venture in Canada would be, but not knowing the most basic rules and expectations about putting up signs in the language of the majority in that city was a blunder. It was quickly rectified and Walmart apologized, but this shows the distinction between uncertainty and ignorance. Moreover, it applies across all industries and sectors of the economy, as well as in all functional areas of companies. Will a newly hired employee be successful? This is uncertain, and we can take measures to compensate somewhat, but lack of knowledge of labour regulations, employee rights, and employer responsibilities are easily rectified. And yet, there are always problems that are caused by incomplete knowledge and information in HR. The founder and CEO of a commercial tool distribution company died unexpectedly in his early 50s. Unfortunately, all of the key information about clients and suppliers died with him because he never codified his knowledge and made it available to his employees. The company had serious difficulties as a result of this oversight on the part of the owner, though it could have been easily avoided by making the information available to those that would need it in the event of his incapacity or death.

Intentions and Capabilities of Opponents

Soldiers are fond of saying that "the enemy gets a vote." You can have a brilliant strategy and the best laid plans to achieve it, but the enemy also has his own strategy and plans. He's not sitting there passively waiting for you to do something. He's trying to out-manoeuvre you while you try to out-manoeuvre him. There are two components to assessing a military threat: capability and intent. During the Cold War, Western military staffs would assess the military threat of the Soviet Union in terms of capabilities and intentions, arguing that their own forces had to be capable of countering Soviet forces, because their true intentions, while subject to estimation, were fundamentally unknown. In some cases, enemy capabilities are fairly easy to assess. Every year on May Day the Soviets would stage a parade on Red Square, which was the premier opportunity for the Western military intelligence services to estimate new and upgraded Soviet military capabilities. Intentions, on the other hand, are much harder to estimate. The Cuban missile crisis resulted from the Soviet decision to deploy nuclear weapons to Cuba, where they could directly threaten the US mainland. President Kennedy couldn't estimate true Russian (and Cuban) intentions with respect to these weapons, so he chose to focus on the capability instead. This led to the decision to blockade Cuba and the eventual negotiated settlement which saw the US removing its own threatening missiles from Turkey in exchange for the Soviets removing their nuclear weapons from Cuba. The Cuban missile crisis showed just how vulnerable the world was to misunderstanding, miscommunication, and misjudgement, and this led Kennedy and Khrushchev to set up a hotline between both countries so their respective heads of government could talk to avert a crisis.

Brilliant Manoeuvre

Each decision a company makes puts it on a road that has particular consequences. This knowledge allows us to narrow the uncertainties surrounding competitors' future actions and decisions.

The same distinctions apply in assessing business competitors. Just as with military capabilities, business capabilities are usually a good way to estimate likely intentions, but they are not infallible. This is because capabilities are hard to acquire and develop. Once a firm has invested in a certain technology or production system, the likelihood that it would make a 90-degree turn to enter a completely different industry or market can be quite low. On the other hand, one can never be quite certain, and this is where surprise is crucial. The company that has made an art of surprising competitors is Apple. But with that said, with every new product category the company enters, the next one becomes more likely. Once you've gotten into desktop computers, laptops, portable music players (iPod), and music retailing (iTunes), the next logical move is into phones. After that, what's left? Tablet computers. And after that? Television? As Winston Churchill said, "first we shape our buildings, and then our buildings shape us." Each decision a company makes puts it on a road that has particular consequences. This knowledge allows us to narrow the uncertainties surrounding competitors' future actions and decisions, even though there will never be absolute knowledge and predictability. This allows us to identify opportunities given competitors' lack of freedom of action. This is also one of the reasons that the point of maximum vulnerability for a company is when it is fully committed to its offensive strategy and has invested heavily in new products, services or markets. It is possible that there may be still some capital and other resources in reserve to react to a competitive counter-move, but it is likely to be almost fully invested in the strategic moves it has made. This creates vulnerability for that company and an opportunity for competitors to launch their own offensive moves.

What is YOUR level of unpredictability?

- Are your plans and operations simple or complicated? Would they lead to greater or lesser potential for friction? Do you have procedures and processes in place to reduce or mitigate friction?
- What risks are you facing? What uncertainties are there in your assumptions and knowledge of markets, clients, products, employees, and competitors? Do you have plans in place to mitigate those risks?
- Is there something you don't know, but should? How can you get that information or knowledge?
- What competitive threats are you facing? What capabilities do your competitors have? Can you estimate their intentions? How would you react to their actions? Do you even care that they might or might not do something to harm your business prospects?

Assumptions

One of the terms that has repeatedly appeared in the foregoing discussion of friction, uncertainty, and risk is 'assumption.' An assumption is a proposition about a state of affairs that enables planning to continue in the face of uncertainty and lack of knowledge. Assumptions are only provisional. They are a convenience to promote common understanding and analysis, but they should be verified or modified as soon as confirmatory information is available. If the information is not easily accessible, then further research must be undertaken to reduce the uncertainty or increase precise knowledge. Assumptions are critical to military staff planning and that is why they are emphasized in the education and professional development of officers at all ranks and in all specialties. Assumptions also have real-world consequences that can be of momentous import. When the US led a coalition of the willing to invade Iraq in early 2003, the assumption was that Saddam had continued the development of chemical, nuclear, and biological weapons (the capability) and that he intended to use them to further his domestic and international aims (the intent).

Assumptions are fuel for planning, but they need to be assayed on a regular basis to ensure they aren't contaminating the efficient and effective functioning of the business' engine.

Assumptions are critical to the formulation and implementation of strategic, operational, and tactical plans. Without assumptions, all planning would stop and organizations would grind to a standstill. Assumptions are fuel for planning, but they need to be assayed on a regular basis to ensure they aren't contaminating the efficient and effective functioning of the business' engine. Assumptions are propositions about planning variables that are held to be provisionally true subject to verification and real-life experience. For instance, when an executive decides to launch a new product, he makes assumptions about the capacity of the organization to manufacture it, about market demand, about competitors' reactions, about suppliers, distributors, and retailers, and many other factors that cannot be known with certainty until it is launched and the business has acquired sufficient experience to confirm or deny the initial assumptions. When assumptions are proven incorrect or inaccurate, the real-life facts must be substituted for the assumptions.

There are four problems or limitations that often arise from making assumptions in business, and it shouldn't be surprising that they correspond directly to the Four Horsemen of the Apocalypse. There is no real way to eliminate the risk of faulty assumptions. The best solution is simply to be aware of them, so they can be mitigated through research, experimentation, intelligence, and reconnaissance. These are:

  ▪ **Relating to friction:** Assuming that strategy, intentions, objectives, and plans are fully understood by everyone in the organization and that all will go smoothly. As a result of this, plans are often detailed like clockwork but the slightest error in estimation or miscommunication can have disproportionate consequences. I helped a client to resolve a dispute concerning sales territories between the managers of two divisions in his company, but then he failed to ensure that the sales people in one of the divisions got the directive that clarified the dispute. The miscommunication kept the dispute alive even though clear direction could have kept it under wraps. This generated needless friction between the two managers.

- **Relating to uncertainty:** Just about any planning assumption in business will be based to some extent on a probabilistic estimation of prices, costs, demand, and sales figures. The problem comes when executives forget that these are just estimations based on likelihood and start treating them as facts. This stems in large measure from the SALY syndrome. SALY stands for "Same As Last Year." It's the syndrome that grips every organization and manager near the end of the fiscal year or during budgeting season. Past experience is treated as the best guide to future experience, and the most recent year's sales and cost figures get plugged into the spreadsheets to produce some kind of budgetary projection. Unfortunately, this approach almost completely ignores the real-world possibilities of managers' current and past decisions on the company's immediate future. Projections are just that: projections. They are just as subject to confirmation and verification as any other estimation.

- **Relating to lack of knowledge:** Making an assumption instead of finding the information. Walmart's signage error is an example of this type of problem. Another illustration comes from the case of the municipal transit service I described in Chapter 4. For years, decisions about bus routes and schedules were made on the basis of assumptions about where riders wanted to go in the city and when they wanted to go there, as well as how fast. This led to inadequate levels of service, which then translated into poor ridership by the most lucrative market segment for a transit service, daily commuters. The decision to hire an operational research firm led to much better information and more detailed knowledge of travel patterns, especially with respect to commuters, thus enabling more effective decision-making about routes, schedules, and investments in transit infrastructure and vehicles. It was knowledge that finally led to key decisions to ensure the service's future success, instead of dilettantish guessing.

- **Relating to competitive threats:** The most egregious and common form of this problem is simply the assumption that your competitors are too stupid, uninformed, or incapable to know what you know and to do something about it. This belief is the basis of all surprise. 9/11 proved once and for all that it is actually pretty simple to cause massive death and destruction, assuming there is a will to do so. Canadian journalist Gwynne Dyer once said that the big secret about military strategy is that there are no big secrets. The same can be said of business strategy, and this can be summarized as follows: Find something you can do better than the competition, package it in a way that customers will feel compelled to buy it, and then execute on that. Simple, right? Well, we know it's not THAT simple. But the point is that most raging successes in business and life look evident once they become successes. That is the essence of Peter Drucker's philosophy and technique for innovation. Look around you; examine your own weaknesses and strengths, your strengths and failures; look at what the competition is doing; listen to what customers are telling you.

Scenarios

Assumptions are an effective way of getting on with business, so long as they are kept in proper perspective and confirmed on a regular basis. They can also be combined into larger entities called scenarios. Scenarios are a way to envisage future changes in the environment so as to develop a better understanding of what could lead to these changes and how to cope with them. Military planners use scenarios to generate insight into the enemy's possible future actions. These are often used to develop new weapons systems based on trends in technology and potential enemy capabilities and intentions. Scenarios are also used to develop operational and tactical level plans, specifically by projecting potential enemy actions and counter-actions as a result of friendly actions. For instance, prior to launching an attack against an objective, a commander and his staff must consider likely enemy force dispositions as well as the possibility of a spoiling attack (when an enemy 'counterattacks' an attacker before it has actually had a chance to launch its own assault) or the possibility of counterattacks or unknown reserves. In modern complex operations such as peacekeeping and counterinsurgency, scenarios are extremely important as they allow the modeling of multiple belligerents, national and international stakeholders and actors (non-governmental organizations, UN agencies, peacekeeping forces, international observers, diplomats, etc.), as well as multiple potential decision points. At their most developed, military scenarios can involve computerized simulations and complex exercises with forces manoeuvring on a mock battlefield in force-on-force war games.

Brilliant Manoeuvre

Scenarios are a way to envisage future changes in the environment so as to develop a better understanding of what could lead to these changes and how to cope with them.

Since the early 1970s, scenario based planning has emerged as a viable means of envisaging potential future changes in the business environment and managing complex chains of events and their effects. It is well beyond the scope of this book to get into the details of scenario based planning, but it is nonetheless instructive to touch on its salient aspects for business management. The Royal Dutch Shell group is one of the first companies to apply scenario based planning in a disciplined and consistent manner. In the early 1970s, the company's senior leadership determined that the economics of the oil business had been favourable for so long to the oil majors that something had to give. A small team of planners was assembled to look into various future scenarios irrespective of whether management thought at the time that they were entirely realistic. The objective was to generate a range of potential futures in order to determine how the company could react and take advantage of the changes. Through this process, Shell management realized that the economics of the oil business rested on cheap oil and that political change made a continuation of that stable situation highly unlikely. For instance, OPEC had been formed a few years before, but without immediate political or economic consequences. What if, the team wondered, the countries of the nascent oil cartel decided to restrict production or raise prices drastically? How would that affect the economics and operations of the international oil business? Because of these questions, Shell decided to start stockpiling oil in the early 1970s. When the Arab oil embargo hit in 1973, Shell had reserves to sell at much higher world prices, thus dampening the financial effects of the crisis for the company.

There are many ways to develop scenarios, but when I'm working with my clients I focus on change dimensions, trends, and variables. A change dimension is an aspect of the business environment that can't be controlled by the company or its management. The economy and political atmosphere of a country are often considered key change dimensions. Others include aspects of technology, demographics, competitive market forces, social trends, and consumer tastes. At any point in time, some of the change dimensions are clearly evolving in a certain direction with little possibility of variation. As an example, many demographic trends of interest to a company in its chosen time frame would be fairly predictable, such as retirement estimates. In this case, the change can be treated as a fairly predictable trend with the assumption that it will continue into the foreseeable future. These trends become background assumptions for each of the scenarios. Other change dimensions can have considerable variability. Economic factors often have this quality and can have a major impact on business outcomes. For instance, a real estate firm would have to keep a close eye on interest rates because these will affect mortgage rates, which will in turn affect demand for housing. A real estate firm's management would therefore do well to consider the possibility of considerable future variation in interest rates. In practice, estimating a worst-case outcome and a best-case outcome achieves this. Managers should identify and estimate best- and worst-case outcomes for three to five key change dimensions and then create combinations of these variables so that there are three to five scenarios that combine various outcomes that would test the resolve of management and the resilience and robustness of the organization. I've used this approach with several consulting clients. In one case, an insurance company, we created four different scenarios based on five change dimensions and a few notable trends. One of the change dimensions concerned the fractiousness of the board, something I had definitely not considered in my initial research in preparation for the scenario development workshop with senior management and the CEO. It did, however, come out in the discussions that this was a major risk factor for the future of the company, one that could have an effect on strategy and operations. Moreover, it was one that senior management didn't fully control. As a result of developing these scenarios, the company was able to create a new insurance product to generate additional revenue and better serve its clients. The CEO also had greater confidence in her ability to deal with eventual disruptions and conflict between board members.

Options

One of the first things young military officers learn in their training is to consider more than one course of action prior to making plans and issuing orders. The reason for this is simple. We tend as humans to default to preconceived ideas and, especially, to rely on force of habit and instinct, rather than to think through the full implications of plans. This is not only dangerous in war, but can lead to mission failure, which is why tactical training includes the learning of a problem analysis and decision technique called the military estimate. The estimate can be formal or informal, and the result of an individual or team effort. The point is to analyze the situation by considering as many relevant factors as possible that may impinge on the decision and outcome. The planner then uses these factors to make observations and draw inferences, and then combines these to form a range of potential courses of action prior to deciding on an optimal one, and then formulating a plan to implement it.

The point here is that there is always more than one way to achieve an outcome. The more options one can consider before making a decision, the more one can expect the decision to be rational and optimal. We see this approach in its most basic form by considering that there are usually three, although not always three, viable options for attacking an objective: left flanking, right flanking, and frontal assault. There might even be a fourth option: going around the enemy's defences to make them irrelevant. Each option must be weighed and compared to determine which one is optimal, even if not perfect. There can never be perfection but, at least, considering the possibility of a range of options, a commander and his staff can have a better idea of the potential success of their plans. When this is combined with careful use of assumptions and scenarios, especially the consideration of possible enemy actions and counter-actions, the plans can be much more complete, thereby reducing the effects of friction, uncertainty, lack of knowledge, including of enemy intentions and actions.

Brilliant Manoeuvre

There is always more than one way to achieve an outcome. The more options one can consider before making a decision, the more one can expect the decision to be rational and optimal.

Options are relevant to all types of business situations and at all levels of an organization, tactical, operational, and strategic. In day-to-day tactical situations, there is usually more than one option available, but one has to take the time to stop and think rather than operating on automatic. One of the reasons negotiations with suppliers or customers fail is that both sides are thinking of only the option that is favourable to each side. Considering many courses of action opens possibilities, and leads to greater success in reaching mutually agreeable terms and solutions. I usually include three options in my consulting proposals. The client is presented with three levels of intervention with appropriate investment. This way, there is a range of returns on investment from which to choose. Customers like to choose amongst options because they perceive, correctly, that they have greater freedom of action in deciding on their future. I'm also always pleasantly surprised at how many options can be generated during a brainstorming session when presented with a problem that seems initially intractable, or with only one viable solution. This is why the first question we should ask consulting and coaching clients when presented with a problem, "What options are there?" There is always more than one option when we take the time to think, and don't stifle creativity through authority or fixation on current methods and habits.

Option analysis is also applicable in operational situations. For instance, organizations should consider more than one technology option and supplier when investing in a new information system. Not only is this prudent governance, it opens up the company to solutions that hadn't been envisaged when the acquisition project had been initiated. I learned this firsthand when I was a young captain working in the Canadian National Defence Headquarters on weapons systems acquisition. A military colleague and I were insisting that we sole-source the development of a new gunnery simulator for an anti-tank missile project, but the project manager insisted that we go to tender. We didn't have to, but he argued that we might be surprised at the variety of technical solutions this would produce. We were initially sceptical, but when we received three, completely different, technical proposals from three, competing companies, we were pleasantly surprised to note that the proposed solutions included ideas that no one on our project team, including our own systems engineers, had even considered. We chose a novel technical solution that eventually proved to be successful. Had we restrained ourselves to going with what seemed, at first blush, to be the logical solution, we would have missed out on what proved to be a more elegant and effective gunnery simulator.

Finally, at the strategic level, we can see from the discussions of previous chapters that the whole point of strategy formulation and strategy implementation is to generate options for the company so it has freedom of action to pursue opportunities that leverage its centre of gravity while undermining that of competitors.

Simplicity

In the Middle Ages, a monk named William of Ockham put forward the postulate that the simplest explanation for a natural or human phenomenon is usually the correct one. This principle, known as Ockham's Razor, is a fundamental tenet of the scientific method since nature works with resources at hand to craft simple solutions to problems of survival and thriving. Simplicity is also an important principle of war. This is because simplicity is the surest means of limiting friction. Complication of plans and manoeuvres tends to lead to mistakes, misunderstanding, and miscommunications since complicated, complex systems have a much larger number of possible ways for things to go wrong. When things are simple, they are easier to understand and implement, and there are fewer, systemic ways to fail. The whole point of communicating the commander's intent and concept of operations as well as clear articulation of the organization's mission is that soldiers and officers be able to react effectively to changes in the heat of battle, and to exploit opportunities because they understand the objectives.

Brilliant Manoeuvre

Simplicity is the surest means of limiting friction.

It is surprising how managers and executives in companies make things needlessly complicated. The main reason for this level of complication, and the consequent increased risk of friction, is that strategies and plans are neither explicit nor communicated in a clear, direct manner to all concerned. With one of my clients, we formulated a fine strategy, but the client failed to communicate the changes that would be required to the rank-and-file of the organization. When the CEO moved one of the key sales people out of a division as part of organizational changes required by the new strategy, the remaining members of that team thought that this was a sign of impending doom. Luckily, I had been brought in to do a follow-up project with the same division. During interviews with two operations managers, they asked me if their division was about to be closed. I knew that the CEO had no intention of doing so, and told them so as well as the fact that the CEO was searching for a replacement for the sales person moved from the division, and that he had hired me to work with the division. These were two, clear indicators that the CEO had no intention of closing the division in question. It was the CEO's failure to communicate the new strategy and plans that created needless friction.

Another frequent cause of complication is a failure to establish clear lines of authority and responsibility. Authority is the formal assignment of power to deploy resources in the attainment of specified objectives. Responsibility is the formal assignment of accountability for the decisions and actions resulting from that authority. Many times, many different people are working on the same project or initiative without a clear chain of command. So, when things don't work out as planned, responsibility is diffuse such that no one person can be held accountable. When one person is designated to be in charge of achieving an objective, the resulting clarity leads to better outcomes because that person has their reputation on the line. Moreover, they know that if something goes right or goes wrong, they will either get the kudos or the blame. Either way, this provides clarity of purpose, and simplifies communication and channels of authority.

Military forces have developed principles to guide in assigning authority and ensuring that plans and manoeuvres are understood, principles that are applicable to any organization and which maximise simplicity.

- **Unity of command:** Is there one person in charge of a unit or project, or are authority and responsibility unclear, diffuse, confused, and confusing?
- **Communication:** Has the situation been communicated to everyone who needs to know? Have the intent, mission, objectives, and plans been communicated to everyone who needs to know?
- **Simplicity:** Are plans, manoeuvres, and procedures simple to the point that an intelligent outsider or layperson could understand them?

Opportunism

We now turn to the last method for turning circumstances to one's advantage. I give it the shortest treatment since it is implied in the whole philosophy described in this book. Opportunism is the mark of successful people in all walks of life and in organizations of all kinds. The great biologist Louis Pasteur claimed that, "In the field of observation, chance favours the prepared mind." You have a much better chance of finding opportunities and threats if you're alert to them, and this requires preparation, planning, and organization. The Normandy invasion could not have been launched without months and even years of training, stockpiling of resources, keen intelligence work to find the enemy's weaknesses and vulnerabilities, and development of technical capabilities, procedures, and systems. In other words, success just doesn't happen. It is created, and it usually relies on preparation plus willingness, and the means to exploit a breakthrough when it is detected. To do so requires a framework that allows one to assess changes as opportunities to be exploited or, alternatively, as threats to avoid.

Brilliant Manoeuvre

You have a much better chance of finding opportunities and threats if you're alert to them, and this requires preparation, planning, and organization.

- **Failures:** Where have we failed recently? What does that teach us? How can we extract value from that experience? What does it teach us about competitive threats and market opportunities?
- **Successes:** What have been our recent successes? What caused them? Were they the result of design, or just plain luck? Did we exploit that luck or success? If not, how can we exploit it now? What does this tell us about market opportunities? Are we poised to exploit them?
- **Surprises:** Have we been surprised recently? What happened that was totally unexpected? Did we exploit it, or shy away from it? What does this tell us about our strategy, objectives, and organizational ability to implement and exploit change?
- **Changing Situation:** Use the mission analysis approach presented in Chapter 4 to analyze the changing situation in order to determine if goals are still appropriate. If yes, then continue with your plans. If not, then you need to rework intent, objectives, and concept of operations to bring them into line with the new realities.

Summary

- Military wisdom is fully applicable not just to the predictable aspects of business, but also the unpredictable. Business and warfare share characteristics of uncertainty, risk, friction, and lack of full awareness and knowledge of the environment and situation.
- There are four principal causes of why the best-laid plans and intentions go off-track. I call these the Four Horsemen of the Apocalypse, because they are not just disruptive to plans and intentions, but also because they actually cause failure and defeat. These are: friction, which is the disruption and confusion that arises as a result of complexity and complication; uncertainty, which is the probabilistic component underlying all risk; lack of knowledge, something that can be rectified, but of which we are unaware; and the capabilities and intentions of the enemy or competition since they are usually pursuing the same thing as we are.
- There are five key ways executives and entrepreneurs can, like any good military planner or commander, identify these hindrances and counteract them to stay on track with their plans and even use them to create

opportunity: make assumptions; create and assess scenarios, which are groups of assumptions that generate insight by presenting a range of possible futures; develop options before deciding on the optimal one, which then becomes the actual plan; make things as simple as possible to minimize friction; and be willing to seek, recognize, and seize on opportunities when they present themselves.

- The five techniques are instrumental to success in business, whether intentions are offensive or defensive, or whether they are at the strategic, operational, or tactical levels of decision-making.

Chapter 7

Is Military Intelligence Really an Oxymoron?

By 'intelligence', we mean every sort of information about the enemy and his country—the basis, in short, of our plans and operations.

Carl von Clausewitz

In turbulent times, an enterprise has to be managed both *to withstand sudden blows and to avail itself of sudden, unexpected opportunities.*

Peter Drucker, Managing in Turbulent Times

The essence of formulating competitive strategy is relating a company to its environment. Although the relevant environment is very broad, encompassing social as well as economic forces, the key aspect of the firm's environment is the industry or industries in which it competes.

Michael Porter, Competitive Strategy

There is an old joke that military intelligence is an oxymoron although, in reality, it is the oxygen that fuels military strategy, operations, and tactics. In common language, intelligence is the capacity to understand, or the power of discernment. We think of intelligent people as quick-witted, as great learners, as capable of discerning patterns where others tend to see a formless mass of data and sense impressions. The meaning of military intelligence is similar, in that it seeks to develop the best possible understanding of the enemy, and the strategic, operational, and tactical environments. The objective isn't to know everything, as that is impossible, but rather to know more than the enemy or the opponent so as to gain the upper hand.

In a nutshell, military intelligence is the process by which commanders and planners generate the information and understanding they require to identify and assess threats and opportunities.

The objective isn't to know everything, as that is impossible, but rather to know more than the enemy or the competition so as to gain the upper hand.

As with military forces, many companies are now operating in dangerous, unstable regions around the world. They must contend with 'messy' business environments, where politics, economics, diplomacy, culture, and demographics play major roles in determining success. This 'messiness' also extends to a company's home environment. Transcanada Pipeline's experiences in recent years are illustrative of this complexity. Transcanada operates an oil and gas pipeline network throughout North America, but its plans to build a new pipeline to transport oil from Northern Alberta's oil sands to the southern United States have repeatedly been stymied by environmental groups in the US and Canada. As of early 2012, environmentalists and citizens groups have successfully lobbied federal and state governments in the US to delay the project or reroute the pipeline owing to ecological concerns. In some respects, Transcanada's real competition is not other businesses but rather environmental groups.

Business leaders can learn from the principles of military intelligence, especially as they are applied and practised in what is known as 'low intensity conflict,' or LIC. There are many similarities between business and military LIC operations such as peacekeeping, counter-insurgency, and counter-terrorism. In both cases, the opponents are competing to 'win the hearts and minds' of people. In LIC, military forces are engaged in struggles with warlords, insurgents, and other belligerents to gain the loyalty and support of the population. Similarly, companies are in competition to win the business and loyalty of customers so they can dominate markets, and generate growth and profit over the long term. To do this, they must consider many factors and events in the environment. They must not limit their definition of competitors to other businesses, but should also consider other groups and organizations that may want to counter the objectives of companies and, even, of entire industries. Companies must also empower managers and employees to be on the lookout for changes, threats, and opportunities.

This chapter is not the place to go into all the details of military intelligence, as it is a highly technical field. However, the principles and philosophy that military planners and commanders bring to bear in assessing the enemy, his capabilities, intentions, and actions, as well as the natural and human environments are highly applicable in business. On the other hand, there are many well-developed and proven techniques for analyzing competitors and the business environment. We won't try to replace these approaches, but rather amplify and illuminate their usefulness further by looking at the most salient and useful principles of military intelligence for business intelligence, especially as they are applied in LIC. We will focus on five key principles, as described in the following text box.

Principles of Intelligence for Business

- **Adopt a wide area of interest.** You can't just focus on what is in front of you at the present time, but must also watch the bigger picture in the future, assessing current threats and opportunities as well as ones that are only nascent or potential.

- **Seek comprehensive understanding.** Intelligence is much more than just understanding the enemy or competition. It also requires a comprehensive understanding of factors and events in the natural and human environment.

- **Intelligence is everyone's business.** Intelligence is too important to be left only to specialists. Everyone must understand the bigger picture so they can signal changes, and see how they might hinder or benefit their business unit and the whole company.

- **Data and information must be interpreted to become intelligence.** Intelligence distinguishes the important from the unimportant, the critical from the insignificant, with the aim of identifying actual and potential threats and opportunities.

> ● **Information is best sought through reconnaissance.** Information just doesn't fall into one's lap. It has to be sought, collected, analyzed, and assessed. This is the role of reconnaissance, which is an active process for searching for significant changes in the competition and the environment in order to reduce uncertainty and friction, as well as to gain useful knowledge for uncovering actual and potential threats and opportunities.

Adopt a Wide Area of Interest

The field of competitive intelligence has developed since the early 1980s, having received its impetus from Michael Porter's seminal work, *Competitive Strategy*. However, as the quote at the beginning of this chapter shows, Porter's main focus was on industry analysis. This is certainly important, but what happens when a company thinks it's in one industry but is really in another or, alternatively, thinks it's in one business when it is really in another? This is what happened to newspapers when Google came along. With its search engine, Google showed advertisers that they could give them precise information about people who were searching for the information that they, the advertisers, wanted to give them. On the other hand, newspapers and other traditional information providers thought they were still in the business of selling mass audiences to advertisers, using editorial and entertainment content to attract them. In fact, Google showed that it was more effective to sell detailed knowledge about searchers who might be open to receiving unobtrusive ads in the form of paid search results on the Google search engine. Google's success has severely undermined the economics of newspapers and of electronic media. Newspapers were focused on each other rather than Google, a competitor that effectively came out of nowhere to undermine their business model and also, as per Chapter 5, their centre of gravity.

Brilliant Manoeuvre

Do not limit your definition of competitors to other businesses, but also consider non-business groups and organizations that may want to counter your objectives.

The best way to understand the importance of taking the widest view is to compare it to the military approach, as depicted in Figure 7.1.

Figure 7.1: Area of Interest

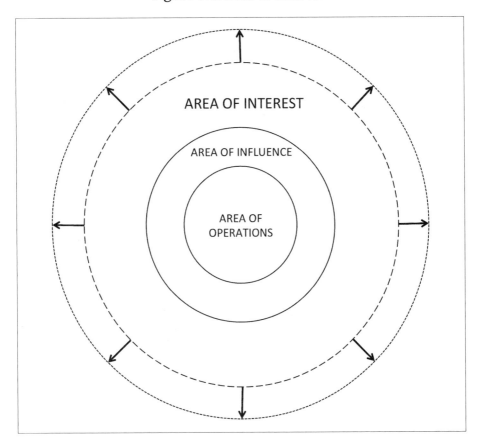

Every military unit has an area of operations. This is the geographical area in which it operates and for which it is responsible. The unit can also influence events outside its immediate area of operations because there are always unforeseen consequences to its actions. At an even higher level, the unit and its commander and planners must also keep an eye on developments in its area of interest, because these can eventually impinge on the unit. This can include intelligence about the enemy's capabilities, actions, and intentions, as well as information relevant to the natural and human characteristics of the environment where the unit is currently operating, or may be operating in the future. In a nutshell, military units rarely, if ever, operate in isolation, and military leaders and planners at all levels must be on the lookout for information and intelligence relevant to their responsibilities and areas of operations and influence, but also to the effects their actions and plans can have on events and stakeholders outside this immediate zone. Military commanders and planners are often pushing the envelope of their area of interest, especially in the context of LIC, since they never know what might be relevant information that can give them an intelligence advantage. This is depicted in Figure 7.1 by the dotted line showing the limits of the area of interest and the arrows indicating the efforts to expand continually that area.

Figure 7.2: Military Organization Areas of Influence and Interest

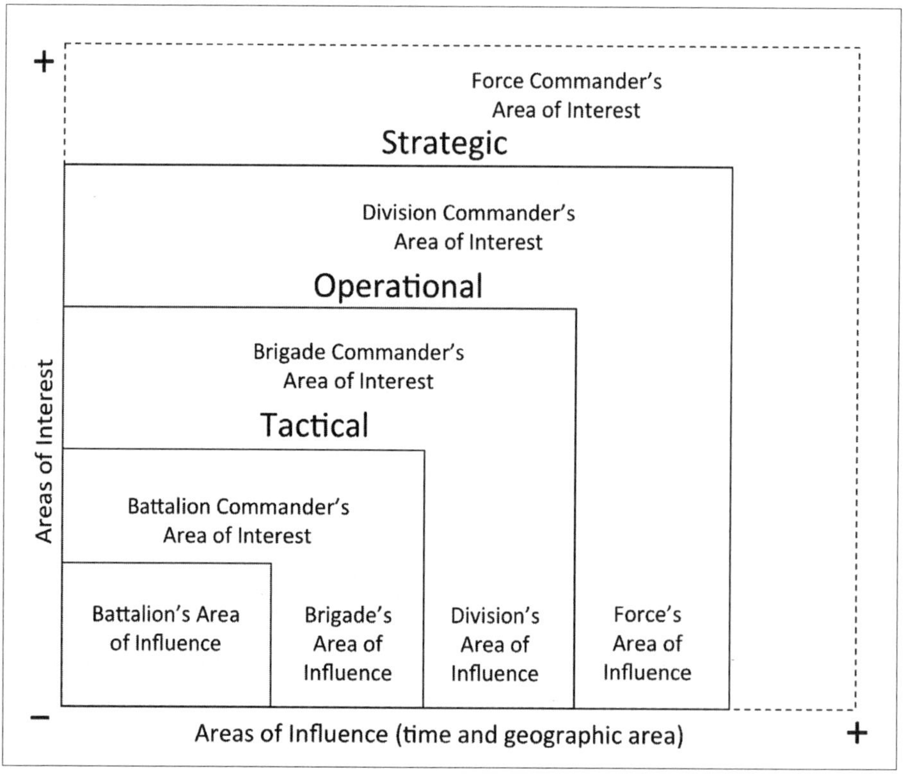

Another way to examine this concept is to relate it to the strategic, operational, and tactical levels of conflict, which in turn relate to the organizational levels in a military force, as illustrated in Figure 7.2.

For the sake of simplicity and clarity, the areas of operations are not shown, but they are included within the respective areas of influence. As a general rule, the area of interest of any organizational level corresponds largely to the area of influence of the next highest level in the organization. The battalion commander's area of interest, therefore, coincides with the area of influence of the brigade of which his unit forms part. The battalion's area of influence is depicted as the lower, left-hand rectangle. Thus, the brigade's area of influence is approximately three times larger, both in physical and in conceptual terms. This is depicted by the brigade's larger rectangle. In sum, the battalion commander has an interest in understanding events and characteristics in the brigade's area of influence because they may affect his unit, and his ability to achieve his objectives and mission, either directly or indirectly. The same applies to all organizational levels: the division commander's area of interest coincides with the force's area of influence; and so on up and down the chain of command. Since the force commander is responsible for the overall strategy of the force, he will have an interest in developments at the national and international level. This logic corresponds closely to the framework of nested hierarchical planning, mission command, and mission analysis described in Chapter 4.

Furthermore, we see that these organizational levels and their respective areas of influence and interest correspond to the levels of war: strategic, operational, and tactical. These levels, therefore, also provide a structure for understanding the parameters that frame a military organization's perspective about operations. A unit that is operating within a tactical context has a very short-term focus, executing a mission with immediate objectives and effects. For instance, if we take the example of the battalion mentioned in the diagram above, it could be clearing insurgents out of a village. The fact that something is happening with another battalion within a neighbouring sector of the same brigade may or may not be relevant to that battalion's commander. This would be all the more the case for things that are happening within the division (operational context) or the force as a whole (strategic context). The same logic applies at the operational and strategic levels of the conflict. At the operational level, the division commander is conducting a whole campaign within a particular sector of the theatre of operations, while the force commander is executing his strategy for the entire theatre of operations, within a context of international diplomacy, national and international politics, and other factors such as economics.

This hierarchical structure consisting of successively more encompassing areas of operations, areas of influence, and areas of interest fitting within the larger framework of tactical, operational, and strategic levels of conflict provides a model for how businesses should structure their own areas of concern. Moreover, while competitive intelligence is usually limited to industry and competitive forces alone, this approach can redefine 'business intelligence' from its current narrow focus on data crunching, and 'competitive intelligence' from a narrow focus on the company's industry and immediate competitors and markets to one that can truly encompass all the concerns of business executives for the achievement of their business objectives. In Figure 7.3, I've replaced the military hierarchy terms with business ones. These show the power of this approach to a business' competitive, natural, and human environments.

Figure 7.3: Business Organization Areas of Influence and Interest

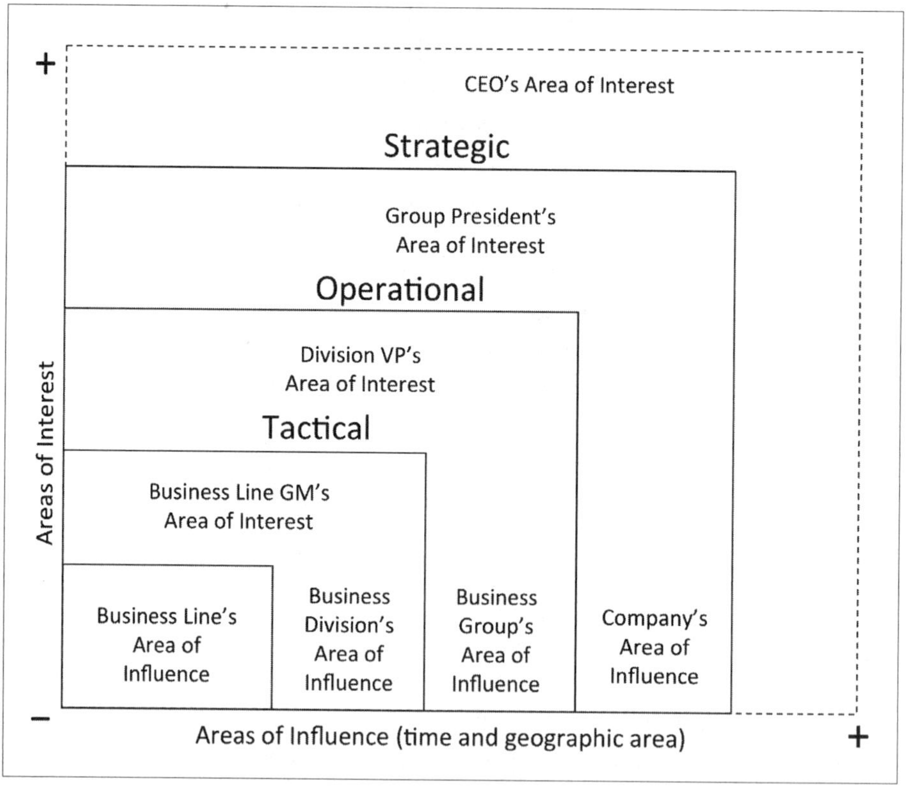

We see that the areas of interest and influence of each successive level of a company have approximately the same relationship in terms of breadth of concern as in the military example. Figure 7.4 shows how this framework can be mapped onto the organization and leadership of a typical, diversified, multi-division company.

Figure 7.4: Areas of Influence and Interest Relative to Company Structure

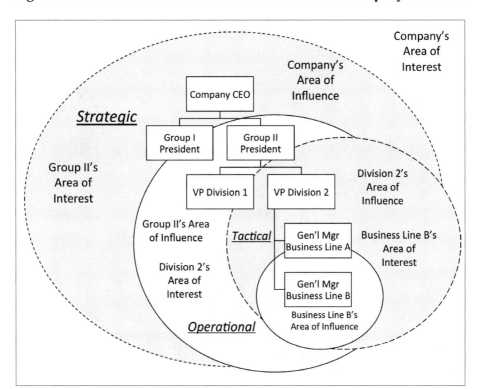

The CEO is responsible for the entire company's strategy. His influence and that of the company are shown by the larger of the two, dark ovals. His area of interest, though, is the entire environment outside the area of influence, with no necessary limitation on its size in terms of time, geography, competition, or domain (e.g. politics, demographics, technology, etc.). The Group II President is responsible for implementing a major thrust of the company's overall corporate strategy, and is therefore working at the operational level of the company. Consequently, Group II's area of interest corresponds to the area of influence of the entire company, and even more in some cases, as we can see by the depiction of the larger of the two, light grey ovals, which extend somewhat outside the area of influence of the company. This shows that groups with operational level responsibilities have to be on the lookout for changes, threats, and opportunities in their environment of which the company's strategic leaders may not even be aware. Each of these groups has divisions headed by a vice-president, each with its own tactical mandate within their respective group's wider, operational mandate. The VP of Division 2 has an area of influence that falls somewhat outside the area of influence of the company and group's respective areas of influence. This is because managers of this division can sometimes see and influence things outside the field of vision of the group president and company CEO. The same logic applies no matter how many structural or business levels there are in the company. The level of influence of the next higher hierarchical level provides a good gauge for the breadth of the area of interest of the manager of that particular level.

Brilliant Manoeuvre

Executives and groups with operational level responsibilities have to be on the lookout for changes, threats, and opportunities in their environment of which the company's strategic leaders may not even be aware.

This approach to determining the areas of operations, influence, and interest also corresponds to the framework that underlies nested hierarchical planning, as described in Chapter 4. We recall that nested hierarchical planning is what enables leaders and planners to conceptualize their respective visions, missions, objectives, and plans within the larger organizational context. We also saw that the process of mission analysis, which requires leaders to consider the widest possible context for their own tasks and roles, also requires them to consider the intent, objectives, and plans of their immediate superior and again at higher levels of the hierarchy. The company's strategy and plans are translated into action and plans throughout the entire organization by this hierarchical process. The final step of mission analysis consists in asking if the situation has changed and, if so, how. We see that this situational analysis depends on understanding the environments and competitors at each successive level of the company's structure. At the strategic level, the company's CEO and his immediate staff must be on the lookout for changes in the company's environment. This much is accepted in all the literature on environmental analysis that supports company strategy. However, executives, managers, and employees at all levels of the organization must also apply the same principles, and have the same curiosity about their respective environments.

Brilliant Manoeuvre

At the strategic level, the company's CEO and his immediate staff must be on the lookout for changes in the company's environment.

Application of Areas of Operations, Influence, and Interest

- What are your responsibilities and level within your company?
- What is your vision and mission? What are your business objectives and plans? This is your area of operations.
- What can you influence outside your immediate mandate and responsibilities? This is your area of influence.
- What is the area of influence of your immediate superior and the organization he or she leads? This may be your area of interest, but it could also be larger than this if you estimate that it is relevant to your mandate and concerns.
- If you are the CEO, what is the area of interest of your company? What dimensions of the external environment are of concern to you and your company?

Seek Comprehensive Understanding

BP has made a strategy of investing in oil ventures in marginal, risky regions of the world. BP's joint venture with the Russian oil firm, TNK, became strained in 2008 as there were accusations of political interference by the Russian government. Fortunately, BP's management successfully manoeuvred to resolve the dispute, thus saving its massive investment in what represents a significant proportion of its worldwide production capacity and proven reserves. Shell wasn't as lucky though because, in 2006, the Russian government forced it out of its holdings in the huge Sakhalin-2 natural gas project, provoking considerable financial losses. Canadian oil company Talisman Energy invested in a joint venture in the Sudan in the early 2000s, but it was accused of supporting and abetting war crimes perpetrated by one of the Sudanese factions. Talisman eventually sold its investment in the joint venture to an Indian company. Whether or not these companies could have prevented or mitigated these risks to their operations and investments, this shows, nonetheless, how critical is the need for timely, accurate intelligence. This is certainly the case in the international environment. In addition, companies in many countries are willing to spy, cheat, and steal technology and information, often with the support of their governments. However, it is just as critical to understand the business environment even when a company is operating on its home turf.

Just as military forces can no longer limit their intelligence efforts to the enemy and the geographic characteristics of the battlefield, businesses must also be aware of developments in all aspects of their external environment. In the previous section, we saw how it is essential to set the areas of operations, influence, and interest of the company and its structural elements. In this section, we will look at how to identify the types of information that we can glean from these areas. Military planners look at two types of information, that concerning the enemy and that concerning the environment. We saw in Chapter 6 that the enemy influences our own plans. The enemy isn't waiting passively while we plan and execute our missions, but is also conducting his own planning and execution. The key means of determining the enemy's intentions and capabilities is to analyze his actions. This provides data and information that can generate intelligence about purposes and capabilities. To do so, military intelligence specialists try to ascertain the strength and composition of enemy forces, their locations and the positions they occupy, their equipment, weapons and logistical support, the quality and morale of their troops, the quality of their commanders and their leadership, and their most recent movements. This information is crucial for it provides indicators of capabilities and intentions. Military intelligence is therefore concerned with understanding the enemy's actions as a means of generating insight into his capabilities and intentions.

Brilliant Manoeuvre

Just as military forces can no longer limit their intelligence efforts to the enemy and the geographic characteristics of the battlefield, businesses must also be aware of developments in all aspects of their external environment.

However, military planners and intelligence specialists aren't just interested in the enemy's actions. There is also a lot of information and knowledge to be gleaned from observing and analyzing the environment in which belligerents operate. The environment includes the physical and geographic characteristics of the areas of operations, influence, and interest, as well as their human characteristics. Physical characteristics are critical to gaining an understanding of the enemy's actions, because they set limits on what is feasible in terms of movement, positioning, supply, and the time and place for battles and engagements. They can also give an indication of possible enemy intentions.

Human factors such as economics, technology, and politics have always figured in the conduct of warfare. After all, it was Clausewitz who said that "War is a continuation of politics by other means." However, other types of human characteristics have become increasingly important since the Second World War, especially in LIC, to the point where an understanding of the human environment is now considered critical at all levels of war, whether strategic, operational, or tactical. In LIC, the belligerents are not so much fighting each other, as struggling to influence groups and factions of the population within their respective areas of concern, which includes the actual battle space, but also the international arena and the domestic populations of military forces operating abroad, even in the remotest parts of the world. This requires military planners, specifically intelligence specialists, to divide the populations of these areas into groupings relevant for analysis.

Then, they analyze each of these groupings for their wants and needs, political leanings, social, cultural and religious characteristics, economic capabilities, morale and willingness to endure hardship and sacrifice, and other factors that may be considered relevant. Military operations are conducted on many battlefields, not just the actual area of operations. There is a physical battlefield, corresponding to the physical plane of war, but there are also multiple moral or psychological battlefields such as local media, international media, and domestic media in belligerent countries. The same applies to political, diplomatic, economic, and social spheres of action.

Brilliant Manoeuvre

The competition for hearts and minds of customers isn't just limited to other companies. There are many other 'belligerents' competing for the attention and dollars of buyers.

What does this all mean for business executives and entrepreneurs? Quite simply, businesses aren't operating in pure, unadulterated, economic space. Business people must analyze and understand the environment in which they are operating. That has always been accepted, and any book on business strategy will include a list of environmental factors that must be considered and assessed in identifying potential threats and opportunities.

The competition for hearts and minds of customers isn't just limited to other companies. There are many other 'belligerents' competing for the attention and dollars of buyers. As already mentioned above, Transcanada Pipelines is relying on the construction of a new pipeline, the Keystone XL, to bring oil produced in Northern Alberta to refineries in the southern US. Without this new pipeline, it will be almost impossible to sell all the oil that will be produced in Alberta. However, environmental groups have joined forces with political stakeholders, some in Washington, some in the states concerned, and some internationally, to lobby the American government to halt the construction of the planned pipeline. Here is the key point from the intelligence perspective. Environmentalists are competing for the hearts and minds of the same people who ostensibly will be using this oil. Canadian supporters of the pipeline, including politicians, economists, oil executives, and even human rights activists, have been arguing that the pipeline will allow the US to reduce its imports of oil from questionable regimes in the Middle East and Venezuela.

My point isn't to argue who is right or wrong, but rather to show that competition is multifaceted these days, and is becoming more complicated and complex. When we combine this with the phenomenon of 'creative destruction' that is characteristic of free-market economies, as illustrated by the example of how Google undermined newspapers' traditional, business model, we can see that simple models to guide in analyzing industries and industry competition are useful, essential even, but they do not exhaust the possible competitive forces that companies and their executives must analyze and understand when assessing threats and opportunities. For instance, Michael Porter's framework for industry structural analysis as described in his influential book, *Competitive Strategy*, is useful for understanding the competitive forces in an industry: rivalry between competitors, bargaining power of suppliers and buyers, threat of substitute products and services, and the threat of new entrants. The problem, however, is that it doesn't tell you who the potential, new entrants or substitutes might be, or whence they come. Moreover, the Porter model doesn't take into consideration factors described above, the possibility that non-economic actors can be in competition with a business, either for dollars or buyers, or for their hearts and minds.

Brilliant Manoeuvre

Models for analyzing industries and industry competition are useful but they do not exhaust the competitive and environmental forces that companies and their executives must analyze and understand when assessing threats and opportunities.

What to consider in analyzing the areas of operations, influence, and interest?

The following table provides a sample of the factors and questions business people should be asking as they assess their areas of operations, influence, and interest. There is no limit on the types of questions and factors that can be considered, other than that they be related to the area of concern, whether the direct area of operations, an area of influence, or an area of interest. Whether the level is strategic, operational, or tactical is also of concern. This list is not meant to be exhaustive, but there are a sufficient variety of factors and questions herein to provide an idea of the type of comprehensive analysis that can be conducted when planning and executing strategy. More conventional factors such as demographics and technology have been omitted from the list for brevity, but they are just as important and need to be considered when analyzing the competitive, natural, and human environments of a business. Not all of these factors and questions are relevant at the strategic, operational, and tactical levels. However, as an illustration, we see that if a company is planning an operational level campaign to launch an existing product in a new country, there is plenty of food for thought and analysis herein to guide effective planning and execution.

Competitive Factors These questions are meant to supplement the more conventional, competitive analysis process.	Identification	Are they in our industry? Do they fit within the categories of industry rivals, buyers, distributors, or suppliers? Are there potential new entrants? Are there potential substitute products and services? Are they outside our industry? Are they local, national, or international? Are they even economic actors, or are they other types of stakeholders, or people or groups who claim they should be stakeholders?
	Actions	What are these competitors doing? What are they saying? How are they investing their capital? Is it possible to ascertain their degree of success? How quickly could they change to meet the threat you pose to them? How quickly could they change to pose a new threat to you? Is there an opportunity in their actions or lack of actions?
	Capabilities	What capabilities do they have? Can they harm or help you? Are they locked in to particular strategies, operations, or tactics by the size and type of investments they have made?
	Intentions	Can you estimate the intentions of your competitors by analyzing their identities, actions, and capabilities? For instance, a business competitor will likely have intentions similar to yours, but a non-business competitor or stakeholder will probably have intentions that adhere to a different value hierarchy than yours.
Natural Factors These are characteristics of the natural environment that may be of concern.	Geography	Are you concerned about a zone that is prone to natural disasters? Is geology a factor? Is distance a factor?

	Climate	Is the climate cold, temperate, arid, or tropical? Can it affect your operations? Are the areas of concern subject to climate and weather disasters and disruptions?
	Ecology	Are there ecological or natural environment factors to consider? Are there fauna and flora that can have an impact?
	Health	Are their public or individual health concerns that can affect your strategy and operations?
Human Factors These are the human characteristics of the areas of operations, influence, and interest that may impact on your strategy and operations.	Social and cultural	Are you at home or in a foreign country? Do you operate nationally or internationally? Are you operating in the same or a similar culture to your own? Are the social expectations and norms different or similar? Is the society structured like a Western country, or is it still essentially a tribal culture? Is it predominantly rural or urban? What is the structure of socio-economic classes? Do business people follow similar business practices, or are they very different?
	Infrastructure	Is the transport infrastructure modern and efficient, or is it antiquated and dilapidated? Are there seaports and airports? What is the road network like?
	Political climate	What is the political climate in the areas of concern? Is it pro-business, anti-business, hostile, or friendly? Could a change of government have an impact? Do lobbyists and non-business stakeholders have a political impact? Do your competitors' host countries turn a blind eye, or even encourage practices such as industrial espionage?
	Economic climate	What is the prognosis for growth in the near, mid, and long term? What is the potential impact of a change in interest rates? What would happen if there were a financial crisis? Can exchange rates impact the success of a foreign acquisition or expansion?

Intelligence Is Everyone's Business

A basic principle of military intelligence is that troops in battle are often in the best position to provide valuable information about the enemy, his dispositions, actions, strength, and capabilities. Fighting troops also have a direct view of the battlefield, the lay of the land, rivers, population, and other factors. This is especially true in LIC since the flow of information comes from the bottom rather than from the top, as in conventional warfare. This is because in LIC there can be a lot of variation in conditions from one area of operations to another. For instance, the Bosnian town where my unit operated, Drvar, was predominantly Croat, and there were tensions between Croats and Serbs. The fact that it was Serbs that had been ethnically cleansed from that area created a situation that was distinctive from other areas in Bosnia. However, in another unit's area about 50 kilometers away, in the town of Bos Petrovac, the situation was completely different. There, the Serbs were dominant and had ethnically cleansed the area of Muslims. We had two contiguous areas with the same type of conflict, but with different social, economic, political, and ethnic dynamics underlying the conflicts. As a result, what might work in Drvar might not work in Bos Petrovac and vice-versa, and the best information and intelligence about each of these locations tended to come from our forces on the ground.

Brilliant Manoeuvre

Field service reps and sales people can bring home valuable information about the competition, customers, and the natural and human environments.

Given the similarities of LIC and business, we can say that intelligence is everyone's business. In business, who is out 'patrolling' and winning hearts and minds? In LIC, even truck drivers delivering combat supplies or mechanics on service calls can be included in the information gathering effort. These soldiers work in the areas of operations. They have eyes and ears. If they know what to look for, they can provide useful information, just like an infantry squad patrolling in towns or meeting with farmers in the hills. The same applies to businesses. Field service reps are everywhere. They are talking to clients and, occasionally, even the employees of competitors. Sales people also attend conferences. They talk to their counterparts in other companies. They all can bring home valuable information about the competition, customers, and the natural and human environments in which they exist. To do this, however, they must be made aware of what might be significant, and must be empowered to look for it and report their findings to company managers. These are the people who are talking to potential and actual customers on a day-to-day basis, asking questions, providing answers, listening to complaints, fixing problems. Who better to gain insight into the competition's actions and whereabouts, thus providing insights into their potential intentions, than the sales force and field service reps?

In order to generate information and insight about competitors, customers, and markets, everyone in the company must be aware of the basics of its strategy and strategic objectives. All must understand the leadership's vision for the company and its mission. The processes of nested hierarchical planning and mission analysis described in Chapter 4 provide the framework for determining the area of operations of each part of the company organization. The concepts of areas of operations, influence, and interest provide the framework for determining what can and should be of interest. The listing of factors in the table in the previous section provides the type of information that they can and should be seeking. It is not enough for employees and managers to do their jobs. They must also be on the lookout for opportunities and threats, and to do so, they need to know what to seek, and how it might fit into the big picture of the company's strategy, or the operational plans and tactics of each of its elements.

Brilliant Manoeuvre

In order to generate information and insight about competitors, customers, and markets, everyone in the company must be aware of the basics of its strategy and strategic objectives.

The best way to imagine this in action is with an example. To do so we need to combine the diagram showing how areas of operations, influence and interest map onto a typical company structure (see Figure 7.4), with the table listing various factors for analyzing the company environment. Let's suppose that Division 2 of this company has a mandate to expand into a new country. The division's area of operations will be the specific products and services it is offering within the relevant market segments it has targeted for expansion in that country. Its area of influence will encompass products and services it offers elsewhere, as well as those capabilities which the wider group offers in that market or elsewhere. Its area of interest will be the entire company's activities. In that way, the division's VP, or more likely, sales people and others working in that particular country, will be able to look for opportunities and threats relevant to their own operations, but also potentially to other parts of the company. Managers and employees have to be on the lookout for opportunities and threats as the eyes and ears of the entire company, not just their own little part of it. This gives a considerable power to the company since everyone is potentially an information gatherer. Managers and employees can also transform some of this information into intelligence since they know their part in the bigger picture of the company's strategy and goals, but also because they know what is relevant and important to others. This can even extend to production people and customer service representatives. After all, they are like an army's truck drivers and mechanics. They work in the company's areas of operation and influence, and sometimes in its area of interest.

Brilliant Manoeuvre

Managers and employees have to be on the lookout for opportunities and threats as the eyes and ears of the entire company, not just their own little part of it.

Making intelligence everyone's business

- Do managers and employees understand the company's strategy and objectives? Can they describe the company vision and mission quickly and succinctly?
- Can managers and employees in any part of the company do the same for the intent and objectives of their part of the organization?
- Do they know their unit's areas of operations, influence, and interest? Could they give a quick overview of what a sister unit is doing, and what is of concern to them? Could they identify opportunities and threats for their own unit, for sister units, or for the company as a whole?

Turning Information into Intelligence

The principles we've discussed so far are instrumental for generating information about competitors and the natural and human environment. However, this information must be transformed into intelligence in order to make it fully relevant. Otherwise, the organization and its members will be drowning in a stormy sea of data and information, rather than swimming in a calm bay of intelligence. Intelligence is the ability to discern differences that make a difference, that are important and even critical. The key distinction between information and intelligence, in conflict and in business, is that intelligence tells us what matters. Intelligence, thus, is about threats and opportunities.

Brilliant Manoeuvre

A threat is a risk that has an intentional component. It results from human action and intention.

What is a threat, and how does it differ from a risk? Risk is the probability that an event will have negative consequences or, more succinctly, the probability of loss or damage owing to the event. It can be defined mathematically as the product of probability and impact. A threat is a risk that has an intentional component. This means that a threat is a risk that results from human action and intention. Risks can result from non-human causes, such as natural disasters and technological catastrophes and accidents. Threats, on the other hand, are always the result of human intention, whether deliberate or not. We can therefore see that one part of the intelligence analysis process is to determine which human actions in the company's environment are indicative of human intention that might be harmful to its ability to achieve its objectives and to carry out its strategy and plans.

Opportunities are, in a sense, the converse of threats. Instead of our side being the potential victim of deliberate or accidental harm from other actors in the environment, it is we who are causing potential harm or benefit to these other actors. Benefit because whether we are talking about LIC or business, our goal is to serve others by our actions. However, these often run against the intentions of others. In LIC, other belligerents, insurgents, and state and non-state actors can be harmed by our strategy, operations, and tactics and, consequently, will react to our actions, maybe even trying to pre-empt them. In business, our actions can prevent other businesses from implementing their strategies and meeting their goals.

The only way to correctly assess whether information is signalling potential threats and opportunities is by analyzing it in light of our own strategy and objectives, and the plans to achieve them. This is why selection and maintenance of the aim, nested hierarchical planning, and the mission analysis process are so critical. They provide the framework for searching for, and assessing, actual and potential competitors, as well as the natural and human environments in which we operate. For instance, a competitor may introduce a new product in a market where we have no presence. It may present a threat if it is subsequently introduced here, or conversely it might be viewed as an opportunity to pre-empt them in our current market once we see that the product is successful there. This doesn't guarantee success, but it at least provides a lens for analyzing changes and characteristics of the environment for their potential to hinder (threats) or advance (opportunities) our vision, mission, and objectives.

Brilliant Manoeuvre

We can't just sit down once every three or four years to examine the environment or conduct a SWOT analysis.

We can also see that this is an interactive, iterative process. We can't just sit down once every three or four years to examine the environment or conduct a SWOT analysis. Strengths, weaknesses, opportunities, and threats only take their meaning from our own goals and objectives. These evolve and grow with time. Consequently, if we wait a number of years to look at the environment, the threats can ambush us and the opportunities can pass us by. This also highlights the need to have multiple time horizons. It is a fallacy, however, to think that strategy is focused only on the long term and tactics on the short term. The reality is that some events and changes over all time horizons can have an impact on strategy, operations, and tactics.

Reconnaissance

Prior to deploying to Bosnia in command of an infantry company in 1999, I went on a reconnaissance mission to the country with the commanding officer and the other company commanders in the battle group. It was a revealing trip that allowed us to adjust our plans and our training. Had we stayed at home and waited for our deployment, we would have been in a passive posture on our arrival in theatre. The fact that we actively sought information prior to our mission gave us an edge to make preparations more effective. As a result, we arrived as peacekeepers but were ready, nonetheless, to fight against any belligerents who might oppose the Dayton Peace Accords.

Brilliant Manoeuvre

Intelligence depends on a constant stream of information that is interpreted in light of plans and objectives to determine threats and opportunities.

Reconnaissance is the active search for information to feed the intelligence process. As we have seen, intelligence is the understanding of actual and potential opponents and the natural and human environment in which all sides must operate. Intelligence depends on a constant stream of information that is then interpreted in light of our plans and objectives in order to determine what constitutes actual and potential threats and opportunities. While it is possible to glean information about competitors and the environment by passively observing events and waiting for changes to occur, it is preferable to take an active stance in seeking out information. There are four basic types of reconnaissance, according to whether they are active or passive, using overt or covert (hidden) means. These four types are depicted in the following table, along with military examples and their approximate business equivalents. The military examples are ones that tend to be used in Low Intensity Conflict, in order to understand the intentions and capabilities of belligerents and opponents, as well as the expectations and intentions of various groups of stakeholders, including local populations.

Types of Reconnaissance		
	Passive	**Active**
Overt Means	*Observation* Military: patrols, talk, media, events, stakeholder actions, reports from troops in contact with enemy Business: industry events, press releases, websites, promotional materials, public financial statements, annual reports	*Probing* Military: reconnaissance by fire, reconnaissance in force, probing attacks Business: experimental products and services (see Chapter 2)
Covert Means	*Stealth* Military: aerial photography, hidden observation posts, electronic eavesdropping Business: shopping the competition, posing as suppliers, reverse engineering	*Duplicity* Military: espionage, posing as enemy soldiers, disinformation (deliberate spreading of false information) Business: industrial espionage, wire tapping

Observation

Simple observation is the most common form of information gathering. It combines a passive stance with overt means. In a sense, it isn't really reconnaissance, as it involves observing the environment, including reading and analyzing as much open-source information as possible. This includes media reports, openly observable actions of competitors and customers, quarterly and annual financial statements of public companies, annual reports, etc. If a sales person attends an annual industry conference and hears in passing of a new product from a competitor, this might be vital information for her company, even if it concerns another division. This is where we see the power and importance of properly framing everyone's understanding of respective areas of operations, influence, and interest.

Brilliant Manoeuvre

A sales person attends an annual industry conference and hears in passing of a new product from a competitor; this might be vital information for the company, even if it concerns another division.

Probing

This is the combination of an active stance using overt means. In the military, this is often called 'reconnaissance in force.' An example is the use of small, controlled, probing attacks against an entrenched enemy to determine potential breaches and gaps. A variant of this is 'reconnaissance by fire,' where a unit fires on the enemy to see if they will react, and then uses this information to estimate dispositions and capabilities. The idea is to use one's own actions to determine threats and opportunities. The business equivalent is the experimental and probing approaches described in Chapter 2.

Stealth

This type of reconnaissance combines a passive stance with covert, or hidden, means. In the military, this is usually referred to as 'stealth reconnaissance,' and it involves taking observation and listening positions to watch the enemy or the environment while hoping to stay undetected. It can also include such things as electronic eavesdropping of radio and radar signals, and aerial reconnaissance. For applications in business, this can include such things as reverse engineering a competitor's products, in order to identify their characteristics and estimate their production and supply methods, but it can also include such legitimate means as 'shopping the competition' by posing as customers or by pretending to be graduate students conducting research. While seeming to be active methods, they are in reality passive, as they do not involve penetrating a competitor's defences, such as with the probing methods described above. Some may view these methods as illegitimate or even unethical, but they appear to be quite common.

In his book *A Class with Drucker*, William Cohen discussed a survey on 'pretexting' practices common in business circles in the early 1980s. Survey participants were asked questions about approaches that companies use to find information about competitors. For example, one of the questions concerned employees posing as researchers who called a competitor's suppliers and distributors. Forty-one per cent of the respondents answered that their company would use such a technique. However, 88 % answered that they believed other companies also used this technique. This pattern of estimating the practice as much more common among other companies than within one's company was consistent throughout the responses. This indicates a widespread belief that such passive, covert means were common. Human nature rarely changes much in a quarter century so it's safe to assume that, even if the reader of this book wouldn't use such tactics, competitors may use them. However, if we think of competition in the wider sense of anyone wanting to win hearts and minds, we can easily imagine environmental or other groups that have other notions about the validity of a company's activities as being willing and able to use these means. Here, we also see the utility of the distinction between capabilities and intent, as assessed through observed behavior. So, even if you are personally 'holier than thou,' that may not be the case with competitors and other stakeholders in your business.

Brilliant Manoeuvre

Even if you are personally 'holier than thou,' that may not be the case with competitors and other stakeholders.

Duplicity

This type of reconnaissance combines an active stance with covert means, and it is usually risky, and more than likely illegal. This is certainly the case in most countries. All countries practise technical, military, and diplomatic espionage presumably because of the high payoff, but the consequences can be devastating if the deceit is exposed to both the persons and the countries involved. In our categorization scheme, industrial espionage is clearly distinguished from stealth reconnaissance by the illegality of the means used. In other words, whereas the legitimacy and ethics of stealth reconnaissance in the business sphere is, at least, open to discussion, duplicity clearly isn't, and is usually viewed as illegal. This includes such means as active espionage, the penetration of a competitor's organization with a view to obtaining valuable information, listening in on conversations through active wire tapping (clearly illegal), or attempting to penetrate a competitor's computer networks. Such forms of industrial espionage are often state-sponsored, or at least tolerated, in certain countries. There have been persistent rumours of such activities emanating from China, as well as outright theft of product designs through the mechanism of joint ventures and through piracy of software, books, and music. Non-business competitors can also be tempted to use such means to advance their own ends. At the end of 2011, the computer networks of Stratfor, the strategic forecasting consultancy, were hacked. Financial and other confidential records of clients were stolen. A group that opposed the activities of the company presumably perpetrated this electronic break-in. Whether or not we agree with Stratfor's activities and the nature of its business, this type of active, covert threat will continue to grow, and companies must be on the lookout for attacks not just from direct business competitors, but also from actual and potential opponent groups.

Brilliant Manoeuvre

Active, covert threats will continue to grow, and companies must be on the lookout for attacks not just from direct business competitors, but also from actual and potential opponent groups.

A final word about ethics is in order. I am definitely NOT advocating any kind of illegal or unethical methods of information gathering and reconnaissance. There are plenty of opportunities to gather information and probe the competition, customers, and the environment without resorting to active, covert means. In fact, even fairly mild, covert means probably only have a marginal effect on the total amount of relevant information. Most of the intelligence that can be generated about threats and opportunities is staring us in the face, and can be readily acquired through ethical, open means. However, the fact that these covert methods exist, both legal and illegal, ethical and unethical, is part of the competitive environment in business. Just because you wouldn't use these methods, even the more benign ones, does not mean that competitors can't or won't. Criminal threats also emanate from these methods.

Summary

- Intelligence is the understanding of the competitive, natural, and human environments in order to identify and assess actual and potential threats and opportunities.
- Military intelligence as practised in various forms of LIC—peacekeeping, counter-insurgency, and counter-terrorism—has many applications for business.
- Intelligence is everyone's business in a company, not just that of specialists or line managers and executives. Companies have employees in contact with competitors, stakeholders, suppliers, distributors, buyers, and sellers. They see and understand things that enhance the company's capacity to gather information, and through their appreciation of their own role in the company, can contribute to the intelligence assessment.
- People at all levels of a company must be aware of and must understand the implications of events and factors in all facets of the competitive, natural, and human environments.
- Everyone in a company can view the environment in terms of areas of operations, influence, and interest, and these can correspond to their particular role within an organization as well as the scope of their activities, whether they are strategic, operational, or tactical.
- Information becomes intelligence through an active process of interpretation, analysis, and assessment, to identify and evaluate actual and potential threats and opportunities.
- Information just doesn't fall into one's lap. It has to be sought, collected, analyzed, and assessed. This is the role of reconnaissance, which is an active process for searching for significant changes in the competition and the environment in order to reduce uncertainty and friction, as well

as to gain useful knowledge for uncovering actual and potential threats and opportunities.

- Reconnaissance through ethical, overt means is largely sufficient to meet the information gathering needs of companies in most circumstances. However, not all competitors, business or otherwise, limit themselves to legitimate, ethical, and legal means. This reality is part of the competitive and human environment in which companies must operate, and is therefore part of the intelligence equation.

Chapter 8

Bucks, Bullets and Bully Beef: Logistics and the Sinews of War

Strategy decides where to act; logistics brings the troops to this point.

Jomini, Précis de l'art de la guerre

Gentlemen, the officer who doesn't know his communications and supply as well as his tactics is totally useless.

General George S. Patton

One of the last big missions I accomplished in the military was when I was assigned as the Canadian Forces Liaison Officer to the land component headquarters of the US-led coalition in the months leading up to the invasion of Iraq in 2003. My task was to provide information about Canadian ground forces should the Canadian government decide to participate in the coalition and represent Canadian interests to the primarily American commanders and staff officers. As it turned out, Canada did not participate in the war, but I was nonetheless able to witness first hand one of the biggest and most impressive logistical build-ups since the end of the Second World War. As leader of the coalition, the United States was not only able to bring to bear large numbers of soldiers, but also their armament, ammunition and just about every type of equipment and supply imaginable. I was integrated into the 'Coalition Forces Land Component Command' located at Camp Doha Kuwait. Every day, for weeks on end, as the build up of forces continued, 747s loaded with troops would pass overhead on their final approach to the airport in Kuwait City. Camp Doha itself was a huge equipment storage depot with thousands of armoured vehicles, guns, and helicopters. Every morning at the planning conference, the force commander, General McKiernan, would get updates on everything from fuel supplies, supply ships in the North Atlantic and Indian Ocean, water pipelines, and heliports being built in the desert. General McKiernan had a very serious disposition, but it could be occasionally lightened, as when a staff officer gave a briefing about 'rhino snot.' General McKiernan stopped the officer in the middle of his sentence and said, "I have to ask, but what the hell is rhino snot?" It turns out it was the chemical compound that was laid down on the desert floor to harden the surface and prevent flying dust and sand so that helicopters could taxi, take off, and land.

The ultimate aim of all of this force build up was of course to prepare for the invasion of Iraq, and that couldn't start until there were sufficient forces, tanks, helicopters and guns, along with all the ammunition that would be needed for the coming battle. This gave me a first hand realization that logistics and materiel supply really are fundamental to war and military operations. There is a common saying in military circles, that "Amateurs study strategy, but professionals study logistics." Logistics is the supply, movement, and maintenance of military forces in peace and war. Although most military forces don't view it as such, raising and recruiting military forces also counts as part of the 'sinews of war.' We saw in previous chapters that strategy requires the balancing of ends, ways, and means. Even if you want to fight, you can't do so if you don't have the means, that is the soldiers, money, weapons, ammunition, and supplies that confer combat power and staying power. We also saw that there are strategies that allow weak forces to continue the fight, and these usually involve guerrilla warfare. However, we must realize that this is only a stopgap measure until a force can muster the means to go back on the offensive.

This chapter is similar to Chapter 7, on Intelligence, in that the study of logistics is a highly specialized field. We will focus on those principles and practices that have the most relevance and importance for business. These principles are summarized in the following box.

Principles of Logistics

- **The necessity of rational analysis:** The underlying focus of military logistics is quantification and rational analysis and calculation. This principle can be applied to supply, transportation, recruiting, and other support activities, but it is also fundamental to planning. Business managers need to apply the same 'logistic' framework to all of their planning, analysis, and decision-making.

- **Marshal forces to maximize probability of success:**
  Ambitious objectives usually require massive levels
  of resources to carry them off. Military forces must
  marshal their resources before launching an offensive,
  and the same applies to business, to be in a position
  to exploit successes and breakthroughs. This is directly
  linked to the twin principles of economy and mass.
- **Establish a bridgehead to expand in hostile territory:**
  You need a secure base area from which to operate, so
  that logistics and supplies can be built up and there
  is a relatively solid and safe springboard for launching
  operations. Expansion is a risky proposition, especially
  in a totally new country. It is best to proceed in phases
  and to spread the risk over several smaller bridgeheads,
  which can then be consolidated prior to further
  expansion.
- **Develop and maintain robust lines of communication:**
  You never know what can happen to your sources of
  supply and your lines of communication. They can
  be cut off or disrupted. Armies and companies need
  alternate sources of supply, optional supply routes, and
  the ability to recover from disruptions in the lines of
  communication.

Eggheads and Bean Counters: Rational Analysis

The scientific approach to business management started in the late 19th century,
but was rapidly taken up by the military during the First World War and even more
during the Second World War and the Cold War. This has been the greatest area of
cross-pollination between military and business practice, because the needs are so
similar. In the business world, 'logistics' usually only refers to the transportation
and storage of goods, as part of the production, manufacturing, and distribution
processes. 'Military logistics' on the other hand, has a much wider application, in that
it encompasses the sourcing and supply of materiel, the movement and maintenance
of military forces, and even the medical care of troops. While military forces do not

traditionally include personnel management—everything from recruiting to pay services—under the rubric of logistics, many of the same principles apply. For the purposes of this discussion, we can encompass all forms of rational calculation to estimate needs and activities as part of comprehensive planning of military strategy, operations, and tactics. In fact, the origins of the word 'logistics' indicate that it is fundamentally the discipline of calculation and logic: the Greek word *logistikos* means 'pertaining to logic.' Logistics is therefore the art of calculation in support of strategy, operations, and tactics. The same 'art of calculation' can and should be applied to all aspects of business strategy, operations, and tactics, and not just the traditional understanding of business logistics, which is focused on transportation and warehousing.

Brilliant Manoeuvre

Logistics—the art of calculation—should be applied to all aspects of business strategy, operations, and tactics, and not just the traditional understanding of business logistics, which is focused on transportation and warehousing.

Much of the education and training of military staff officers involves making calculations so that supplies, transportation, and maintenance can be planned and stockpiles can be created. I quickly learned as a young officer that most activities and tasks could be broken down into component parts and that each of these components could be quantified in various ways. For instance, there are fairly standard rates of movement by troops on foot over rough terrain, in forest, desert, or on roads and trails. These standard rates can be used to calculate speed of movement, and then integrated into a tactical battle plan. If I needed to lead my infantry platoon on foot through a dense wooded area, I could calculate the duration of the movement with great exactness, simply from knowing these standard rates of movement and the distance to be crossed. Conversely, it was possible to calculate distances by the time it took and multiplying by the known rate of movement. This type of dead reckoning is used all the time by military planners to calculate expected ammunition usage, movement times, vehicle usage and consequently requirements for spare parts. The standardized rates are consigned into 'staff tables' that then provide the basis for making calculations. No military planning can occur without these basic calculations. There are tables for speed of movement, ammunition usage, expected casualty rates, vehicle spare parts, and so on and so forth. Most of these 'staff tables' are now built in to databases, but they used to be kept in a book called 'Staff Officer's Handbook,' or some variant thereof. The point is that anything and everything that can be quantified in military processes and activities, as well as anything and everything that can be standardized, is analyzed and put into a readily accessible format for planning and estimation purposes. This doesn't obviate the requirement for intuition and experience, but it certainly helps in overcoming the lack of detailed and specific information needed to create effective plans, especially their support aspects.

We've already seen how a municipal transit service was able to use the data and information that was generated through operational research to determine travel needs of the population in their city. This gave management the information they needed, in combination with known standardized data about ridership rates and travel times by buses over certain types of road networks, and the estimated population, to estimate potential travel requirements by bus riders. Through quantification and rational calculation, managers of the transit service were able to estimate demand, numbers of buses that would be required to meet the demand, the types, routes, and frequencies of bus routes, and the infrastructure that would be required to support the needs of the travelling public. This example also shows that every business organization must go through a phase of what can be called 'professionalization' of management. This doesn't necessarily mean that everyone needs to get a MBA, but it does mean that at a certain point, the growth of the enterprise will require a certain level of quantification and calculation of means, so that the business can continue on its path of growth.

Brilliant Manoeuvre

The traditional ways of estimating on the basis of gut feel, past experience, and personal interactions between managers and employees are no longer enough to make timely and effective decisions.

Another example is a small business that is making the transition to medium sized operation. The traditional ways of doing business, of estimating on the basis of gut feel, past experience, and personal interactions between managers and employees are no longer enough to make timely and effective decisions. I worked with just such a company. The aim was to increase sales in one of the divisions without necessarily increasing the number of people involved in the sales process. The first point that was noted in our deliberations was that there was no basic financial information from which to compare results from one year to the next. Improvements must always be based on knowing the starting point for improvement. Consequently, the company president decided to invest in detailed and timely financial figures on revenue, cost of sales, and company overhead, so these could be imputed to the division to calculate its revenue, fixed and variable costs, gross margins, and net margins.

The same logic must be applied to calculating the profitability of each client and each project that the division implements for its clients. This allows the staff and managers to get away from discussions such as these: A project manager says that her gut tells her project A with client X was not profitable. Company president says he thinks the contrary. The sales person who closed on the deal says she thinks the project broke even. Who knows what the truth is, since they're all going by the seat of their pants? Only rational calculations to estimate actual revenue, fixed, and variable costs that can be imputed to the project and the client can give them the information they need to have an intelligent conversation. Once they have that information, they are also able to determine the costs of each component of their services that they provide to their clients for their various projects. This allows them to improve their pricing models, generate more detailed and accurate resource estimates, and generally make more informed decisions on whether to even put in a proposal to the client. If they estimate beforehand on the basis of their best calculations that they can't possibly break even on the project, then they need to decide if they want to bid or not, under the conditions that the client wants. They can then propose alternatives to the client that are based on actual data, rather than hope and conjecture.

As we saw in Chapter 6, "hope is not a method," and this applies as much to the sales process as that of calculating production inputs and transportation logistics. Furthermore, in working on this problem, we determined that the company was wasting an enormous amount of its resources just securing business from its clients. With the downturn in the economy, the company's clients, who were other businesses, were increasingly wary of committing to a particular project without having the detailed schedule of activities and cost breakdown. This had two consequences for my client: they were delivering value to their clients for free, and they were leaving a lot of money on the table as a result. The whole 'logistical' approach we took to analyzing their situation and coming up with viable solutions to improve performance was based on the need to get valid data and information and to infer from that what the real options were to improve performance.

▨ What aspects of your business, strategic, operational, and tactical, are amenable to quantification and rational calculation? There are probably many more than you think.

▨ What is the current state, in quantitative terms, of your business, division, or team?

▨ What are your objectives? What data and information do you need to make informed and timely decisions to support your plans to achieve them?

▨ How have you created your plans? Are they based on rough 'guesstimates' or are they based on actual historical figures that give you the information you need to calculate realistic resources, time, and personnel requirements?

Marshal Forces to Maximize the Chances of Success

Warren Buffett has the reputation of being one of the best investors in history. He has taken the public company he controls, Berkshire Hathaway, from struggling textile manufacturer to one of the largest insurance companies and diversified conglomerates in the world. Berkshire generates enormous amounts of cash, which has led to outstanding stock market returns over decades. Berkshire is a cash machine, and this has fuelled Buffett's ability to buy companies, in whole or in part, largely without any kind of borrowing. This is largely because of his uncanny and unique talent for calculation, and stringency in waiting for the right time and place to make investments. Buffett only moves when he fully understands the business he is acquiring, as well as its underlying economics and business model, and when he is convinced that he can acquire it wholly or mostly for cash, with a minimum of financial engineering. In other words, Buffett knows how to restrain his appetites and to marshal his company's forces for the right kind of investments. Had he been more undisciplined throughout his history at the helm of the company, it is highly unlikely that he would have made so many successful investments. However, the willingness to wait and to build up financial reserves has given him the ability to strike when the time is right and to acquire companies that will generate even more free cash flow with manageable levels of risk and a cash investment.

Buffett's overall approach to investing can be likened to the principle of marshalling of forces. He seems to understand intuitively that it is concentration of force, the ability to economize in non-decisive areas in order to mass in decisive ones, that generates the greatest success potential. The successful application of this principle has been demonstrated time and again in military history. This is a lesson that Stalin had to learn the hard way during the Soviet Union's struggle against the German army in World War Two.

In the early part of the war, he would order incessant counter-attacks, believing that this was the way to stop the German thrusts and encirclements. The problem with this approach, however, was that the Soviet forces would not have the time to build up sufficient forces and reserves to exploit the surprise of their counter-attacks. The Germans knew that if they held out against the initial, disorganized Soviet counter-attacks, they would be able to destroy more Soviet forces and then resume their assault. The first time the Red Army was truly successful in pushing back the German army was at Stalingrad. It's true that the Germans were badly overextended, but the Soviet field commander, Georgi Zhukov, was able to convince Stalin to build up massive forces to the east of Stalingrad before launching the final encirclement of the German 6th Army and the counter-offensive which threatened to cut off German forces in the Caucasus. This was the first major defeat of the German army in World War Two, and it was as much a logistical victory as a tactical and operational one. We also saw in Chapter 3, on Defence, how the same philosophy of marshalling forces was applied by the Red Army prior to the Germans' planned offensive at Kursk, in July 1943. The experience of Stalingrad had sunk in. After that, the Soviets always ruthlessly calculated what they called the 'correlation of forces,' especially for their major offensives. The idea was that they would not launch a major operation unless they were certain of overwhelming material superiority.

Brilliant Manoeuvre

Marshalling of forces is the logistical aspect of the twin principles of mass and economy. In order to concentrate mass for the main effort, you have to economize forces in other areas of the battlefield.

Marshalling forces is a critical component of strategic, operational, and tactical planning, both in battle and in business. Marshalling of forces is the logistical aspect of the twin principles of mass and economy that we explored in Chapter 5. In order to concentrate mass for the main effort, you have to economize forces in other areas of the battlefield. You then have to actually move these forces from one part of the battlefield to the other, while ensuring they are properly supplied and maintained in the field. This principle applies at the strategic, operational, and tactical levels of business. For instance, when you take resources from an underperforming line of business, or one with lower expected growth, to one with higher growth potential, this is equivalent to marshalling forces at the strategic level. Similarly, the decision to launch a product in a new market will require the marshalling of resources prior to the campaign and then during its early phase so there is staying power to weather initial setbacks, such as competitors responding to your moves and initial customer resistance. This is an example of marshalling of forces at the operational level. Finally, at the tactical level, a sales manager has to judge when to become involved in a sale with a major client, so as to preserve resources for her many responsibilities and not become exhausted in trying to accomplish everything for everybody.

There are three main benefits of marshalling resources for the main effort. These are illustrated Figure 8.1.

Figure 8.1: Why Marshal Forces?

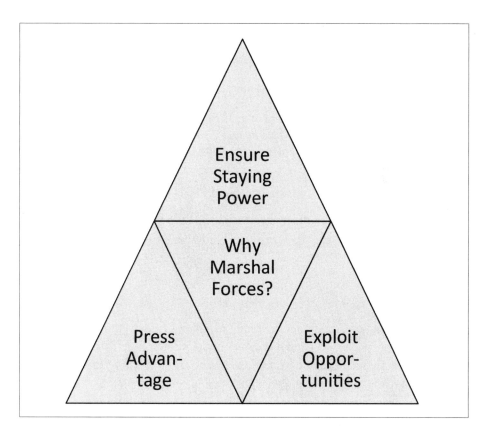

Exploit Opportunities

You can't exploit opportunities unless you have the resources available and waiting, or you can reallocate them quickly from underperforming areas. This is the concomitant of the principle of probing we explored in Chapter 2. When you launch a campaign or an attack, you don't necessarily know ahead of time where all the opportunities will be. That is why it is better to probe forward with smaller forces and then to reinforce the successful incursions by following up with additional resources once opportunities appear. For example, suppose you decide to launch an existing product in a new geographic market. You select three retail stores in different towns of that region. However, from your sales data, you realize that 50 per cent of the customers in one of the stores come from a nearby town where you don't yet have a distribution arrangement with any of its local retailers. You had intended to finance further expansion in this region by the additional cash flow generated in the first three locations. Instead, you decide to move up the introduction of your product in that town in order to take advantage of this unexpected opportunity, but you can only do this if you have sufficient resources to hand or easily accessible. The resources would likely include the working capital to fund accounts receivable with the retailers in the newest location, but you may also have to ramp up production, transportation, and warehousing quickly and efficiently. This means your initial plans must include not just the cash needed to fund the operations, but also the logistical and production capability to exploit targets of opportunity.

Brilliant Manoeuvre

Initial plans must include not just the cash needed to fund the operations, but also the logistical and production capability to exploit targets of opportunity.

Press Advantage

The second benefit of marshalling resources prior to launching a campaign is that you can press the advantage of your initial successes and turn them into breakthroughs. In practice, though, you can only do this if you have sufficient forces lined up and ready to pour through a breach that has been created by the vanguard elements of your forces. Let us extend the foregoing example, and suppose that the campaign to introduce the product to a new geographic region was only one of three such attempts by the company to establish itself in a new country. The division VP responsible for this thrust analyzed that country's environment and decided to launch the product in three different regions, in a similar manner to that described in the previous paragraph, and then to give priority to the top market after a period of three to six months of sales, based on which region is experiencing the fastest and broadest growth in sales. There is a sales manager in charge of each of the regions, and they have the mandate to expand sales as fast as possible by seeking out opportunities and exploiting them to the hilt, as described above. The country sales director has the green light to send product to the regions that are experiencing the greatest success at penetrating their markets. Naturally, this plan can only work if the division VP has made provision to ramp up production with the concomitant logistical arrangements in order to meet the increased demand. If the company can't exploit the initial success and then press its advantage, local competitors might see the opportunity and the company's initial success and counter with their own products. The only thing the company would have succeeded in doing then is showing local companies that there is a market for that type of product, at considerable cost, while not necessarily reaping the full benefits of its initiative.

Brilliant Manoeuvre

You can only press your advantage if you have sufficient forces lined up and ready to pour through the breach that has been created by your vanguard.

Staying Power

The third benefit that comes from marshalling resources is staying power. This is the capacity to continue the campaign once initial successes have petered out and the competition catches up or counterattacks. This is the phase of the campaign where many expansion strategies fail, simply because companies run out of cash or production and operational capability to meet demand to the greatest extent possible, or simply to invest in innovation and to meet competitive threats. Competitors can launch a counteroffensive to squeeze the newcomer out, or at least put them on the defensive. This is what has happened over the years to many Canadian retailers that have tried to expand into the US market. The Canadian company has a stellar reputation in Canada, highly profitable, with limited competition from Canadian and foreign retailers. The company acquires a US retail chain, intending to grow its base in the United States from the initial incursion. The problem is that the US chain that is acquired is usually an also-ran, with low growth and low margins; it is a company that is already having a hard time competing against larger chains. The Canadian company doesn't have the financial backbone and economies of scale of the larger US-based chains, so it struggles to revamp its newly acquired US operations, often trying, unsuccessfully, to import a retail model that works well north of the border, but not in the cut-throat US market. The Canadian company then acquires other struggling US chains in the hope that this will give it expanded market reach and greater economies of scale, but it eventually gives up and sells its US operation after meandering around the profitability line for a number of years.

Brilliant Manoeuvre

Staying power is the capacity to continue the campaign once initial successes have petered out and the competition catches up or counterattacks.

This is what happened to Canadian Tire Corporation in the 1980s after it tried to expand into the US. Jean Coutu Group, one of the leading pharmacy chains in Canada, also tried a similar expansion through the 1990s and early 2000s. The company is a highly successful brand in Quebec, and has been a consistent innovator since its founding in 1969. In 1994 it acquired the Brooks drugstore chain, but the US operation struggled for the next decade. In 2004, it acquired over 1,500 Eckerd drugstores in the Northeast, but continued to be unprofitable, and couldn't sustain the investments needed to be truly competitive. In 2006, the company withdrew from the US, selling most of its stores. Other Canadian retailers have struggled in the same way, such as the Tim Hortons coffee franchise, although the jury is still out on whether the chain can continue its US growth. US retailers entering the Canadian market have fared considerably better because of their massive size relative to Canadian companies. This gives them the resources to expand and sustain competitive counterattacks, to the point where most of the large retailers in Canada are US owned or controlled, such as Walmart, Sears, Best Buy, and other more specialized retailers.

There have been success stories, such as Alimentation Couche-Tard, another

Quebec-based retail chain, but this one concentrated in convenience stores and gas bars. The company has grown aggressively in the US by progressively acquiring smaller convenience store chains, becoming the largest such chain in North America. So, it is possible for a Canadian retailer to succeed in the US market, but the company must find a way to create staying power. Canadian banks have been successful expanding in the US over the decades, primarily because their prudent practices have led them to expand more slowly by biting off smaller pieces to chew. Nonetheless, this strategy has served Toronto Dominion Bank extremely well, as its operations in the US have expanded to become TD Bank, which is now a major retail banker in the eastern United States.

Strategic Application of the Marshalling Principle

- What are your expansion or sustainment plans? Do you have sufficient financial, production, logistical, and operational capability to exploit opportunities? How can you free up such resources? Have you empowered your managers to seek out and exploit these opportunities? Have you given them the tools and resources to do so?
- Have you developed contingency plans and capabilities to press an initial advantage, whether offensively or defensively? Do you have resources and capabilities on standby, or can you reallocate them from underperforming areas of the company? Are your people empowered to press your advantages so they can turn initial incursions into breakthroughs? Do they have the resources to do so?
- Do you have the staying power to survive and thrive beyond the initial push into a new product-market segment? Can you sustain the advance and turn tactical and operational victories into strategic ones?

Establish a Bridgehead to Expand into Hostile Territory

The concept of a bridgehead is implicit in the previous discussion on the marshalling of forces. In fact, the concept is fundamental to all of military logistics, and it can be extended to business. A bridgehead is a secure base of operations. The success of the Normandy landings in World War II depended on the Allies' ability to gain a foothold in France and expand it into a bridgehead. One aim of a bridgehead is to create a defensible area on which to anchor subsequent operations. That way, when the enemy counterattacks, the attacking force will be able to keep a foothold in enemy territory. A second and more important reason is to create a support base for building up supplies and to which forces can repair for maintenance and refitting. In other words, the bridgehead is a little bit of secure territory from which to expand the offensive. Without such a base of operations, it would be almost impossible to establish a permanent presence in enemy territory.

Brilliant Manoeuvre

Whether the intention is to expand the range of products in an existing market, or to extend the market of an existing range of products, it is always more prudent to proceed in phases, from the known to the less known.

The bridgehead principle is crucial for expanding business, as it provides a notional and physical anchor point in the new territory. Whether the intention is to expand the range of products in an existing market, or to extend the market of an existing range of products, it is always more prudent to proceed in phases, from the known to the less known. This is prudent risk management, as it allows the company to develop the necessary intelligence and experience with a new product-market mix. It also enables it to build up the reserves that will be needed to exploit opportunities, press its advantage, and sustain expansion and the inevitable competitive counterattacks. This is illustrated in Figure 8.2 on the next page.

Figure 8.2 shows a company's campaign to expand into a new country, using the example given in the discussion on the marshalling of forces. The main effort of the expansion campaign is city A, which is the largest in the region, with the aim of establishing an initial bridgehead and, then, expanding it to encompass a progressively wider area, either by design or by exploiting opportunities as they appear. The company is also trying to establish smaller, secondary bridgeheads in cities B and C, with the understanding that it doesn't want to put all its eggs in one basket. After all, its original analysis on the best city to focus on could be wrong, so the company's executives want to be poised for unexpected opportunities while prudently managing risk. Once these initial bridgeheads are established, they can be consolidated into a combined bridgehead, which then provides a secure base for further expansion, either by introducing additional products into these markets, or by offering the same products in markets that are in close proximity.

The notion of proximity can be geographic, such as when the company decides to infiltrate another region nearby, or it can be conceptual, as when it first focuses on a particular population demographic, then extends its offerings to other

Figure 8.2: Company Expanding into New Market

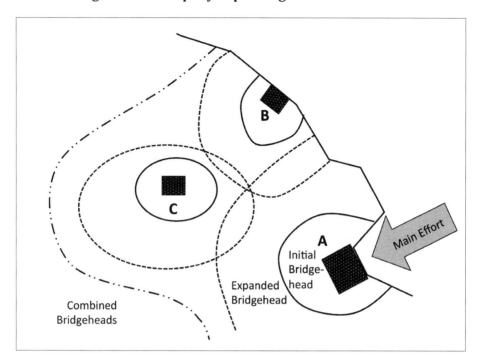

demographic or behavioural segments in the same geographical market. Either way, the idea is to expand sequentially, first by creating a bridgehead as a secure base of operations, and then by expanding outwards according to design and opportunity. The key is to have sufficient resources in reserve so that targets of opportunity can be exploited, the initial advantages of surprise and novelty can be leveraged, and the resulting successes can be recycled into additional resources to fuel further expansion.

Brilliant Manoeuvre

Expand sequentially, first by creating a bridgehead as a secure base of operations, then by expanding outwards according to design and opportunity.

One of my consulting clients is planning to expand its operations from Eastern to Western Canada, and this is exactly the outline strategy that it has adopted. The idea is to select a Western Canadian city and then decide on whether to acquire a small local firm operating in the same field or to build it from scratch. The main advantage of the acquisition option is that it minimizes risk while maximizing speed. There is no need to develop local market and competitive knowledge, as this will come with the target company's existing owners, assuming they are kept as local managers. The investment is also reasonable, and allows the acquiring company to husband its resources for further expansion as required and as opportunities arise.

This prudent approach to expansion has served Toronto-Dominion Bank extremely well as it has taken a phased and controlled approach to expansion in the US from its strong base of operations in Canada. Toronto-Dominion Bank (TD) established a US bridgehead in the US Northeast by acquiring Bancnorth Group of Maine in 2004. It then added Hudson United Bank with operations in New Jersey and Philadelphia in 2005. TD Ameritrade, the result of a previous expansion of TD into US based discount brokerage operations, was integrated into TD Bank. TD acquired Commerce Bank with branches all along the eastern seaboard in 2008, further expanding out of the initial bridgehead in the Northeast. In 2010, TD Bank acquired a series of banks headquartered in South Carolina and Florida. By 2011, TD Bank had become one the 10 largest banks in the US, with over 1,200 branches from New England down to Florida. Throughout the period, Toronto-Dominion never overextended itself and was able to marshal resources in phases for further thrusts into the US market. Moreover, the knowledge and experience that was gained in each phase of the expansion campaign became useful intelligence for the next phase. We can contrast this with the over-ambitious expansion of the Jean Coutu Pharmacy chain described in the previous section. The key difference was in the more prudent and step-by-step approach of the Toronto-based Toronto-Dominion group as opposed to Jean Coutu biting off more than it could chew. TD had the resources to meet the competitive challenges, whereas Jean Coutu basically shot its load in acquiring the Brooks and then Eckerd chains. Jean Coutu Group has had to withdraw from its American adventure, whereas TD Bank is still growing.

Brilliant Manoeuvre

Toronto-Dominion marshalled resources in phases for further thrusts into the US market. Moreover, the knowledge and experience that was gained in each phase of the expansion campaign became useful intelligence for the next phase.

Strategic Application of the Bridgehead Principle

- What are your expansion intentions?
- Will you offer existing products to new markets, or new products to existing markets?
- If you are extending your market, is your expansion geographic in scope, or is it instead conceptual, and focused on a new market segment in an existing geographical market?
- Are you intending a major push by acquiring a competitor in the new market? If so, do you have the resources and staying power to fight off the inevitable competitive counterattacks and initial lack of knowledge and experience in this market? Do you have the resources to invest in continual upgrades in your products and marketing in these markets or will you prematurely run out of resources, having shot your load in the initial takeover campaign?
- Have you considered a phased, prudent approach based on the bridgehead principle, first acquiring a small company in a smaller market with less competition?
- What other areas or market segments could you consider that would allow you to spread some of the risk and to identify and exploit targets of opportunity for further quick expansion, while demanding fewer resources and exposing you to more manageable levels of risk?

Develop and Maintain Robust Lines of Communication

Money, supply, and transportation have always been considered the 'sinews of war,' but economic warfare reached its apogee during the Second World War. The Germans tried, using submarines, to cut off Britain from its North American sources of supply, and very nearly achieved their objective for a brief period in 1942. The Allies bombed Germany relentlessly from 1942 onward, aiming at disrupting industrial production, fuel production and distribution, railways and marshalling yards, bridges, and a multitude of other logistical and supply targets. The aim was to whittle down Germany's ability to fight by destroying its industrial base and its lines of communication. The campaign wasn't totally successful, but it did have a marked impact on its war fighting capability. After the war, the German armaments minister, Albert Speer, admitted to Allied interrogators that the US Air Force raids on the ball bearing production facilities in Schweinfurt had almost brought war production to a standstill.

Manufacturing and distribution companies also rely heavily on safe and secure sources of supply for materials, components, and sub-assemblies. Vertically integrated enterprises were once the rule in manufacturing. Henry Ford developed one of the first large-scale, integrated production facilities at his River Rouge complex near Detroit. This became the paradigmatic approach to manufacturing and production, as it allowed the company to control all aspects of sourcing of materials, supply, transportation logistics, and component manufacturing. The reality nowadays is that few companies own the entire value chain going from natural resources to final product, and even the distribution and retail sales channels. Companies are just nodes in a continuous chain of manufacturers and suppliers, with transportation logistics firms providing the glue that holds the whole process together. Apple may design its products in California, but they are manufactured by armies of factory workers and sub-contractors in China and other parts of Asia. This is the rule rather than the exception in manufacturing in the early 21st century.

Companies are vulnerable at multiple points and in many different ways in their supply chain. For instance, a car manufacturer has a final assembly plant, but the sub-assemblies are manufactured in other plants owned by the company, or by sub-contractors. These in turn have their own sub-contractors manufacturing components and parts that go into the fabrication of the sub-assemblies. These can be separated geographically, and even sometimes in different countries. In aircraft manufacturing, sub-assemblies can even be made on different continents. Bombardier Aerospace's aircraft might have wings built in Ireland, engines in Britain, engine nacelles in Japan, cockpits in the United States, with the tail and body manufacturing, and final assembly occurring in Canada. This creates multiple vulnerabilities because of time, distance, geography and climate, culture, and the hazards of transportation. These vulnerabilities can be compounded by the fact that many manufacturers now have concentrated sources of supply for components and materials, either in terms of the number of different suppliers, or their geographical spread.

As an example, the massive earthquake that occurred off the eastern coast of Japan on 11 March 2011, and the resulting tsunami and damage to the Fukushima nuclear power plants, disrupted the manufacturing and supply of parts and components of thousands of Japanese manufacturers. Car manufacturers around the world, but especially Japanese companies such as Toyota, Honda, and Nissan, had concentrated their sources of supply in Japan. This exposed their vulnerability to supply disruptions, especially as it quickly became evident that in many cases, there was only one supplier of a particular component, often supplying more than one car company. There are clear financial and operational advantages to having a limited number of suppliers, and to have them in close proximity. If, however, something happens to disrupt the supply chain, or one of those component manufacturers goes under or its products are no longer functioning properly, the company would need to find new sources of supply.

Military forces of course face exactly the same type of vulnerabilities. Geological and climate events can threaten an army's supply chain, but it is actually the enemy that takes the major role in disrupting lines of communication and supply. In fact, as we saw in the discussion on German submarine warfare and Allied bombing in World War II, attacking the enemy's lines of communication and sources of supply is a major part of military strategy and tactics. This is why military forces have developed principles and practices for protecting their lines of communication and supply trains. Military forces therefore aim for resiliency and robustness in their logistical systems. Resiliency is the ability to bounce back and to adapt to threats against lines of communication and disruptions of supply. Robustness is the ability to avoid or withstand these threats in the first place.

Four Keys to Logistical Resiliency and Robustness

- **Redundancy:** Multiple means of supply and transportation, routes, stockpiles, etc. In other words, there should always be multiple logistical means in effect, or at least the possibility of alternatives that can be put into action quickly.
- **Reaction:** Rapid detection of changes in logistical conditions, new threats and risks, and the ability to react and spring into action quickly with contingency plans and/or problem solving.
- **Responsiveness:** Capacity to adapt to changing requirements and conditions, especially those that are generated internally by the company or supply chain as a result of new products or processes.
- **Anticipation:** The foresight to imagine potential future scenarios in order to create contingency plans or adapt in advance of changing requirements and conditions.

The contrasting reactions of Ericsson and Nokia to the same disruptive event in 2000 highlights how companies can apply these four principles of resiliency and robustness to their logistical operations, as well as what can happen when a company doesn't apply them adequately. These facts are taken from Yossi Sheffi's excellent book on supply chain vulnerability, *The Resilient Enterprise* (MIT Press, 2007).

On 17 March, 2000 there was a small fire in a semiconductor fabrication plant operated by Philips NV in Albuquerque, New Mexico. Plant employees were able to extinguish the blaze. While the fire had been relatively small and heat damage was minor, smoke and water and the fire fighting activity itself had damaged much of the work in progress and rendered the plant unusable for further semiconductor fabrication until a major clean-up operation could be completed. This is because semiconductors must be manufactured to exacting standards in an uncontaminated environment.

Forty per cent of the production of the Albuquerque facility went to the cell phone manufacturers Ericsson in Sweden, and Nokia in Finland. The two companies reacted very differently to the initial news and, especially, the growing realization that the Philips plant would not be coming back on line within days, but rather within weeks or even months. Nokia immediately started working with Philips to ascertain the full extent of damages to the Albuquerque plant. Nokia engineers and executives sprung into action when they realized that the fire could potentially disrupt the manufacture of 4 million or so cellphones, which was about 5 per cent of the company's production. Nokia's chief component-purchasing manager, Tapio Markki, saw that the company's limited reserves of components could only last a few days, so he led a team of 30 or so engineers and supply chain experts in searching the world for alternate sources of supply to tide the company over during the Philips facility's down time. They were quickly able to find alternate sources of supply in Japan and the US, but for certain components, Philips was the only manufacturer. Nokia managers convinced Philips to reallocate production from some of its other facilities to compensate for the shortfall. Nokia maintained production and, more importantly, its ability to continue serving its customers, throughout the disruption. This was largely due to its executives' and engineers' skill in reacting to the plant fire and then anticipating further disruptions and difficulties. They were also able to leverage existing redundancies of supply and relationships to remain responsive to the ongoing need for production. Moreover, they worked closely with Philips executives and engineers to ensure alternate sources within that company so that they could also be responsive to the needs of their customer, Nokia. Nokia could have shown more robustness by anticipating their vulnerability to one particular manufacturer, Philips, but on the other hand, there is no mistaking its team's high level of resiliency in the face of disruptions to its supply chain.

Brilliant Manoeuvre

Resiliency is the ability to bounce back and to adapt to threats against lines of communication, and disruptions of supply. Robustness is the ability to avoid or withstand these threats in the first place.

Ericsson's reaction and response couldn't have been more opposite to Nokia's. Ericsson's engineers were notified at exactly the same time as Nokia's, but there was no initial reaction. As Sheffi points out, it was "one technician talking to another." There was no immediate impact assessment, and higher-level management was not apprised of the incident until much later, once it was realized that the Philips plant wouldn't come back on line quickly. When Ericsson management did realize what had happened, they went back to Philips for assistance, because, contrary to Nokia, they had no pre-existing alternate sources of supply. Philips couldn't help though, because Nokia had already commandeered all of Philips' extra capacity. Ericsson suffered the most from the disruption caused by the fire. In the subsequent quarter, the company had losses on the order of half a billion dollars, mainly due to lost production because of the inability to find alternative sources of parts in a highly competitive industry. Sheffi claims that the hit to Ericsson lingered for another year and may have played a role in its eventual team up with Sony. Regardless, the immediate effects were enough to show that Ericsson's lack of redundancy of supply and slow reaction led to poor responsiveness. Had Ericsson shown more anticipation it would have been more resilient in the face of adversity, with less negative effects on its competitiveness.

Strategic Application of Logistical Robustness

- How vulnerable is your supply chain? Do you have a limited number of suppliers, or multiple ones, with potential alternatives for an emergency situation?
- How long could your company withstand a supply chain or other form of logistical disruption?
- Do you have contingency plans in place to deal with such disruptions?
- What could you do to prevent or protect from such disruptions?
- How quickly can you react to a supply chain or logistical disruption? Do you have emergency operations teams and procedures in place to manage such a crisis?

- Do all your supplies originate from one company or one geographical region? Do they pass through one transportation route or port of entry? Do you use only one transportation logistics company?
- What could you do to diversify your sources of supply and transportation?
- Are you well linked in with suppliers' operations, and those of your internal clients who need the supplies and support?

Summary

- Logistics isn't just about transportation. It is about using rational analysis and quantification to solve business and organizational problems of all kinds so that you can achieve your strategic, operational, and tactical objectives.
- You must marshal your forces to achieve success with your main effort. This also means you must be ready to take resources and means away from secondary and tertiary fronts to reinforce the successful thrusts.
- If you've successfully marshalled resources, you have the means to exploit opportunities and to press your advantage. You also have the staying power to continue with the campaign, even when the competition counter-attacks or your initial estimations prove erroneous or the inevitable friction causes plans to go awry.
- Any major campaign into new territory, whether that is a new geographical market or a new clientele, requires a prudent, phased approach. This is why a bridgehead is so critical. It allows you to gain a secure footing in a new market and to build up (or marshal) your forces prior to making a break out.
- All complex undertakings require resiliency and robustness in the supply and logistical chain in order to absorb and spring back from threats and disruptions. Resiliency is the ability to absorb a shock and to spring back. Robustness is the ability to prevent and protect oneself from such threats and disruptions.
- Resiliency and robustness are achieved through the four key logistical principles of redundancy, reaction, responsiveness, and anticipation.
- Resiliency and robustness of the supply chain and logistics can reinforce your competitive advantage, or damage it irreparably.

Chapter 9

"The Moral is to the Physical as Three is to One"[3]: Morale, Cohesion and the Motivation to Perform

Success is not final, failure is not fatal; it is the courage to continue that counts.

Never give in. Never, never, never, never. In nothing great or small, large or petty, never give in except to convictions of honour and good sense. Never yield to force; never yield to the apparently overwhelming might of the enemy.

Winston Churchill

The best morale exists when you never hear the word mentioned. When you hear a lot of talk about it, it's usually lousy.

General Dwight D. Eisenhower

What we need is to replace the externally imposed spur of fear with an internal self-motivation for performance. Responsibility—not satisfaction—is the only thing that will serve.

Peter Drucker, The Practice of Management

---

[3] The maxim "The moral is to the physical as three is to one" is attributed to Napoleon.

We've often heard the expression, "war is hell." War is destructive of humanity and its material comforts. It calls up the most atavistic of human tendencies: hatred, fear, anger, and pure destructiveness. It also can bring out the noblest of emotions and virtues: courage, perseverance, cooperation, *esprit de corps*, and self-sacrifice. I certainly won't claim that war and business can be considered equivalent on this front, but there is a certain quality of perseverance, courage, and dogged determination that is required to succeed in business. In the previous chapters of this book, we've seen many of the ways in which military principles and practices can be useful for overcoming obstacles and reaching business objectives. However, these approaches are all rational and technical in nature. It is time now to turn to the moral plane of war and business. This is the battlefield of emotions and group dynamics, where intangible factors play a role in determining the outcomes of strategies and plans. Material and technical factors are important—critical, even—but ultimately it is the human qualities that lead to victory or defeat.

We usually study the overnight business successes, or what we think are overnight successes. What we fail to see are all the instant successes that have been twenty years in the making. Sure, there will always be examples of a Mark Zuckerberg who founded Facebook in his dormitory room at Harvard, but these cases are few and far between. In fact, the reason we find them so remarkable is because of their rarity. Even in such cases, though, the so-called overnight sensation still has to show considerable perseverance and determination to succeed. This chapter is about the ability and will to fight and persevere in the face of obstacles, opposition, threats, and difficulties. It is also about what it takes to create great teams and organizations that have strong morale, cohesion, and unity of purpose.

Organizational Dynamics from a Military Standpoint

- **The real test of morale is adversity.** It's not what you do when you're successful that counts, but rather what you do when you're facing adversity and obstacles; this is the real test of morale.
- **Morale is different from mood, and is built on unity and cohesion.** Strong morale is built upon unity of purpose and action, determination to succeed, and cohesion in the face of opposition, disruptions, uncertainty, friction, and obstacles.

- **Perseverance and courage come from faith in the mission.** No one can call up the reserves of strength, courage, and motivation needed to persevere without total belief in their mission and vision, and in the nobility or validity of their cause. Powerful metaphors can rally people around the mission and vision.

- **People need to feel they are part of something bigger than themselves.** Strength comes in numbers, but the group must be made up of the right people, and have a structure and purpose that resonates at all levels of the organization.

- **True motivation and discipline come from within.** Individuals perform at their best when they are impelled to do so from within themselves. External rewards and punishments only go so far in influencing behaviour.

The Real Test of Morale Is Adversity

When France was conquered by Germany in the Second World War, the French army had been defeated in battle, but it could have continued to fight. The Maginot Line, which faced Germany in the east, was still relatively intact and many of France's finest divisions, including thousands of aircraft, tanks and guns, were still capable of fighting. France surrendered not because it was completely defeated, but rather because its leadership was demoralized by the German attack, and the apparent futility of resisting a German war machine that appeared unstoppable. This was why the French historian, Marc Bloch, called his history of the first days of the war, *Strange Defeat*. It was in recognition of the incompetence and demoralization in the high command and political leadership of the country.

Once France had been defeated during the Second World War, Britain and her Commonwealth allies and empire possessions stood essentially alone against Germany. Churchill's resolve and leadership were instrumental in continuing the struggle against Germany. Without Churchill at the helm, it is quite possible that Britain would have sued for peace, which was what Hitler had assumed it would do. It is hard nowadays to imagine just how dark the period 1940-41 was for Britain and her allies, before the U.S. and the Soviet Union entered the war. When Germany invaded the Soviet Union on June 22nd 1941, Churchill's spirits rose, because he knew Britain would no longer be alone in the struggle. The Japanese attack on Pearl Harbor that brought the United States into the war on December 7th 1941 was the decisive event that turned the tide of the war. With the US in the war, Churchill knew then that victory for the Allies was but a matter of time. Throughout the dark days of uncertainty when Hitler ruled Europe, and Britain sustained daily night time bombings, Churchill rallied Britain's military forces and her people. He would walk the streets of London the morning after a bombing, he would visit troops on exercise, factory workers, Home Guard volunteers filling sandbags, and observing the skies for German bombers and the beaches for German invasion forces. The Royal Air Force and its Commonwealth allies were able to defeat the German air attacks during the Battle of Britain in the late summer of 1940 but through this whole period, it was Churchill who kept the morale of the British people alive. The times were hard and fearsome, but the British never lost hope that eventually they would defeat Nazi Germany.

I believe one of the main reasons so many businesses fail in their first few years of operations is that their owners and managers hit a wall. They run out of money, can't find enough clients, make mistakes in their strategy and operations. This leads them to lose their motivation to succeed and their morale to persevere in the face of difficulties and obstacles. If entrepreneurship were easy, more people would be in business, and the failure rate of new businesses wouldn't be as high as it is. Napoleon Hill, one of the founders of success literature wrote a book in the 1930s called *Think and Grow Rich*. Many who have dreamed of making it big by starting a business have read this book, in some cases, several times. Hill's basic message is very simple: one must really believe in one's goals, and persevere in achieving them even against the most daunting of obstacles, setbacks, and failures. Pretty much everything else in the book is an elaboration on that theme.

Brilliant Manoeuvre

You have to really believe in your goals, and persevere in achieving them even against the most daunting of obstacles, setbacks, and failures.

That is certainly the meaning of the Churchill quotes I included at the beginning of this chapter. "Success is never final, failure is never fatal." That just about sums up life, in general. Successes are fleeting because the world continues to change around you. If you're in an oppositional or a competitive situation, others want what you have, and they are willing to fight or compete intensively to take it from you. On the other hand, you can always spring back from failures and defeats, unless you lose your will to persevere and to fight back. As I mentioned in the chapter about defensive strategy, guerrilla warfare is a defensive strategy designed to keep fighting when everything objectively tells you to give up. It is a strategy of weakness that refuses to accept defeat. Call it a blend of realism and optimism.

Brilliant Manoeuvre

You can always spring back from failures and defeats, unless you lose your will to persevere and to fight back.

As an entrepreneur, I myself have hit the wall when I seriously considered giving up my business aspirations. The problem was that I knew I would never be happy working for someone else. I had spent almost 26 years in the military, and though I am proud of my service and of my accomplishments in the military, I just feel that I have to continue and persevere no matter what business obstacles I face. As Nietzsche said, "What does not kill me makes me stronger." Nothing that happens to me in business can harm me, although it is likely to make me stronger if I work through the difficulties, and find ways to achieve my goals when what I try doesn't work the way I anticipated. Moreover, as my business mentor, Alan Weiss, often says, "If you're not failing, it's because you're not trying hard enough."

A friend of mine has had the same type of experience. This friend I'll call Norm joined a start-up company that had acquired the right to commercialize a novel process for manufacturing bio-diesel. However, just because this company had a great idea, and there was ostensibly demand for its product, it didn't mean that everything was peachy. Norm told me that the founder-president and principal shareholder once dug into his own pocket to cover the payroll for the company because they had one of their numerous cash crunches in the first years of operations when everything was still experimental. This was when there wasn't much demand because of the initial, high price of the company's product as compared to traditional sources. The technical advantages of its process and product can speak for themselves, but these don't lead self-evidently to business success. This was not easy when key investors had told the president and his key executives that they had had enough. They wanted immediate returns, and when they weren't forthcoming, they were ready to pull the plug. The president found new investors, and the race to build a fully operational production facility continued, and it was Norm's main responsibility to oversee that project. They worked 18 hours a day for months on end. Norm told me the company finally became profitable the year before our meeting, and that prospects were good. Did they meet all of their initial goals and milestones? Of course not, but they at least know now that the business model can succeed. The company is now consolidating and perfecting its operations in its first production facility, and hopes to expand within the next few years.

What this story and many, other success stories in business show, is that defeat is only temporary if you are resolved to stay in the fight no matter what. Norm is adamant that the main reason the company is still in business is due to the resolve, perseverance, and leadership of its founder. He was able to convey to all in the company this sense of optimism and determination. His willingness to dig into his own pockets to make payroll showed that he believed in the company and its product and production process. The key element in keeping morale and persevering was hope. Hope that the company would succeed. Hope that the economics of bio-diesel would eventually become more favourable to the company. Hope, also, that the 18-hour days and uncertainty would lead to success in the future.

Brilliant Manoeuvre

Defeat is only temporary if you are resolved to stay in the fight.

How Is Your Perseverance?

- What obstacles have you faced in business that appeared insurmountable at the time but that in retrospect were not so?
- How did you overcome them? Where did you find the reserves of will and perseverance to overcome them?
- What role did your co-workers and business colleagues/partners play in supporting you or pulling together to overcome them?
- Did you ever lose hope? What did it feel like? How did you gain it back?

Morale is Different from Mood—It's Built on Unity and Cohesion

Many if not most people confuse true morale with superficialities such as mood. They take good humour and happy, peaceful feelings as signs of strong morale when they are nothing but an adjunct to strong morale, and a peripheral one at that. When I was at Canadian Army Staff College in 1997, we did a battlefield tour in Italy to study the Battle of the Gothic Line, a major Allied offensive against one of the Germans' main defensive lines in Italy. A number of Canadian veterans who had participated in the battle as officers accompanied us. One morning, one of the students on the course asked a seemingly innocent question. How was morale during this operation? Tom DeFaye was one of the veterans who had commanded an infantry company throughout the hard-fought battle. As we stood on a hillside with a magnificent view overlooking vineyards, he felt compelled to answer the question. It was my first real lesson in what morale really is: "I'm hearing a lot of questions about whether our morale was good, and whether the troops had the stomach for the fight. Let me be clear. Morale was excellent, but the troops complained constantly. The troops bitched and moaned about anything and everything. It was too hot or too cold. We were advancing too slowly or too quickly. We didn't have the right equipment. The food was terrible. There was nothing they didn't bellyache about but they fought, and we had no doubt whatsoever that we were going to win the fight and the war."

Brilliant Manoeuvre

A good humour and happy, peaceful feelings are nothing but an adjunct to strong morale.

In other words, just because people complain, doesn't mean that morale isn't good. I was also able to experience this myself subsequently during my own command of an infantry company in Bosnia. The only valid measure of morale is whether the troops are willing to fight, to make the sacrifices and effort needed to ensure final victory. Everything else, whether they are complaining, or whether they are in a bad mood or a good mood, is tangential. Good morale depends on the technical competence and leadership of the chain of command, especially the immediate superiors. It also requires a mission and objectives in which the troops can believe, and believe that they are noble and right. Finally, good morale thrives on cohesion, unity of purpose, and a belief that the organization as a whole as well as its leaders have the welfare of its members at heart, that they won't needlessly squander or waste them in useless battles and incompetent manoeuvres.

The only valid measure of morale is whether people are willing to fight, to make the sacrifices and effort needed to ensure final victory. Everything else, whether they are complaining, or whether they are in a bad mood or a good mood, is tangential.

I was working with a small family-owned business, and the founder's son had just taken over as managing director of the company. One of his objectives was to improve morale as part of a general business turnaround, to get everyone pulling in the same direction and jazzed again about working for the company. However, as I started to work with the management team, I quickly came to understand that morale wasn't the core problem. The managers and employees were quite willing to work hard, and wanted to persevere in the face of difficulties. They were also highly committed to the company and wanted it to succeed. Rather, what was at stake was their ability to function effectively and efficiently as a team and an organization. This started at the level of the managing director and his four managers, and included many of their basic operational, management, and communication processes. The company had reasonably good morale and sense of unity, but it lacked cohesiveness. People were willing and well-intentioned, but they lacked the skills and capabilities to work effectively as a team. They didn't have effective processes for generating leads and qualifying prospects, for creating client proposals, and for tracking all of this information. They lacked effective means of identifying and communicating plans and objectives, assigning resources, and measuring progress. The company was a body, but it functioned in a sub-optimal manner because it needed a tune-up. The sub-optimal functioning had led team members and managers to the belief that their morale was low. However, it was really a question of creating greater cohesion so that the *esprit de corps* and morale could be exploited to the fullest. On the other hand, the inability to operate effectively did undermine the mood in the company, and there was a temporary attitude of exasperation with the lack of progress in bringing in new business.

Brilliant Manoeuvre

There is a need for nuance and understanding of all the components that go into making a strong organization where everyone can perform at their peak, are fully motivated and engaged, and where there is satisfaction and the feeling of being part of something special.

Figure 9.1: Components of Group Dynamics

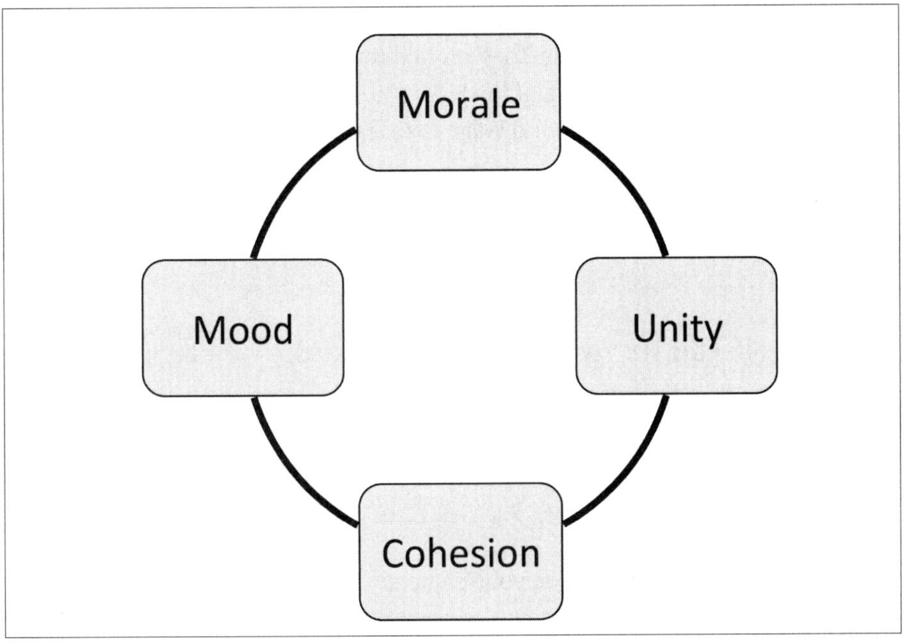

Morale

Mood

Unity

Cohesion

This example shows that it is risky to put all organizational and cultural issues under the umbrella of poor morale. There is a need for nuance and understanding of all the components that go into making a strong organization where everyone can perform at their peak, are fully motivated and engaged, and where there is satisfaction and the feeling of being part of something special. Military wisdom makes a distinction between four interacting factors that are often just subsumed under morale. These are morale proper, the sense of unity, cohesion, and mood. None of these components of group dynamics can be viewed in isolation as they are all related, and function as a whole to create well-functioning teams and organizations. This is illustrated in Figure 9.1, and we will explore each of its elements in turn.

Morale

Morale is the willingness of an individual, a team, or an organization to win and to succeed. There is a relationship to other personal and group factors such as mood, but it is a different beast. Morale is best described as a grim determination to soldier on despite hardships, obstacles, and failures. When morale is high, organizations and individuals keep focusing on a positive outcome. There is a hope and, even, an expectation that final victory and success will be attained. Thus, morale can survive even in the presence of a temporary mood of discouragement. However, if an atmosphere of defeat persists, then morale can quickly deteriorate to the point where only an extraordinary act of leadership or luck can pull it up again. This is what we saw with the Second World War examples and the experiences of my friend Norm.

Brilliant Manoeuvre

Morale can survive even in the presence of a temporary mood of discouragement.

How is the morale in your organization?

- Do you sense that people in your company have hope? Is the language they use optimistic and hopeful, or pessimistic and despairing?
- Are people making plans for the future with themselves in the plans, or are they instead making plans to abandon ship?
- Do people have a lot of idle time, or are they working on ways to continually improve the organization and its performance?

Unity

Unity is the willingness to subordinate individual goals to those of the team, group, or organization. In the military, unity is often referred to as 'esprit de corps,' French for 'spirit of oneness,' or 'sense of unity.' To function as a coherent unit, the members of an organization must subordinate their goals and aspirations to those of the whole. Individuals can draw motivation and satisfaction from their role in a team or organization, but it is the latter's good that should come first. Individuals must have unity of purpose and a sense of belonging to something that is both greater and more powerful than themselves as individuals.

Brilliant Manoeuvre

Unity is the willingness to subordinate individual goals to those of the team, group, or organization.

How united is your organization?

- Is your organization or team riven by unhealthy conflict and competition, or is there a healthy rivalry and exchange of different viewpoints?
- Is everyone aware of the mission, vision, goals, and plans of the organization? Do they know what they are doing and why they are doing it? Have they conducted their mission analysis and planning to know how they fit into the greater scheme of things?
- Is everyone pulling in the same direction, or is there useless competition for resources and senior management attention?
- Do people believe in your mission and vision? Do they live the values of your organization or merely pay lip service to them?

Cohesion

Cohesion is the ability to function as an organic whole, as a well-oiled machine. Whether you prefer a biological metaphor or a mechanistic one, cohesion is literally the glue that holds the team or organization together in a dynamic equilibrium. Well-led military units in combat are highly cohesive, usually characterized as having strong *unity of purpose*. Poorly-led units usually suffer poor cohesion and have low unity. When this happens, units often disintegrate. A non-virtuous cycle of poor morale and even lower cohesion ensue. Consequently, military commanders zealously guard the morale and cohesion of their units, lest they fall apart under the strain of combat. Most of the principles and techniques discussed in this book are designed to improve the cohesion of business organizations and teams, so they can perform at their peak in as many situations as possible.

Brilliant Manoeuvre

Cohesion is the ability to function as an organic whole, as a well-oiled machine.

How cohesive is your organization?

- When is the last time you spoke to your whole team, to tell them what is happening and why it's happening?
- Are things in your company managed consistently in an ad hoc manner, or is there deliberate analysis and planning prior to making decisions and executing them?
- Do you follow set procedures for communicating objectives and measuring progress in achieving them?
- Do you conduct regular meetings to talk about strategy and tactics, and to solve real problems that will get you closer to your goals?
- Do people feel free to come forward with suggestions to improve performance, or do they expect those above them in the hierarchy to solve all their problems for them?
- Do people know what is expected of them? Do they know the mission and vision of the organization? Do they know the objectives and performance metrics? Have they conducted their own mission analysis and planning, so they know how they fit into the bigger scheme of things?

Mood

Just because people are complaining doesn't mean that they have bad morale. In fact, the opposite is often quite true. If they stop talking, that's when you should be worried. One of the factors that can lead to a bad mood is poor leadership by the organization's executives, especially a belief that they don't have the welfare of members at heart. Another factor that can contribute to a poor mood in an organization is an insufficient amount of work. It's like the old expression, "Idle hands make the Devil's work." In other words, when people have too few things to do or to keep them busy, they easily fall prey to troublemakers or even just rumour mongers. In the military, there is a type of soldier called the 'barrack room lawyer.' This is someone who fancies himself an expert in all the rules, and encourages others to contest the authority of officers and NCOs. The less there is to do for people, the more these people can have the run of the place. This is why experienced military commanders always keep their troops busy, if not in operations, then at least through constant training and retraining. Not only does this produce more cohesion and unity when it is needed, thus contributing to strong morale, but it also prevents the deterioration in mood that often accompanies idleness and boredom. The example of the small, family business I gave above shows that it was mood that was the issue, not necessarily morale, although the two are obviously linked.

Brilliant Manoeuvre

Just because people are complaining doesn't mean that they have bad morale. In fact, the opposite is often quite true. If they stop talking, that's when you should be worried.

How is the mood in your organization?

- Are people happy to be working together? Do they joke around or are they morose?
- Do people complain a lot in your organization? What do they complain about? Do they complain about superficial things and minor creature comforts, or are they more focused on substantial issues?
- Do people feel free to approach management with issues, or do they let them fester and lead to grievances?
- Are people making suggestions to improve things as a whole, so the company can achieve its mission and goals, or are they focused on improving things for themselves?
- Is there a major discrepancy in perks and privileges between executives and the rank and file of the organization? Large differences in this regard can breed resentment and anger in employees and lower level managers.

Faith in the Mission and Vision

Although I served in Bosnia after the end of the civil war, helping to enforce the Dayton Peace Accords, I knew many who did serve during the war. Many of my own soldiers and NCOs had experienced the difficulties of the UN missions between 1992 and 1995. One of the things that struck me, both with those who had served there during the fighting, and during my own deployment there in 1999-2000, is how much we all believed in the mission and the vision for Bosnia. We felt it was important to provide protection and succour to those who were in need. We also felt deep in our bones that the former belligerents, in the case of my sector, the Bosnian Croat militia known as the HVO, had to be kept in check. I was willing to do everything in my power to do so, even to the point of engaging in combat with them if they tried anything against the Serbs who were attempting to return to my sector to live in peace. In fact, I was surprised on several occasions during my tour at my own willingness to fight. I also observed the same beliefs and determination in my officers, NCOs, and soldiers, as well as my colleagues in other units. In other words, we all believed deeply in our mission, and were committed to executing it to the best of our abilities. The same faith in the mission and the purpose of military actions is present in Afghanistan amongst the troops having to serve there. Whenever we hear from American soldiers who have served in Iraq, we hear the same conviction in the basic goodness of the mission. Whatever else we may think of all these military operations, whether peacekeeping, counter-insurgency, or outright war, there can be no doubt that a deeply held conviction of the rightness and justice of the mission are at the base of the morale of military forces.

Peter Drucker said that the basis of any organization's mission statement is the passion that people in the organization have for helping their clientele. In fact, Drucker defined the mission of an organization as the intersection of market need, competence, and passion. Without that passion and willingness to meet the needs of customers and other stakeholders, it is extremely difficult to sustain the motivation and drive to succeed over the long term. This is especially true in business. You have to believe that you can provide outstanding value to your customers. There is a common belief that entrepreneurs go into business in order to earn profits but in my experience, this is usually not the case. Yes, profits are needed to grow and invest in the business. They also represent a gauge of success in achieving goals. However, the ultimate aim of a business is, as Drucker would say, to serve a customer. The better that customer is served, the greater the chances that the company will see its revenues grow, and its profits along with them.

Brilliant Manoeuvre

The mission of an organization is the intersection of market need, competence, and passion.

In their survey of highly successful companies, *Built to Last*, Jim Collins and Jerry Porras found that one of the key ingredients of visionary companies, ones that have had a long run of success, is that they have a purpose beyond just earning money. As they put it: "Profitability is a necessary condition for existence and a means to more important ends, but it is not the end in itself for many of the visionary companies. Profit is like oxygen, food, water, and blood for the body; they are not the point of life, but without them, there is no life." (p. 55 in the Collins Business Essentials edition, 2002)

The story we saw above about my friend Norm and the bio-diesel manufacturer is a case in point. The company did not have profits for many years, but the owners were able to find investors, and keep the company's employees engaged because they fully believed in the vision of producing bio-diesel using their proprietary process. They were able to demonstrate that the market would eventually develop, and that they would have a highly attractive solution to meet the need. Moreover, they felt that it was only a matter of time before market conditions and government regulations evolved in such a way that they would have an advantage against bio-diesel manufacturers that used other processes and ingredients. The owner had to rally the troops often because the situation was indeed precarious.

Metaphors and other forms of imagery are extremely effective at conveying a new vision and mission, a purpose for an organization. When General Rick Hillier became Canada's Chief of the Defence Staff in February 2005, he convinced then-Prime Minister, Paul Martin, that he had a compelling vision for the roles and purpose of the Canadian Armed Forces. He chose to rally the troops to his new vision of highly deployable and flexible military forces for Canada by creating an image. He said that during the Cold War, Canada and its allies in NATO had been structured, trained, and equipped to fight the Soviet bear. This made the job of identifying threats and reacting to them very easy. Everyone knew who the enemy was, and he was big and loud and very threatening. It was relatively easy to motivate people to see the threat, and to do something to counter it. However, with the end of the Cold War, the world went from basically two camps, US-led NATO and the other Western countries against the Soviet Union and its Warsaw Pact allies during the Cold War, to the realities of a multipolar world. What's more, the threat of global nuclear war having lessened considerably, and with Russia being weak through most of the 1990s, created opportunities for military adventurism and civil war that had been kept under wraps during the Cold War. The paradigmatic struggles in the 1990s were in the former Yugoslavia, Rwanda, and Somalia. After 9/11, the front switched to Afghanistan, but the struggles were very similar. General Hillier invoked the image of a bundle of poisonous snakes. The threat was no longer monolithic and large, but rather a large number of smaller threats who were willing to do whatever it might take to achieve their political and social objectives. By creating powerful metaphors and images, General Hillier was able to communicate a fundamental change in mission and a vision to all ranks of the military and, perhaps more critically, to politicians, the media, and the public. In the Cold War, Canada and its allies were focused on the Soviet Bear. In the post-9/11 world, the focus was on the snakes, with everything that implied in terms of new structures, organizations, and equipment.

Brilliant Manoeuvre

Metaphors and other forms of imagery are extremely effective at conveying a new vision and mission, a purpose for an organization.

We rarely hear business leaders use such powerful metaphors to communicate their company's mission or vision, much less a change or evolution in that purpose. Instead, they repeat mantras about profitability and hitting targets. Many company missions are vapid statements that could apply to many other companies as well. Moreover, many company visions make motherhood statements such as "employees are our most important asset," and that the company is a "forward-looking and innovative place to work and grow." The problem with these is that they are usually artificial and superficial, having been arrived at through a process of 'fill in the blanks.'

In *Built to Last*, Collins and Porras recount how all of the visionary companies they studied had highly original and deeply held beliefs and values. The companies' founders and leaders also felt they were on a mission to help the world, and this was communicated and believed by all the rank and file. They contrast Sony, which at the time the book was published in 1994 was the world leader in consumer electronics and entertainment technology, with Kenwood. Sony had an ideology called the "Sony Pioneer Spirit." It started thus (*Built to Last*, p. 51), "Sony is a pioneer and never intends to follow others." The image of a pioneer, heading out into the wilderness to tame and colonize new lands is a powerful metaphor for how Sony's founder, Akio Morita, viewed the company. Compare this to their experience with Kenwood. Collins and Porras could find no evidence of any ideology or fundamental purpose or vision for the latter company beyond the usual financial objectives and strategy statements in annual reports. Sony has been much more successful over the years than Kenwood, although it has been facing many challenges in recent years.

Brilliant Manoeuvre

Many company missions are vapid statements that could apply to many other companies as well. Moreover, many company visions make motherhood statements such as "employees are our most important asset," and that the company is a "forward-looking and innovative place to work and grow."

This type of faith in the purpose of a company is, once again, exemplified in Apple Inc. Steve Jobs was fond of saying that Apple was at the intersection of technology and art. This is why every new product that Apple imagines, as we have argued earlier, has panache and a unique design philosophy. Everything in the company is oriented to producing beautifully designed and highly functional devices that work with a minimum of fuss and that are fun to use. The metaphor of being at the crossroads between technology and art powerfully conveys the idea that one doesn't have to be sacrificed to the other. You can have extremely powerful electronic devices incorporating the latest technology without them looking like a clunky box with mysterious appendages and cavities. Conversely, the artfulness of design isn't at the expense of technological capability and functionality. Beyond this metaphor of the crossroads, moreover, even the name and logo of the company evoke archetypal imagery. The apple is the biblical symbol of knowledge, also the forbidden fruit, but someone indeed has taken a bite out of it. What Apple is telling us is that what life is all about, and that you have to take a bite out of life. With these kinds of images and metaphors, Jobs created an ideology and purpose that transcends any particular technology, device, market, or application. Moreover, this ideology resonates not only with employees, but also with customers and competitors. The brand, ideology, vision, and mission are all one entity expressing the purpose of Apple.

Building Faith in Your Company's Purpose

- What are your company or organization's mission and vision?
- Have you articulated your values and deeply held beliefs, that is, your ideology?
- Does everyone in your company adhere to this purpose? Can they express it in their own words to themselves, their colleagues, and their customers?
- Is there passion for this purpose? Do people come to work excited to find new ways to serve the company's customers according to this purpose?
- Do you use strong imagery and metaphors to convey this ideology or purpose, or the mission and vision?
- Take the time to articulate your purpose using a metaphor or image. Start to communicate it to your entourage, your subordinates, your colleagues, and your customers.

We All Need to Belong to Something Bigger than Ourselves

There is a story, possibly apocryphal, about a visit by President John F. Kennedy to one of NASA's facilities where important work was being done on the Apollo moon-landing program. Kennedy supposedly goes up to a janitor, and asks him what he does; the janitor leans on his broom and answers, "Why, I'm helping to send a rocket ship to the moon, Sir!" As I said, it's possibly apocryphal, but it conveys, nonetheless, the idea that whoever we are, and whatever our role in an organization, we have a deep-seated need to feel a part of something greater than ourselves. In fact, the bigger and greater, the better. When we are part of a great undertaking, we feel we can achieve things we wouldn't have thought possible otherwise. This also creates cohesion and unity of purpose, as well as strong morale and the resolve to work through obstacles and difficulties. Everyone in the organization, from the chief executive to the line worker, is involved in achieving the overarching goal. They also know what role they have to play, even though it may appear relatively unimportant or tangential to the main mission.

Brilliant Manoeuvre

We have a deep-seated need to feel a part of something greater than ourselves. In fact, the bigger and greater, the better.

In Chapter 4, we saw how selection and maintenance of the right aim is crucial to achieving overall success. We also saw that this overarching goal must be broken down into successively smaller pieces so that everyone knows what is expected of them, and how they can contribute to its accomplishment. This philosophy of mission command harnesses the creativity and initiative of as many people as possible, so they can contribute their particular strengths and competencies to the team. In a nutshell, you tell people the ultimate objective, and give them the parameters within which they are to work, and then you let them figure out the best ways to get to where you want to go.

Most of the time, though, the goals aren't monumental in scope. Finding a way to send men to the moon, and bring them back safely, is pretty extreme as goals go. During the Second World War, there was a clear goal: defeat Germany, Japan, and Italy. Such undertakings only come along once every 40 or 50 years. Moreover, these are national goals, intended to motivate an entire society. A business can be confronted with a major financial crisis, and this can be enough to rally everyone for a while, at least. However, you don't want to wait until you're at the brink of failure to rally the troops around a life or death undertaking. The key is to create an overarching vision for the future of the organization that will give direction, while not being too unrealistic so as to discourage everyone at the first signs of difficulty. Competition, changing customer needs, evolving technology, and all the other changing factors of the company's environment provide the incentive to constantly reinvent what a company does to serve its customers, and how it does this. Therefore, there should be no lack of goals and incentives to keep people moving forward, to get them engaged and committed to the growth and prosperity of the company. But they do need to be articulated.

Tell people the ultimate objective, and give them the parameters within which they are to work, and then you let them figure out the best ways to get to where you want to go.

An important aspect of being part of something great is also the need to be part of a team. Humans are inherently social animals, and they function at their optimum when they are working together to achieve their aims. The military has recognized this from time immemorial, and this has been translated into a universal, hierarchical structure that has stood the test of time. The names may have changed, but the basic structure of squad, platoon, company, battalion, and brigade has existed since Roman times. The idea is that there is a maximum span of control that any one leader can have, usually eight to ten people, the basic squad of soldiers. To create larger units, you have to start combining them into organizations with multiples of the lower level. Thus, a platoon consists of three squads, a company is made up of three platoons, and so on. This also ensures that there is leadership at every level of the organization. Most types of organizations have adopted this typical, hierarchical organization structure, and it isn't just a case of wanting to imitate army structures. It's deeply rooted in human evolution. Anthropologists have discovered that hunter-gatherer peoples have always been organized into bands of approximately 30 people, which are in turn part of larger groups of approximately 500 people. A platoon is about 30 people, and a battalion is usually between 500 and a thousand people. So these aren't just arbitrary groupings. There is obviously a natural reason for these structures. The military may have reproduced them because of the intense needs of survival and camaraderie in combat.

The lesson here is that it is crucial to create these types of teams, notwithstanding theoretical models which encourage businesses to 'flatten the organization' by eliminating intermediate levels of structure, or creating 'self-organized' structures and other supposedly non-hierarchical organizations. The problem with these approaches is that people get lost in a sea of other people, with very little structure and guidance. People need to be part of groups and teams. If you don't create them deliberately according to what you're trying to achieve, then they will form spontaneously. Some may see this as a good way to proceed, but they may not like the results it generates. With a hierarchical structure, you can also create a hierarchy of goals and plans, as we saw in Chapter 4. This ties the work and effort of everyone in the organization to its overarching goals. You might be able to generate unity of purpose and cohesion in flattened structures, but it might only be happenstance or, in fact, informal and temporary.

Brilliant Manoeuvre

If you don't create teams deliberately according to what you're trying to achieve, then they will form spontaneously, and you may not like the results.

One thing that tends to happen if you let people just gravitate together is that like tends to attract like. 'A-teamers' congregate, as do 'B-teamers' and so on down the line. Just creating teams of high performers, or allowing them to form spontaneously, doesn't always lead to great results. We can just look at professional sports teams that are made up of free agent stars without any team spirit or cohesion. They usually get beaten by more balanced teams that only have a few star players but also many other types of players. The military has traditionally gotten around this problem by creating balanced units with a mix of types. This is because an army is only as good as its average units. If you take all of the best soldiers and put them in elite units, you end up with a few units of high performers, and a lot of units of average and under-performers, unleavened by any stars. This reduces flexibility and tends to undermine the morale of normal line units.

All militaries have elite units, but it is a myth that they are made up exclusively of high performers. The common element in elite units isn't so much the raw talent and ability of their members but rather their motivation, and the fact that they are all seeking extreme challenges. We can call them high performers if we want, but the reality is that it is more a question of physical and personality type than relative performance. I have personally known and seen individuals of all types in all types of military unit. Skimming the top performers off the top of all the units and putting them into one elite unit is not the solution to an organization's problems. In fact, it would probably exacerbate them, for the same reasons that a sports team made up of all stars isn't necessarily the best and most balanced team.

On the other hand, creating elite or special teams within an organization to carry out special missions or functions, and then asking for volunteers, does make sense. In business, this can be done through the creation of a 'skunk works' team. This is a group that is given a special mission, usually to solve a highly complex problem, then given resources and hived off to work separately from the main organization. Lockheed Aircraft was able to create a number of successful aircraft designs over the years by putting together special teams of designers and engineers apart from everyone else. They created the F-104 Starfighter interceptor and the SR-71 Blackbird strategic reconnaissance plane in this way. For these teams to work, they must have goals that are different or highly specialized from the rest of the organization. It helps if the problems they address are particularly thorny, or if there is a severe time limit to respect. This creates a challenging environment to which volunteers can be attracted. The volunteers won't necessarily be the people with the highest performance or potential in normal circumstances, but they will likely be well adapted to the needs of the 'skunk works' team. The advantage here is that mavericks and people with unusual talents will also have a unique role and place in the organization to stretch and reach their full potential. This is excellent for morale and leverages the unique characteristics of more types of people.

Creating Something Bigger than Ourselves

- What are your organization's goals? Are they monumental in scope, or more mundane?
- Do all the members of your organization know what team they are part of? Do they have a clear chain of command?
- Are your teams balanced in terms of talents, skills, and personality? If not, could you make them more balanced?
- Are your people allowed to gravitate into teams or do you deliberately create them?

True Motivation and Discipline Come from Within

You can't motivate someone else. True motivation comes from within oneself. It is an impulse to action, a motor. Motivation is linked to discipline, in that all discipline is fundamentally voluntary in nature. You read that correctly. In the final analysis, discipline cannot be imposed from without, but rather must come from within the person. Etymologically, discipline is a body of learning, a doctrine. It is related to the word 'disciple,' which is a follower of a teacher or body of learning. In other words, discipline is followership, and you can only follow someone for any length of time if you have an interest in doing so.

Brilliant Manoeuvre

Discipline cannot be imposed from without, but rather must come from within the person.

I have lived this relationship between discipline and motivation myself, as an officer in command of troops. As I mentioned earlier, I learned at a certain point in my military career that there can be a bad mood in an organization, with complaining and griping, but that it doesn't necessarily indicate the level of morale. This is because they are related to two different types of influencers. Morale is the ultimate expression of motivation in the face of adversity, the willingness to fight and continue the struggle no matter what sacrifices must be made, the risk, and the level of discomfort. To achieve that level of motivation, there must be a very strong motivator that acts as an attractor for people in an organization. On the other hand, the mood in an organization tends to be much more dependent on external influences, such as creature comforts, pay, access to food and drink, rest, recuperation, and recreation. Students of organizational psychology will recognize the basic elements of Frederick Herzberg's two-factor theory of motivation, as described in his book *The Motivation to Work* first published in 1959, co-written with Bernard Mausner and Barbara Bloch Snyderman. Herzberg and his associates conducted a series of experiments and surveys in various work settings to discover that factors governing working conditions external to the person, what he called 'hygiene factors,' tended to be related closely to the mood in the group, and had a short-term impact.

For instance, if you increase someone's pay, that person's work satisfaction rises quickly, but then it fades quickly and reverts to what it was previous to the pay rise. On the other hand, if you increase the inherent satisfaction of the work, or make it more interesting and challenging, then the rise in satisfaction is more deeply felt and also persists as long as the person feels more engaged and challenged in the work. This is exactly what I observed over my military career. The true motivators for soldiers are the challenge and difficulty of the job, the chance for learning and progressive development, and the ability to work in a team environment where everyone is pulling in the same direction. Time and again, soldiers would tell me that their motivation for joining the military, and remaining for a career was the possibility of challenging work and advancement, meaning personal development and the recognition that comes with promotion and increasing responsibilities.

Brilliant Manoeuvre

Large discrepancies in welfare and creature comforts among elements within an organization lead to a lot of griping and a sour mood.

Conversely, hygiene factors—the military uses the term 'welfare'—are clearly secondary in determining work satisfaction and motivation. No one joins the military expecting to get rich, but they do expect a decent level of pay and benefits. Napoleon said that "an army marches on its stomach," and meals tend to be the high point of the day for soldiers, especially on deployed operations. On the other hand, this is clearly a short-term, creature comfort. If there is a compelling reason or a challenging and difficult mission, soldiers will put up with considerable disruption to normal creature comforts because they realize the necessity and gravity of the situation. If there is no apparent reason for skimping on welfare amenities, however, that is when the griping starts. If there are large discrepancies in welfare and creature comforts among units or among elements within a unit, this tends to lead to a lot of griping and sour mood. If the officers have a lot more comfort than the soldiers and NCOs, then it is even worse. Soldiers will accept these differences, within limits, but if their superiors are treated royally while they have little, or even worse, if their superiors are relatively safe while they are exposed to danger, then it is likely that the mood will deteriorate to the point of insubordination.

The relationships between hygiene factors, motivators, and the various elements of group and interpersonal dynamics in an organization or team are illustrated in Figure 8.2 on the next page. What we see is that hygiene factors tend to have a temporary effect, mostly on the mood of people in an organization. Various elements of welfare, such as quality and availability of food, pay, health and the overall safety and quality of the workplace play a role in how soldiers or anyone in any organization for that matter view their surroundings. These exert a push on people. In other words, they are an external form of influence that pushes people to behave in a certain way. Interestingly, punishment and rewards are also forms of external influence that are based on hygiene factors. Material and physical rewards and punishments can influence people in a certain way, but the effects tend to wear off relatively quickly. This is why what people tend to consider traditional forms of discipline are actually fairly inadequate to motivate people. They come from outside the person affected. They may have an effect, but it is only on external factors. They can make people angry and resentful and, when they are administered differentially, they tend to

Figure 9.2:Intrinsic vs. Extrinsic Motivation

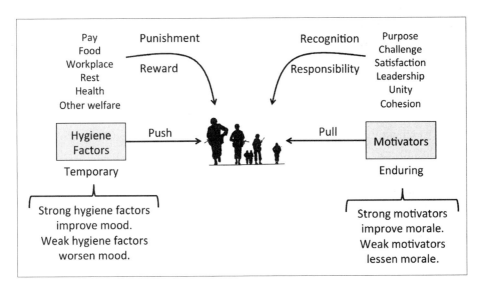

undermine cohesion, unity and, occasionally, morale. Conversely, motivators are those moral factors that work on deep motivation of individuals, from within individuals. Motivator is related to motor, and a motor is inside the vehicle, not outside it. Motivators exert a pull on individuals, and they are drawn to excel and perform together as a cohesive body to achieve their collective purpose. Factors such as purpose, challenge, satisfaction, cohesion, and unity interact to create strong motivation, and these, in turn, lead to a willingness to persevere in the face of difficulty and adversity, what we call, in the final analysis, morale.

Brilliant Manoeuvre

Material and physical rewards and punishments can influence people in a certain way, but the effects tend to wear off relatively quickly. Purpose, challenge, satisfaction, cohesion, and unity interact to create strong motivation.

This leads us finally to the assertion by Drucker quoted in the opening to this chapter: "What we need is to replace the externally imposed spur of fear with an internal self-motivation for performance. Responsibility—not satisfaction—is the only thing that will serve." Drucker was pointing out that fear (i.e., punishment and reward) and other external, hygiene factors are not sufficient motivation to perform in a sustained manner. Only motivation from within individuals, what he calls responsibility, will serve the purpose of impelling people to perform well over the long term. Also, his use of the term satisfaction can be taken to mean external satisfaction, for instance, the satisfaction that comes after a fine meal, rather than the deep, internal satisfaction that results from taking on a challenge and a job well done.

The military philosophy of mission command is designed to create this type of intrinsic motivation and responsibility. When people truly believe in the purpose, mission and vision of the organization, and that they can participate and be responsible for outcomes by using their initiative to find ways of achieving the goals, then they will have strong work motivation, cohesion and unity will be high, and morale and resilience in the face of adversity will be strong.

How Is Motivation and Discipline in Your Organization?

- Are people motivated to perform by intrinsic motivators such as the mission and vision, challenge, and morale and cohesion of the organization? Or, are they motivated by external, hygiene factors?
- Do you take care of your people? Do they have the creature comforts they need? Would they be able to function in an emergency situation without worrying about their safety, security, and welfare?
- Does your organization function by punishment and reward, or by recognition and responsibility?
- Is there a true spirit of cooperation and mission command in your organization, or are people expected to do as they are told, and nothing more?

Summary

- The moral plane of business is just as important as the rational and material planes. This is because business is a human undertaking; moreover, one that requires the cooperation, cohesion, and unity of purpose of groups of people under strong leadership.
- The real test of morale is adversity. You only know the mettle of your people, your organization, and yourself as a leader when you are facing difficulties and obstacles. There is nothing better for morale than

winning, but it is what you do when you're failing that determines your true level of morale.

- People often confuse morale and mood. Morale is the determination to fight until final victory. It is the will to persevere despite obstacles, opposition, and adversity. It is linked to factors such as group mood, cohesion, and unity, and it is strongly influenced by the quality of leadership.

- Mood on the other hand, is the collective attitude and tone of everyone in the organization. Mood can be influenced by the objective performance of the organization and the morale of the group, but it is possible for an organization to have a bad mood, yet still be determined to persevere and fight until final victory. In other words, you can be in a bad mood, but still have high morale.

- Cohesion is the degree of structure and organization of a group. It is the glue that holds the group together to achieve things collectively. It depends on collective competencies and processes, and is revealed in the ability to perform efficiently and effectively, to get things done.

- Organizations need unity of purpose to ensure that individuals subsume—or, at least, align—their personal goals and interests to those of the greater whole.

- All people need to feel part of something bigger than themselves. The hierarchical structure of organizations is intended to harness this sense and need for belonging to the achievement of objectives. The greater the purpose, the more people will sense that they belong to something bigger than themselves.

- Metaphors and other forms of imagery are essential to convey a sense of uniqueness, purpose, and destiny, so that people understand the message of the mission and vision, and feel special.

- Real motivation tends to come from within people, and discipline is essentially a voluntary act. The mood of a group is dependent on external influencers, called hygiene factors, which impact the welfare of people in the organization. The changes from external factors are ephemeral.

- The ultimate motivation comes providing a compelling vision and mission, intrinsically satisfying work, in a cohesive and united team. These factors have a lasting impact on the morale and performance of a team.

Chapter 10

Follow Me: The Art of Leadership

Leadership is the art of getting someone else to do something you want done because he wants to do it.

General Dwight D. Eisenhower

No leader should put troops into the field merely to gratify his spleen; no leader should fight a battle simply out of pique. But a kingdom that has once been destroyed can never come again into being; nor can the dead ever be brought back to life. Hence the enlightened leader is heedful, and the good leader full of caution.

Sun Tzu

Leadership is lifting a person's vision to higher sights, the raising of a person's performance to a higher standard, the building of a personality beyond its normal limitations.

Peter Drucker, The Practice of Management

Leadership is needed in all aspects of military and business life to get things done. It is required to formulate a vision and mission, select priorities and objectives, make decisions, create plans, give direction, and influence others to implement all of these. Leadership is weaved into the very fabric of military wisdom, from the bottom up and the top down. So, why wait until the last chapter to talk about it? The main reason is that military leadership, like business leadership, is built on a framework of technical and professional competence and knowledge. Yes, leadership is needed to implement these skills, but the converse is also true; these skills and competencies are needed to be a truly effective and inspiring leader. We needed the previous chapters to describe the basic skills, techniques, and knowledge before tying everything together with a discussion of leadership.

The military definition of leadership is the art of influencing others to accomplish a mission. Leadership is fundamental to military effectiveness because it is based on competence, on the ability to get things done, and to get them done right with the right people and resources at the right time and place. You can't just guess your way to military success, and you can't fake your way through military command—even if it has been tried to no avail. It is the same in business. To be an inspiring and effective leader, you have to produce results both for yourself and for others. The core of competence and performance is what attracts followers, and gives confidence to superiors, subordinates, peers, investors, and customers that you can get the job done in a timely, efficient, and effective manner.

Exploring the Art of Leadership

- **Competence is the heart of leadership.** Truly effective leaders, leaders who are inspiring and visionary, have the means and will to balance style and substance effectively. They realize that leadership is based on substance, i.e. competence, but effective leaders also need a personal style and attention to people.

- **Transformational leadership leads to exceptional performance.** Traditional forms of transactional leadership based on conditional rewards and punishments are no longer effective to generate the performance needed in today's world, whether in business or any other field. Leaders must transform how their followers see themselves, the world, their organization, and what they can achieve as individuals and as groups.

- **Leadership must be ethical.** Leadership and ethics are really two sides of the same coin. A leader must be worthy of followers' loyalty, confidence, and respect. Superiors, peers, and the wider society that is served by the organization must also believe in leaders. Ethics

There are ten principles of military leadership that
anyone can use. Military forces around the world
have developed lists of leadership principles to guide
their officers, non-commissioned officers (NCOs, for
example sergeants and corporals), and soldiers at all
ranks and levels of responsibility and authority. Leaders
and managers in all fields, and especially in business,
can use these same principles to diagnose, teach, and
improve leadership, both their own and that of their
followers and colleagues.

Competence Is the Heart of Leadership

The requirement for professional competence was brought home to me early in my
military career. I was assigned command of an infantry platoon of about 30 men,
including four NCOs. The truth, though, was that I was not particularly effective
at the beginning of my career. I didn't follow the procedures I had learned and,
consequently, my decisions, plans, and orders were not clear and convincing to my
subordinates. One day while we were on exercise, my second-in-command sat me
right down, and gave me the 'what-for.' This is one of the many advantages of the
military system of command, where an older and experienced NCO provides advice
and backing to a young officer even if the former is his subordinate. He told me I
wasn't using the knowledge and skills I had been trained to employ in leading my
platoon. He reminded me that I was the tactical expert in the platoon, and that
my job was to create effective tactical plans and to give clear and cogent orders
to the platoon. In other words, my job was to be a competent platoon tactician,
and to command my platoon accordingly. That's what everyone expected of me. I
didn't accept his assessment at first but after a few hours, I realized he was right.
I needed to get back to basics. I took out my platoon commander's aide-mémoire
and started to create plans and orders according to correct procedures. I started
to follow what is called battle procedure. As I did so, my tactics and plans became
more effective, and my orders were more direct and clear. My NCOs and soldiers
knew what was expected of them, and how to do it. As I gained in technical and

professional proficiency, I became a more effective leader, and after a few months, I had earned the respect of my NCOs and men, as well as the confidence of my company commander. The soldiers were prepared to follow me; I had to be worthy of their loyalty, respect, and confidence.

Professional competence is also essential to be an effective leader in business. It is fundamental because people, by and large, will follow those who have a claim to leadership, but only if they obtain results. Nobody wants to follow a loser, or someone who meanders aimlessly without purpose or ability. As humans, we are inherently drawn to others who know what they want and where they are going, and who can communicate it well. We are also drawn to leaders who persevere in the face of obstacles and setbacks, and who can influence others to accomplish what they didn't think possible. Human beings have a deep-seated desire to follow, because leaders help them to achieve their own aims and to get results.

Brilliant Manoeuvre

People will follow those who have a claim to leadership, but only if they obtain results. Nobody wants to follow a loser, or someone who meanders aimlessly without purpose or ability.

We've talked a lot about Apple Inc. in this book, the driving force of which was Steve Jobs. By all accounts, Jobs was not a pleasant person. It was even harder to work for him. There was no lack of volunteers, however, who wanted to work for the company he founded and led masterfully. Why? They knew he would get them to perform in a way that they couldn't even imagine prior to working for him. He knew how to get the best out of people for his particular objectives. Steve Jobs was a great business leader and chief executive of Apple because he was a business genius. It was his professional competence that drew people to follow him, and definitely not his pleasant personality.

This question of competence is so important for leadership because it is often forgotten. Sometimes there is just too much emphasis on style over substance. In actuality, to be a truly effective leader requires both substance and style. Substance is basic, professional competence. It is the ability to get things done, to plan, to analyze, to make decisions and, most importantly, to achieve the mission. Substance is the content of leadership. Style is the way in which a leader leads. This is the interpersonal component of leadership. Someone can be a superb technician but a cold fish when it comes to inspiring, communicating intent, or learning about other people. During the 1950s and 1960s, researchers identified two basic leadership orientations: task orientation, i.e. focus on the job at hand and results; and people orientation, i.e. making sure that everyone feels part of the team, and providing personal attention to everyone. Substance in a leader is task orientation. Style is people orientation. We can say that if substance is the steak, then style is the sizzle. Sacrifice one or the other, and you don't have optimal leadership. Sacrifice both, and you have totally ineffective leadership. This is illustrated in Figure 10.1.

Figure 10.1: Style vs. Substance

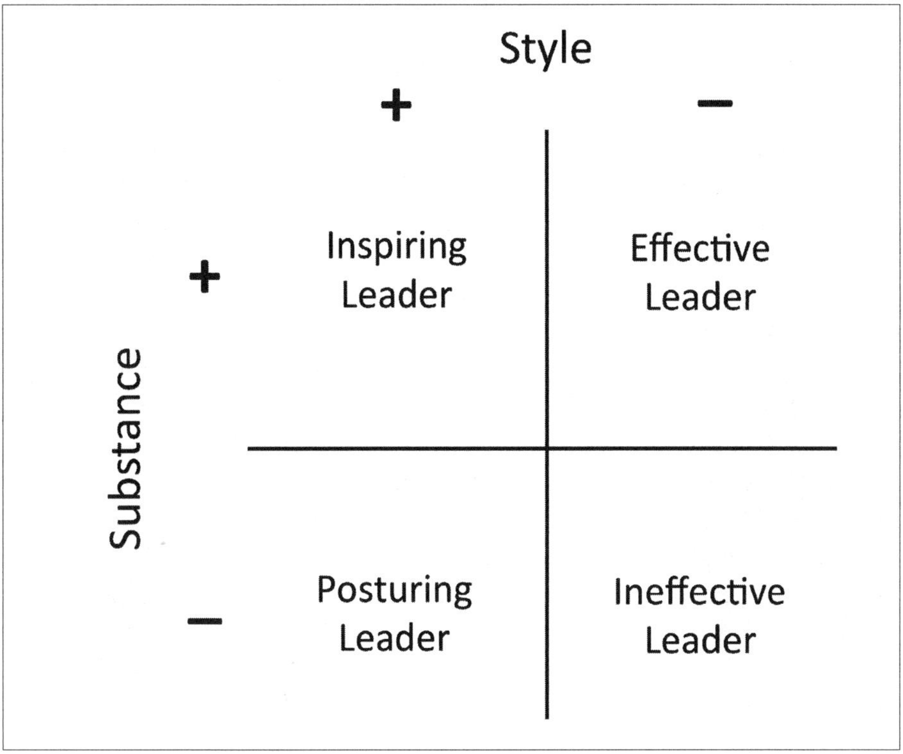

Inspiring, Visionary Leader

The inspiring or visionary leader has it all, or at least enough of both components of leadership, i.e. style and substance, to be remarkably effective. Inspiring leaders tend be respected for their competence, temperament, and influence by superiors, subordinates, and peers. They are almost always admired, and sometimes even loved by the people they lead. Inspiring leaders can be very demanding, but they are respected and followed because they draw the best from their people, both individually and as a team. This is the ideal form of leadership for most people. The inspiring leader manages to combine task and people orientations to a greater degree than most. Some inspiring leaders are downright charismatic, and most can be considered transformational to some extent. They can get their followers to perceive themselves and the world in a different way. We will explore this in more detail below when we discuss transformational leadership.

Effective Leader

The effective leader has substance but little or no style. My mentor, Alan Weiss, talks about "all steak, no sizzle," which describes these leaders. They are effective because they can get the job done, organize their team, make decisions, give direction, and follow up to ensure execution. They tend to be task-oriented in their approach to leadership and management. The most important thing is the mission and results, and people are simply one of the resources at their disposal. They can often forget about social and interpersonal niceties, but this doesn't necessarily mean that people won't be motivated to work for them. However, they will do so either out of obligation, or because they themselves are highly task-oriented. They are usually caring and compassionate leaders, even though they don't make a fuss about it. Effective leaders are usually respected by their superiors, subordinates, and peers. They are often feared or held in awe by subordinates, but this is usually attributable to hierarchy, and the fact that they don't spend a lot of time on the social aspects of leadership. The military approach to leadership development is focused on getting people to be effective leaders and, then, giving them a few tools to help them become more inspiring leaders. This is the most common military leadership style.

Posturing Leader

This is the most problematic type, because the posturing leader often misleads himself and others into believing that he is more effective than he really is. More often than not, the posturing leader is someone who has reached his level of incompetence. It's the effect of the Peter Principle: sooner or later, everyone is promoted to a level where they can't really perform adequately. Problems occur, however, when that leader still believes he's effective, or when he tries to fake it by using personality and style to compensate for a lack of professional competence and skill. There is also a type of posturing leader who is deliberately manipulative and, worse, surrounds himself with personal favourites and yes-men. This stems from poor self-worth because that leader knows that he doesn't have the competence needed for the level of responsibility he's been given. So, he compensates by insulating himself within a personal admiration society. Dictators, whether of the political or business ilk, are just posturing leaders. They are often bullies to anyone who opposes them, in addition to being incompetent.

Ineffective Leader

The ineffective leader isn't really a leader at all because he lacks both substance and style. It is included here because there are people in all organizations with this profile. We can only hope that such individuals will be detected early enough to learn the skills and knowledge to become effective leaders. Alternatively, they have to be weeded out because they may turn into posturing leaders when they see they are ineffective. Trying to find a way to climb the ladder of success, they will adopt the outer trappings of leadership, often relying heavily on punishment and rewards to get their way, or surrounding themselves with relatively competent associates, while still lacking in basic, professional competence. They can survive for a time, but sooner or later they are discovered.

Transformational Leadership Leads to Exceptional Performance

We alluded to transformational leadership in the discussion about inspiring leaders. We noted that they are often highly respected, not just for their technical proficiency and professional competence, but also for their ability to get things done, and because they have charisma, and are considered visionary. In the late 1970s, a political scientist called James MacGregor Burns described the complementary notions of transforming and transactional leadership. He developed the hypothesis that some politicians had an uncanny ability to transform the way the electorate viewed them, the polities of which they are part, and what could be accomplished collectively. He distinguished such politicians from ones who relied on a more traditional, transactional relationship with the electorate. Essentially, transactional political leaders say, "Vote for me, and I'll build a road in your county." Burns found a new way to conceptualize what people viewed as charismatic, political leadership, for good or ill, as history has shown, as well as the 'pork barrel' politician. The former is the transforming leader, whereas the latter is the transactional leader.

In the early 1980s, one of the foremost leadership researchers, Bernard Bass, started a research program into these two types of leadership.[4] A natural, first place to start was the U.S. military. Through his research, Bass confirmed Burns' intuitive understanding of transformational and transactional leadership types. He was also able to identify the components of each broad type of leadership. Transactional leadership is composed of three behavioural approaches :

- *Management by exception – passive*: The leader restricts his actions to correcting mistakes and problems when he notices them, but he is not particularly aggressive in identifying them. Most people would call this laissez-faire leadership but, in actuality, Bass identified laissez-faire as a distinct form of leadership or, rather, as an absence of leadership.
- *Management by exception – active*: The leader actively seeks out problems and mistakes to correct, but is happy to leave well enough alone. This is the philosophy of "If ain't broke, don't fix it."
- *Conditional rewards*: The leader provides rewards for a job well done, or punishments for not doing things properly or for not following direction. This is probably what most people would call punishment and reward, and psychologists call this operant conditioning. It seems to work well for rats in a lab, but isn't a good way to inspire motivation in people, as we'll see below.

Bass was also able to identify the four key factors that make for transformational leadership. Each factor represents a particular facet of this type of leadership, and they have to be viewed together as a whole. The factors are:

- *Inspirational motivation*: The degree to which a leader is able to inspire motivation in his followers through emotional, cognitive, and moral connections.
- *Idealized influence*: The degree to which a leader is viewed as a model of behaviour and performance. The ability to lead by example, obviously, is a key in this factor.
- *Intellectual stimulation*: The degree to which a leader challenges his followers to come up with novel solutions, and to apply their cognitive skills and knowledge. This is an oft-overlooked factor, but intellectual stimulation is the basis for what the military calls 'mission command,' the philosophy that espouses giving subordinates a mission and then letting them get on with it in the best way possible.

---

[4] The best source for this material is Bass, Bernard M. and Ronald E. Riggio, *Transformational Leadership*, 2nd edition, Mahwah, New Jersey and London: Lawrence Erlbaum and Associates, 2006, as well as Bass's Multi-factor Leadership Questionnaire he developed with Bruce Avolio (2004).

■ *Individualized consideration*: The degree to which a leader recognizes and develops each follower's potential by acknowledging and building on individual strengths and limitations. This also includes caring for the welfare of subordinates and followers, not just professionally, but also as people with other wants and needs in life.

Brilliant Manoeuvre

If you want extraordinary results and commitment, then you have to lead in a transformative manner, to get people to buy into a vision, and transform their relationship to it and to their work.

Transformational leaders have an uncanny ability to get others to perform in a certain way, and to do things they never would have conceived themselves doing without the leader's influence. Moreover, transformational leadership is usually presented as an alternative to transactional leadership, which emphasizes punishments and rewards as a means of influencing people. It is also interesting to note that Bass considers the first two facets of transformational leadership—inspirational motivation and idealized influence—to be the essence of what most people call charisma. In Bass's model, charismatic leadership is a subset of transformational leadership. Whether this is true in any ultimate sense or not, it is an interesting consideration, and it helps to explain why highly effective and inspiring leaders usually are viewed as charismatic.

This philosophy is represented graphically in Figure 10.2.[5] The basis of the theory is that transactional leadership, consisting of both kinds of management by exception, both active and passive, and conditional rewards and punishments, leads to a normal level of effort which, in turn, generates a normal or expected level of performance. In other words, transactional leadership leads to average results, which is what can be expected given average leadership. On the other hand, transformational leadership leads to increased motivation by subordinates and followers to achieve exceptional results, primarily by providing outstanding, additional effort toward the mission at hand. This leads to performance beyond expectations, to exceptional performance. If you want mundane results, then you can limit yourself to transactional leadership; however, if you want extraordinary

---

[5] Based on a similar diagram in Avolio, Bruce J. and Bernard M. Bass, *Multifactor Leadership Questionnaire Sampler Set: Manual, Forms and Scoring Key*, Third Edition, 2004, p. 20

results and commitment, then you have to lead in a transformative manner, to get people to buy into a vision, and transform their relationship to it and to their work.

Figure 10.2: Transformational Leadership

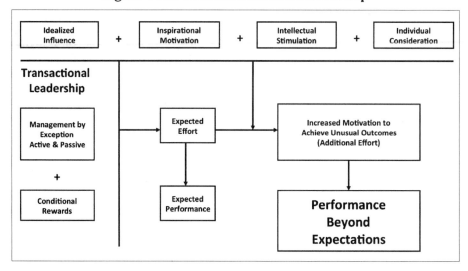

This is a fine theory, but does it really lead to performance beyond expectations, to exceptional performance? In my personal experience, I have found this to be the case, both in the military and in business. I would be surprised if readers of this book would have a different experience. However, Bass and his associates have done a lot of research to validate this model. When you combine all of the research results (through a special, statistical approach called meta-analysis), the overwhelming success of transformational leadership is evident. What is interesting is that laissez-faire leadership (actually an absence of leadership that corresponds to the ineffective leader described above) and passive management by exception are actually counter-productive. Such practices make leaders less effective. Active management by exception, and conditional rewards and punishments are moderately effective when leader and team performance are assessed objectively. On the other hand, transformational leadership, at the least, tends to add 50 per cent to a leader's effectiveness, and can even double it in extreme circumstances. Research over the years has shown that transformational leadership is highly effective in the military and other dangerous professions such as firefighting owing to the need to get people to perform beyond expectations. When facing physical danger and risk, a monetary bonus just doesn't cut it in terms of inspiration. By the same token, the fear of punishment can induce obedience in people, but everyone has a breaking point, beyond which no threat of punishment can overcome the fear of the enemy or of entering a burning building. When that happens, it is intrinsic motivation that counts, and that only comes from transformational leadership.

Brilliant Manoeuvre

Fear of punishment can induce obedience in people, but everyone has a breaking point, beyond which no threat of punishment can overcome the fear of the enemy or of entering a burning building. When that happens, it is intrinsic motivation that counts, and that only comes from transformational leadership.

This is illustrated in Figure 10.3 (next page), which shows the relationship between transactional and transformational forms of leadership, and the hygiene factors and motivators we described in Chapter 9, which cover organizational and individual morale, cohesion, and motivation.

As we can see, transactional leadership basically uses transactions on the basis of hygiene factors to get people to act or work in a certain way towards the accomplishment of a mission. It is a "you scratch my back and I'll scratch yours" approach to motivating and inspiring people, and as we saw above and in the previous chapter, it is only moderately effective and even counter-productive. This is because hygiene factors have an evanescent effect. They fade relatively quickly compared to deep-seated motivators, which impel people to act from within as a motor does. Transactional leadership is 'push' leadership: you try to push or compel people to act in a certain way. This is the classic view of military leadership and command, but it is by and large obsolescent, if not downright obsolete, at least in Western societies.

During my military career, which lasted from 1980 to 2006, I saw a definite evolution in how military discipline and leadership were interpreted and implemented. At the beginning of my career, punishment and stringent discipline were still quite common. As a young platoon commander in 1985, I had to visit the base jail when I was unit duty officer to make sure that our unit's 'delinquents' were being treated well and didn't need anything. Soldiers were regularly arrested and incarcerated for routine, disciplinary matters, such as brawling, talking back,

Figure 10.3: Leadership and Motivation

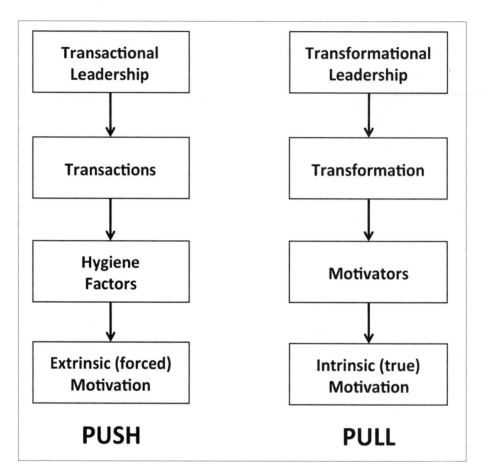

or not reporting for duty on time. By the time I was a company commander in the late 1990s, these minor incarcerations were almost unknown. Discipline was much more voluntary as described in Chapter 9, and there was a definite shift towards motivation by other hygiene factors, such as pay and benefits, but also towards the inherent rewards of military service and the need for inspirational and visionary leadership. In the early 2000s, there came the recognition of the need for transformational leadership, and that is now the fundamental leadership doctrine in most Western countries' military forces, certainly in the English-speaking world. Along with this came recognition of the efficacy of mission command as opposed to directive command. The former encourages senior officers to give mission-type orders to their subordinates, to tell them what to achieve rather than how to achieve it. Directive orders are now seen as less effective, because superiors have to give detailed instructions for them to work.

Turning to the right side of the diagram, we can see that transformational leadership aims at transforming people, how they view the situation, how they work, how they interact with each other and with their leaders, and also how they interact with and serve their customers, stakeholders, or constituencies. Where the currency of transactional leadership is transactions on the basis of extrinsic, hygiene factors, in transformational leadership, it is human transformation. This works at the level of motivators, which improve intrinsic motivation, and thus lead to performance beyond expectations. We can call this 'pull' leadership.

Leadership Must Be Ethical

It is common in Western military forces to develop in parallel the ethical and leadership capabilities of officers, NCOs, and even soldiers. This is certainly the case in the Canadian military, where leadership training at all levels includes a heavy component of ethical education and discussion. In fact, leadership and ethics are always taught together, and are seen as inseparable. There are three main reasons for this. Firstly, a leader must be an example of professional competence, good conduct, and probity to earn the full respect, loyalty, and confidence of the people under his or her responsibility. Hypocrisy and other forms of unethical behaviour tend to undermine respect. People also seem to have a sixth sense for this type of thing, and they can easily detect hypocrisy and poor ethics. The second reason that leadership and ethics are inseparable in the military is that leaders require their followers to put themselves in harm's way. Consequently, they must be able to assess the military and human dimensions of their decisions and orders. Asking others to do something that goes against human nature—to put themselves in potentially mortal danger—is inherently a moral and ethical decision, and not just a question of rational calculation. Ethics is the art of weighing the moral and psychological consequences of one's actions and decisions. Leaders in our society can be informal, but more often than not they have been vested with authority to achieve collective goals and missions. Leaders make decisions and give orders on behalf of other people, so ethics is woven into the act of leadership. Finally, the third reason that military leadership and ethics are intertwined is that military forces hold a monopoly of state-sanctioned violence along with the police. The means at their disposal can destroy people, their livelihoods, their means of sustenance, and even threaten the survival of future generations. This is a massive burden to bear, even in low intensity military operations such as peacekeeping and counter-insurgency warfare.

A leader must be an example of professional competence, good conduct, and probity to earn the full respect, loyalty, and confidence of the people under his or her responsibility.

In sum, leadership is ethical practice because people will only voluntarily follow leaders who are worthy of their respect and loyalty. Followers must have confidence in the professionalism, morality, and probity of their leaders, so they can trust them to employ them judiciously without needlessly risking their lives or livelihoods. Finally, followers are led into dangerous, collective actions with potentially enormous consequences for society. Ill-considered and immoral actions undermine the morale and morality of individuals and the organizations of which they are part, but they also undermine the morality and vitality of the societies these same organizations and individuals are meant to serve.

One means of ensuring that ethical considerations are constantly kept at the center of leadership and decision-making is to grant officially sanctioned authority only to those individuals who have proven capable of leading others at lesser levels of responsibility. The military does this extremely well since everyone must progress through the ranks. You can't expect someone to command a platoon without having experienced the command of a squad. The same goes for a company commander, a battalion commander, a brigade commander, and so on up the line. You prove you are worthy of commanding a unit exercising the appropriate leadership at that level by doing so at lower grades of the organization. This takes time and training. The process can be accelerated for the very best or during times of emergency, but the sequence must be followed for the majority. Authority and responsibility, therefore, must be constantly in balance to ensure effective leadership.

Ill-considered and immoral actions undermine the morale and morality of individuals and the organizations of which they are part, but they also undermine the morality and vitality of the societies these same organizations and individuals are meant to serve.

The other essential factor that contributes to ethical leadership is accountability. Accountability is the willingness and obligation to answer for one's decisions and actions. Personal responsibility and official authority are toothless without accountability. Accountability is built into the military discipline system. Accountability is also built into the disciplinary systems of most professional bodies. For instance, national bodies in most countries govern the practices and ethics of medical practitioners of all kinds, legal practitioners, engineers, and many others. The common element is whether the profession or practice can harm or help others directly. There is also a wider form of accountability through the criminal legal system. We can't just do what we want when we want in the manner we want. We have to answer for our actions.

The relationship between responsibility (the willingness to lead), authority (the official power to lead), and accountability (the obligation to answer for decisions and actions) is depicted in Figure 10.4. All three go together. Responsibility and authority without accountability can lead to corrupt leadership, dictatorship, and abuse of power. This can include everything from a posturing leader who abuses subordinates with the complicity of superiors and close advisors such as Lieutenant William Calley in Vietnam, who led his company in perpetrating the My Lai massacre, to the Nazi regime, wherein state-sanctioned murder and slavery ran amok. Responsibility and accountability without authority is ineffectual leadership, unsanctioned and unsupported by properly constituted bodies, either of government or the judiciary or, in business, the board of directors of a company. Finally, authority and accountability without responsibility result in ineffective, laissez-faire leadership. This usually happens in organizations or countries where punishments for mistakes, even minor ones, are disproportionate to the importance of the act supposedly being corrected or punished. This naturally leads to a culture of risk avoidance, and a docile group of yes-men and sycophants carrying out the supreme leader's every wish and whim. Witness any dictatorship, whether political or organizational.

There have been numerous, well-publicized cases of major ethical and legal wrongdoings in the business world in the last decade and more. Enron, WorldCom, and other companies have gone under because of the questionable ethical and professional practices of CEOs and their immediate collaborators. It need not always be at the highest levels of an organization. Barings Bank, one of the oldest and most esteemed investment banks in the UK went broke because of the questionable dealings of a fairly low-level trader, Nick Leeson. Even Steve Jobs and Apple came under deserved critical scrutiny for the backdating of stock options for

Figure 10.4: Balance in Leadership

Jobs. If the company had been less of a darling of the public, the issue might have been resolved with greater legal and civil consequences for all concerned.

Leaders give the ethical tone to an organization by their own ethics. If these are questionable, they will soon undermine morale, and permeate the organization at every level, producing perverse results in individual and collective behaviour. I once worked with an NCO who would frequently say, "Organizations run the way they are led." If the boss is a crook, or even if he just arrogates a bit of questionable privileges to himself and his closest advisors, soon that will be the culture of the company. If, however, the CEO is just and ethical in deciding and acting, then this will percolate throughout the company, and become part of its culture of leadership and accountability.

Brilliant Manoeuvre

Leaders give the ethical tone to an organization by their own ethics.

I don't claim that the military is perfect in regard to ethical leadership. A cursory study of military history, even very recent, will reveal no lack of ethical and professional blunders by military commanders of all ranks. The difference though between the military and other walks of life is that the consequences of error and mismanagement are that much greater in war and other types of military operations. Soldiers can be killed as well as civilians. Wars can erupt because of military errors. To illustrate, the greatest fear during the Cold War was that an error in a missile launch sequence would cause a global, thermonuclear war.

In business, investors can lose their capital and customers can be dissatisfied, or even defrauded. These can be matters for civil litigation or criminal accusations. There are also important consequences of business mismanagement when thousands of people can be thrown out of work, left without a livelihood. This goes beyond plant closures and lost business opportunities. When Nortel Networks went bankrupt in the early 2000s, thousands of former employees saw significant portions of their pension earnings evaporate. Many, if not most of these people were counting on this money for a reasonably comfortable retirement. Now they are left holding the bag, but there is nothing in the bag. We can blame the government for not making rules and laws against this kind of outcome, or the financial markets for fluctuating, but those who are really responsible are the executives who were in charge of the company. Frank Dunn, the former CEO of Nortel Networks, has been indicted, along with some of his associates, for financial fraud in the downfall of Nortel. As he defended himself in early 2012 against these charges, he argued that he sought to instill a culture of ethical behaviour as the company struggled to recover from staggering losses in 2002 and 2003. Whether he is proven guilty of fraud or not, his defence shows that even he realizes the critical nature of ethics to leadership and a company's culture.

Ten Principles of Military Leadership that Everyone Can Use

I'd like to end by presenting and discussing the military principles of leadership. These ten leadership principles are the ones I learned as a young officer cadet in the Canadian Army in 1980, and applied subsequently throughout my 26-year military career as a field commander, trainer, mentor, and staff officer. They are meant to provide the framework to teach leadership, to guide in leader development, and for evaluation on a regular basis of everyone from the private to the highest-ranking general. Thus, they are applicable whether you are leading at the strategic, operational, or tactical levels. These principles have since been modified by the

Canadian military, but they remain the same in substance. As to applicability and relevance beyond my own country, in my experience and my research, I have noted that just about every military force in the world follows a similar set of maxims, either explicitly or implicitly. I give a brief description of each principle, along with diagnostic questions to assess your own leadership or someone else's. Each principle also includes some skill building techniques to better apply that principle in everyday situations.

10 Timeless Leadership Principles

1. Achieve professional competence.

2. Appreciate your own strengths and limitations, and pursue self-improvement.

3. Seek and accept responsibility.

4. Lead by example.

5. Make sure that your followers know your meaning and intent, and then lead them to the accomplishment of the mission.

6. Know your followers and promote their welfare.

7. Develop the leadership potential of your followers.

8. Make sound and timely decisions.

9. Train your followers as a team and employ them to their capabilities.

10. Keep your followers informed of the mission, the changing situation, and the overall picture.

Leadership Principle # 1: Achieve professional competence.

We discussed this principle in detail in the first part of this chapter. Professional competence is fundamental to leadership. This is why it is listed as the first principle of leadership. As mentioned, the definition of leadership is the art of influencing others in order to accomplish a mission. **The most powerful means of influence is not reward and punishment, contrary to popular belief, but rather to show** that it is in the person's best interests, intellectually, materially, emotionally, and socially to follow a particular person. As already pointed out, people gravitate to leaders that can get them to achieve successful outcomes. They will even put up with quite a bit of inconvenience and personality quirks in the leader in order to get the success that rubs off on them.

- Do people follow you willingly because they believe you will lead them to success, or do they follow you out of obligation and compulsion?
- Do you have the skills and knowledge you need to carry out your leadership functions well? Do you have the right attitude?
- What must you do to acquire more professional skills and knowledge?
- Do you have the right blend of substance and style? What quadrant would you put yourself in on the graph of style versus substance?
- Skills building techniques:
  - Find a role model with advanced, professional competence and emulate their methods.
  - Deepen your understanding and knowledge of your professional field.
  - Read and write about your professional field; become a leading thinker in your field.
  - Work closely with proficient practitioners in your field to gain vital skills.

Leadership Principle # 2: Appreciate your own strengths and limitations, and pursue self-improvement

Whereas the first principle is very hard-nosed and realistic, the second one is more like something you would see in a twelve-step list for personal growth. However, it is the essence of realism to know what makes you tick as a person as well as a leader. Moreover, you can't really evaluate others and the influence you have on them—you can't really be a practical psychologist, which is what a leader needs to be—unless you have some insight into human nature. The best method for developing this principle is to have insight into your own strengths and limitations, as well as your motivations and states of mind. This takes self-knowledge, self-awareness, and motivation to modify your thinking, emotions, and behaviour to become more effective. In a way, this principle is the direct corollary of principle #1, for **you can't achieve professional competence unless you're continuously working to improve your performance and competencies.**

- What are your key professional and personal strengths? What do superiors, subordinates, and peers appreciate the most in you? What do you most enjoy doing? What are your best talents?
- What are your key professional and personal limitations? What do people tease you about, or make jokes about your quirks and behaviour? What consistently takes you longer to do? What requires more effort, or drains you of energy and passion? These are indications of weaknesses and limitations.
- Skills building techniques:
  - What changes can you make in your skills, knowledge, and work that would most leverage these strengths?
  - What changes in your skills, knowledge, and work can you make to minimize or manage these limitations?
  - Can you compensate for your limitations in some way, by avoiding situations that bring them out or by allying yourself with others who have complementary competencies?

Leadership Principle # 3: Seek and accept responsibility

This might appear to be a truism, but you can't be a leader if you're afraid to seek and accept responsibility. **By definition, a leader is in front, which implies a willingness to accept responsibility and be accountable for his or her decisions and actions, as well as those of the people he or she is leading.** There will always be people who are ready to take on leadership responsibilities, no matter what the situation. However, most people need to know that the organization they are part of will support them in their leadership, especially if the going gets tough, or if their followers start challenging them. There must also be an attitude of prudent risk taking whereby leaders are allowed some margin of error in trying new things without having the wrath of the organization or their superiors come down upon them in the event of failure.

- What missions or tasks do you take on without hesitation? Which ones do you avoid?
- Does responsibility and authority scare you, or are you invigorated and challenged by taking on more responsibilities?
- Skills building techniques:
  - Think of a time when you willingly took on responsibilities. What did it feel like? How did it turn out? What are the characteristics of this particular experience? Could you repeat them?

- For each of your top three strengths, find a responsibility or task that would allow you to fully exploit that particular strength.
- For each of your three principal limitations, find a responsibility or task that would allow you to manage that limitation in a novel and effective manner.

Leadership Principle # 4: Lead by example

It bears repeating that a leader must provide a positive example for followers, subordinates, peers, and even superiors. Followers will model their behaviour on their leaders especially if they, the followers, have little experience of the undertaking. **The leader sets the tone for the entire organization by how he or she thinks, acts, speaks, and decides. If the leader is weak and indecisive, the whole organization will often be of the same complexion. If the leader acts ethically and with integrity, then this attitude will tend to permeate the organization.** The leader gives a license to his or her followers to think and perform in a certain way; so all actions and words must be assessed for their impact on followers, superiors, peers, and those the organization is meant to serve. In the final analysis, the leader must be worthy of the loyalty, confidence, and respect of followers, because they will mimic the leader's performance.

- Have you ever been forced to work for or follow a leader of dubious competencies and integrity? How did you feel? How did your co-workers feel? What mechanisms did followers adopt to compensate for the leader's weaknesses?
- Conversely, have you ever had the pleasure to work for a leader who was competent and who provided a superb example of professional excellence and ethical integrity? What was it like? How did you and your co-workers feel and act? What were the mood, morale, and cohesion like?
- Are you always a good role model and example for your followers and peers? Are you truly worthy of their loyalty, confidence and respect at all times?
- Skills building techniques:
  - Make a list of all the leadership qualities and practices that you have always admired. Decide to apply these to your own leadership in a conscious and deliberate manner.

- Make a list of all the poor leadership practices that you've always disliked in others. Observe yourself in action and try to avoid these practices in yourself.
- Look at your speech, decisions, actions, and performance from the perspective of others, especially your followers. What do you think they expect in a leader? What do they *need* in a leader? Work to balance their expectations and their needs in everything you do and project.
- Have you ever said one thing but done the opposite? Why did you do so? How could you have avoided it? What will you do to avoid it in the future?

Leadership Principle # 5: Make sure that your followers know your meaning and intent, and then lead them to the accomplishment of the mission

This is directly related to the principle of selection and maintenance of the aim that we discussed in great detail in Chapter 4. The philosophy of mission command espouses giving a task or a mission to a subordinate, and letting that person come up with the best means of achieving it. This provides intellectual stimulation while recognizing the individual strengths and potential of each person under your influence and authority. To truly work, this philosophy requires that followers understand the leader's intentions and objectives, why they are doing what they are doing, and how this all fits into the greater scheme of things. In other words, this is the leadership aspect of the technique of mission analysis we explored in Chapter 4. However, as they say in the military, "no plan survives contact with the enemy." **While objectives must be fairly constant, leaders and followers must be sufficiently resilient to adapt their plans and means to the realities of the situation as it evolves.** They must adapt to competition, friction, uncertainty, and other obstacles that arise as a result of trying to achieve their mission. The leader must be present at the right time and place to exert personal influence, and to make timely and effective decisions. You don't just give orders, then disappear into your bunker. You have to make sure the orders are carried out. One must lead from the front.

- What are your objectives for your team and your organization? Have you communicated these to your people? Could they repeat and interpret them in their own words? Would they be able to continue with the mission if something went wrong in the original plan? Would they have the confidence and the means to do so?

- When is the last time you spoke to your team? When is the last time you just walked around, and asked people what they were doing, why they were doing it, and how it fit in with the over-arching mission and plan?
- When you give direction, do you then disappear to your bunker, or do you stick around to see how things are going to provide encouragement, advice, and timely decision-making to make sure you stay on track while adjusting plans and means to meet the objectives?
- Skills building techniques:
  - Re-read Chapter 4 closely and use the techniques given to formulate your objectives, then plan for a project. Call a team meeting to explain your intentions in detail. Don't let yourself off the hook with an email or a memo. You need to do this in person and orally. Let them ask questions about anything they don't understand or on which they need clarification. Ask them questions about your direction to ensure they have understood.
  - When you've given your direction, stay involved in its execution. Be available for questions. Ask people how things are going. Ask them if they need more resources or clarification. Ask them how they are doing things without necessarily criticizing or trying to change it if you think it will indeed work. Be ready to provide advice, encouragement, and to push people if you think they need it.
  - Hold a team meeting for no reason other than to let your people ask you questions about anything they want. Tell them anything is on the table. Answer honestly and openly. If you don't know the answer, tell them so, and promise to find it, and get back to them. Do this on a regular basis. Once a month is probably a good frequency.

Leadership Principle # 6: Know your followers, and promote their welfare.

The best way to promote the welfare and the development of your troops is to get to know them. If you know them, you will be in a better position to assess their strengths and limitations, to provide advice and encouragement, and to give them assignments that will use their competencies and exploit their full potential. As we saw in Chapter 9, however, welfare isn't just about external, hygiene factors. In fact, **the best form of welfare for subordinates is to provide them with a clear vision and mission, the tools and resources they need to do their job well, and the leadership they deserve to reach their full potential individually and collectively,**

and also to achieve the mission and objectives of the organization. The German World War II general Erwin Rommel said that the best form of welfare was first-class training. By this, he meant that the ability to function as an effective and well-oiled machine or healthy organism is the best form of welfare for the members of a team or organization.

- Do you know every one of your immediate subordinates by name? Do you know their background? Where are they from, what are their goals, what are their particular strengths and limitations? If you can't answer these questions about your immediate followers, then you don't really know them.
- What do your subordinates want? What do they need? How can you balance the two, and communicate the results of this balance?
- Skills building techniques:
  - On a regular basis, walk around your office or facility, and just shoot the breeze with your people. Ask them about themselves. Find out what makes them tick. Ask them what they think of what they are doing, of the vision and mission and objectives, of the plans. Ask them if they would do anything differently. An amazing thing happens when you ask questions, and listen to the answers.
  - Assess what your people need, tell them, and, then, within the limitations of time, resources, and operations, give it to them.

Leadership Principle # 7: Develop the leadership potential of your followers.

The military expects attrition in the ranks and the hierarchy owing to combat losses, retirements, and releases from service. There is a built-in requirement for redundancy, relief, and succession planning. All military personnel are called upon to do the job of their immediate superior or to supervise a group of peers in a task at some point in their service. This could be very temporary, a question of minutes, or for weeks and months on end. The best way to see leadership development in the military is as a perpetual motion machine. Raw recruits come in at one end, are given increasingly challenging assignments leading others, progressing in rank and responsibilities as their competencies and performance increase. Higher-ups are constantly on the lookout for potential leaders because they know they will be needed. They are continually educating, advising, and training new leaders at all levels. The assumption is, therefore, that **everyone is a potential leader, so the earlier and more comprehensive the leadership development, the better.**

- Do you give extra responsibilities to your highest potential subordinates? Do you force them out of their comfort zone? Do you give them the skills, knowledge, and tools they need to do their supervisory or management job?
- Do you have a process to identify, select, and groom high potential leadership candidates in a formal way?
- Are people encouraged to take initiative and responsibility, or do you punish them—implicitly or explicitly—for doing so?
- Skills building techniques:
  - Make a list of all of your immediate subordinates. Put them in order of highest to lowest leadership potential.
  - Over time, validate your impressions by discussing with your peers, superiors, and selected subordinates, and by personal observation of them in action.
  - Give additional responsibilities to your people in a fail-safe environment to see how they perform. As they become more confident and inspire trust, give them greater responsibilities and authority.
  - Ensure that your subordinate leaders have the competencies and tools, both individual and organizational, that they need to do their leadership job well.

Leadership Principle # 8: Make sound and timely decisions.

Just as there is no such thing as a leader who doesn't take responsibility, there is no such thing as a leader who doesn't make decisions. Decision-making is fundamental to leadership. There are two components: the decisions must be sound, and they must be timely. Sound decisions have the following qualities: they are appropriate given the level of resources and the intended effects; they are arrived at rationally, if possible, after considering various options and their potential direct and indirect effects; they can be hasty or intuitive, providing there are means in place to manage the inherent risks of decision-making in uncertainty; finally, they are sound if the majority of the followers buy into them, and there is no major resistance to their implementation. The final characteristic requires that decisions be explained and understood by everyone involved in carrying them out or supporting them. **Timely decisions are ones that are taken at the right time to have the best effect. The best decision taken and implemented at the wrong time is useless. Timely decision-making requires assurance and boldness.** Most of this book is about sound, timely, efficient, and effective decision-making in support of business objectives.

- Do you make decisions or defer them as long as possible? Are you a maximizer or a satisficer? The former waits for the perfect plan and the perfect time to implement it, often wasting valuable opportunities because of perfectionism and consequent hesitation. The latter acts when there is sufficient information and then adjusts the plan and its execution as more information comes to the fore.

- Are your decisions usually sound and effective? Do your subordinates, peers, and superiors routinely support your decisions, or do they often or occasionally contest them?

- Do you find yourself having to constantly change or reverse your decisions after the fact, or are they sufficiently robust to survive the first contact with reality?

- Do you make decisions quickly when you have just enough information, or do you wait for just a little more information and the perfect time to act?

- Skills building techniques:

  - If you think you're a decision maximizer, and realize you need to temper this trait, take a minor decision that requires your attention and make it quickly even if you don't have all the information, and it's not the perfect time. Afterwards, react to the situation; assess the decision's impact. Was it good or bad; did you survive making this hasty decision? Were you able to live with the consequences? Adopt this stance with progressively bigger decisions.

  - If you think you're a decision satisficer, and realize you need to temper this trait, do exactly the opposite from the previous technique. Take a minor decision on which you are tempted to move hastily but, instead of moving quickly like you usually do, slow down to analyze the situation. Act, then assess. Repeat with progressively bigger decisions until it becomes natural to give greater consideration, and to not shoot from the hip so much.

  - There is little danger of becoming completely opposite, because these are ingrained personality traits. We're working on tempering them to make your decision-making more balanced, not to throw the baby out with the bath water.

Leadership Principle # 9: Train your followers as a team and employ them up to their capabilities

A well-trained, well-functioning team displays cohesion and unity, which means it functions better. This generates better performance, which contributes to morale and keeps people in a better mood. When people are busy, they are less prone to gripe and whine. Busy people are generally a lot happier than bored ones. In a well-trained team, everyone has a particular role to play, which means they can work to their full potential. The corollary to sound training in a business is sound organization and structure. **Well-organized and structured businesses function more effectively and efficiently. There are well-defined roles and responsibilities for everyone, with clear lines of authority, communication, and accountability. This generates opportunities to employ individuals up to their full capabilities and potential.** The larger the business organization, the more there are opportunities for varied and challenging employment, opportunities that correspond to the unique strengths and competencies of employees and managers. This includes possibilities for advancement for those with high leadership potential.

- Is your business organized and structured to provide clear lines of authority, communication, and accountability?
- Are people employed in the right roles with responsibilities, authority, and training that are commensurate to their talents, strengths, competencies, training, education, and personal goals in addition to the needs of the organization?
- Do employees and managers know the vision, mission, objectives, and overall strategy of the organization? Have managers and supervisors conducted their mission analysis to know how they fit into the big picture? Have they communicated their objectives and plans to their teams? Does a philosophy of mission command and initiative prevail, or is everyone hesitant to decide and act for fear of retaliation and punishment?
- Skills building techniques:
  - Review the structure of your business to conduct the organizational diagnosis implied in the foregoing questions.
  - Sit down with each of your immediate subordinates to ask them if they feel they are being employed to their full potential. If not, ask them for suggestions that would meet that need better.
  - Hold a team meeting to ask for suggestions on improving the functioning and structure of the organization. You can also discuss the clarity of lines of authority, communication, and accountability.

- Make progressive changes in how your business is organized and structured to implement the best solutions emanating from your diagnosis and enquiry with your team.

Leadership Principle # 10: Keep your followers informed of the mission, the changing situation, and the overall picture.

People are not mushrooms; they don't grow best in the damp and the dark. You have to let in the light so they know what is happening, why it's happening, and what needs to be done , both individually or collectively. We've already been over this several times, but **people and teams perform best when they know what the mission and objectives are, what the leader's overall intent and plan are to achieve them, and what is expected of them as members of the organization.** Moreover, when they know what the mission and goals are, what the overall situation is—are things going well or poorly; why—and what is required to keep things on track, or get them back on track, then they can use their native intelligence and initiative to work towards the most effective and efficient resolution and achievement of the mission. This principle supports the philosophy of mission command, that it is better to lead a group of motivated and fully engaged, intelligent, and passionate followers than a bunch of passive robots.

- Do your team members often come to you wondering what is happening? Worse, do they simply do their job in the dark without letting on that they haven't a clue as to where the organization is going, what is happening with the overall situation, how things are progressing, or what is expected of them?

- Do your people feel empowered to fulfil the objectives of the organization, or do they see it as someone else's responsibility?

- Can they paraphrase the company's vision and mission, its major objectives and strategy, the means and plans to achieve these?

- Skills building techniques:
  - Hold a meeting to give overall direction to your team along the lines we've mentioned.
  - If the situation changes radically for the business or a particular project, convene a team meeting to bring everyone up to speed, answer questions, clarify direction and guidance, solicit feedback and suggestions, and provide encouragement and congratulations for a job well done, as the case may warrant.

- Periodically, at either specific junctures such as monthly or quarterly, or at project milestones, convene a team meeting to review progress, highlight successes and failures, identify lessons learned, generate ideas for improvement, and to underline good work by particular individuals and groups, or the team as a whole. Close with a general word of thanks for a job well done and encouragement for the future.

Summary

- Leadership is the art of influencing others to accomplish a mission.
- Leadership is fundamental to any complex, collective undertaking, whether in war, business, or life in general.
- Competence is the heart of leadership. Truly effective leaders, leaders who are inspiring and visionary, have the means and will to balance and optimize style and substance. They realize that leadership is based on substance, i.e. competence, but that they also need a personal style and attention to people.
- There are basically four categories of leader, depending on the particular combination and strength of style (people orientation) and substance (task orientation): inspiring leader; effective leader; posturing leader; and ineffective leader.
- Traditional forms of transactional leadership, based on conditional rewards and punishments are no longer effective to generate the performance needed in today's world, whether in business or any other field. Leaders must transform how their followers see themselves, the world, their organization, and what they can achieve as individuals and as groups.
- Transformational leadership is what leads to exceptional performance. It consists of four key facets, or factors: inspirational motivation, idealized influence, intellectual stimulation, and individualized consideration. Inspirational motivation and idealized influence when combined are what most people understand to be charismatic leadership.
- Transactional leadership reinforces hygiene factors, as described in Chapter 9, which generate extrinsic motivation. Transformational leadership seeks to transform individuals so they are motivated intrinsically to perform in an exceptional manner, and to achieve outstanding results.

- Leadership must be ethical. Leadership and ethics are really two sides of the same coin. A leader must be worthy of followers' loyalty, confidence, and respect. Superiors, peers, and the wider society that is served by the organization must also believe in leaders. Ethics and professionalism must be part of every leader's development, education, and accountability.

- Ethical leadership requires a balance between responsibility (the willingness to lead), authority (the officially sanctioned power to lead), and accountability (the obligation and willingness to answer for one's decisions and actions, and those of one's subordinates).

- There are ten principles of military leadership that anyone can use. Military forces around the world have developed lists of leadership principles to guide their officers, NCOs, and soldiers, at all ranks and levels of responsibility and authority. Leaders and managers in all fields, and especially in business, can use these principles to diagnose, teach, and improve leadership, their own and that of their followers and colleagues.

Conclusion

My intention in this conclusion isn't to repeat or summarize what is included in each of the chapters of this book, but rather as a call to action. I find in my own reading that I often enjoy the insights a book provides but then tend to forget them or file them away 'for future reference' when I need them or when I get the chance to review them. Unfortunately, much of the time I only retain a small proportion of what I've read, perhaps ten per cent, and I tend to use even less on a regular basis, because I've forgotten what I've learned in the first reading.

I believe the material in Brilliant Manoeuvres represents a significant departure for many readers, possibly pushing them out of their comfort zones. To really 'get' this material, you have to reread it frequently, and experiment with it on a daily basis in the exercise of strategic, operational, and tactical management, as well as the leadership of your team and organization.

It is my wish that you use Brilliant Manoeuvres as a handbook to develop your skills as a business strategist, planner, and tactician, and even more as a leader getting others to accomplish things they didn't think possible. So, my call to action is that you use this book to actually manage your business and lead your organization in the 'heat of battle.'

We've explored many different aspects of military wisdom in this book. It is encapsulated in examples, explanations, exercises, diagrams and various tools and techniques that you can use to formulate strategy, create plans, and lead others in achieving your goals on a day-to-day basis. You can use the chapters as a guide in helping you develop strategies, plans, and tactics for the challenges you face and the goals you set for yourself and the organization or team you lead. In fact, the chapters are a good sequence to follow in making your own assessments and plans, whether for your individual actions or those of your organization or team:

- For any situation you're facing, ask yourself if you have the initiative or are in a leading position. If you don't have the initiative and wish to gain it, then you must apply chapter two's principles of offensive action.
- If you've lost the initiative because of a temporary setback and want to regain it, or alternatively if you already have the lead and wish to maintain it, then you must apply the principles in chapter three on defensive action.

- To be sure of your objectives and to create commitment at all levels of your business, chapter four provides a detailed approach for selecting and maintaining your overarching aim, and then for ensuring that everyone in the organization is aligned to that objective through the processes of nested hierarchical planning, mission analysis, and mission command.

- Chapter five provides the tools to balance your objectives and plans within the inevitable constraints of time and resources that everyone faces in seeing their plans through to fruition.

- Chapter six provides guidance for when things don't go the way you originally planned or expected, which, if you're like everyone else on the planet, should happen several times a day, a week, a year. Do not underestimate the power of the 'Four Horsemen of the Apocalypse' to undermine and derail your best laid plans. Adopt the military mindset and go into battle assuming that things will not go as expected and that your opponents and competitors will try to defeat you, or at least hinder your actions and your chances of success.

- Chapters seven and eight provide further guidance in developing your plans, first by creating a culture where everyone in the organization is looking out for the smallest of changes and characteristics in the environment so that you can gain an intelligence advantage, and then by using a logistical framework of rational calculation and phased action to achieve your goals within the constraints of time and resources.

- Chapters nine and ten should be a constant reminder to you of the human dynamics of your business (or any type of organization for that matter). I recommend rereading these chapters on a regular basis until they become second nature to you, in particular your ability to assess your team's mood, morale, and cohesion, and your own abilities to lead them through thick and thin. Cycling periodically through the ten leadership principles I described in chapter ten is a good way to continually improve your leadership, as well as your ability to assess others and yourself. It will also help in developing self-awareness, which is probably the number one leadership skill, particularly as it concerns seeing one's effect on others.

I see this as the beginning of a journey and that is why I've created a special blog to add information as it becomes available, update some of the exercises and tools, and provide a forum for discussion and questions. The address is brilliantmanoeuvres. com, or brilliantmaneuvers.com, if you prefer American spelling.

Index